WHITE HA

Reasons. Seasons. Lifetimes.

Ian Cooper

Legal / Copyright

Acknowledgments

To Mum and Jon – miss ya always.
To Pickle (Charlotte) – just, always.
To Jules and Siobhan – there for you always.
To Belle and Aurora – always and forever.
To family – as always, thanks for the memories.
To friends – couldn't have done it without you.
Oh...and the pets – ever after.

To everyone else – I could never forget you.

Foreword

That's life. That's what all the people say, you're riding high in April, shot down in May (as Sinatra once said).

Births, exams, road trips, first hellos, the greatest of love stories, weddings, work, last goodbyes and death.

All those life experiences! They ebb and flow as the very best of games do: tentative, hopeful openings; structured, tactical middles; frantic, messy or emotional ends. All get defined by time and you can only play or react (for better, for worse, for richer, for poorer) to what's in front of you.

Oh...and you are only as good as your last one...exam, wedding, game. Whatever.

We are all blessed with some degree of skill and talent, whatever the situation. How we deal with what's around us, pressure situation or otherwise, is more often than not defined by where our heads are at. Not music and lyrics.

Regular physical activity helps keep our key mental skills sharp. Conversely, poor mental health can adversely affect performance. Many a recognised sportsperson...Oscar De La Hoya, Serena Williams, Kelly Holmes and Danny Rose have spoken of their mental travails. They are as human as me, you, all of us.

It takes courage, both mental and physical, to fight your own battles, your demons, your own inner turmoil...when you tumble and fall, on a pitch, a court, a ring or a track. Or anywhere else. We get help along the way. People lift us as we seek to overcome our obstacles and find the courage to fight another day. Supporters, writers, readers, listeners.

Sport also lifts us. It has an innate ability to transport us away from our moment, to take us on a journey to another place, however transitory. We escape to a world of dreams (and the occasional nightmare)...and, once in a blue moon, we get the whole Disney experience, just to prove that fairy tales really do exist.

If Tottenham Hotspur were a Disney character they'd probably be Mickey Mouse. They have had great matches, their fantasy football games, but once a decade or so they'll take us on a trip, giving us the full monty of gut wrenching, mentally exhausting drama. They are Mickey now, not in any slang expressionist way that depicts trivial, amateurish, small-time, inferior quality or counterfeit. They are Mickey now because time requires reinvention. He evolved, with a lot less emphasis on his friendly, well-meaning personality, more the menacing and stubborn sides of his persona. *Epic Mickey*, the video game, kicked it all off.

Once upon a time I wrote another sports biography, set in altogether different days, the Victorian and Edwardian era. Forget 'rebrands', forget technology (making a game 'fairer' now), forget the fact that in today's elite sport money talks. Back then it was mostly amateur, everything built on ethics.

Immortal Harlequin was fascinating to research. Cathartic as well. The reviews were kind, even the one that also came with a word of criticism…a wish that specific players were referenced by surnames rather than their Christian names, as I had. When I self-published the second edition of that book I sold my soul. I reverted to surnames…and wished I hadn't. I realised that in doing the research I had got close to these guys, their personalities and their characters. They were the book's heartbeat and, having written it in a boy's own style, I always felt that the reader should see them the way I did too. Endearingly, as you would a friend.

Personalities.

We all have them. Sometimes more than one. Either emanating from within ourselves or, because of our deeds and actions, nicknames and monikers that are then foisted upon us. Sport, particularly, is littered with sobriquets. You can take the sport out of personalities but you can't take the personalities out of sport. Their characters become us and we play up to them, we become them.

Whether as a means of intimidation (Psycho, Chopper), through physical appearance (The Fridge, The Albatross), from a unique skillset (The Scorpion, The Whirlwind, The Cat), a comedic play on words (The Turbanator) or earned by endeavour and achievement (The Greatest).

Simply also, just because (The Beast).

My own personal favourite…'Whispering Death', that of one of the greatest of West Indian fast bowlers, Michael Holding. It captured his very essence…graceful, rhythmic, deceptive, frightening.

Me? I was the Headless Chicken.

Never going to be an Oscar or a Danny. Or a Serena or Kelly for that matter. I have, however, walked into a fridge, owned a cat, used an axe and lovingly been called 'Beast'.

Did I have a skillset? I ran around bloodied, covering an awful lot of ground in a game. Worth an extra two or three players. It was a defining characteristic that never worked in a tactical game of chess…it did if you wanted someone to both get the ball back…and to cover yours.

I've played many sports for the better part of fifty years. Good games and bad games, highs and lows. All surfaces, all weathers with mud being the great leveller. All seasons too…the sounds, the smells and the feel of winter, spring, summer and autumn are evocative reminders of a whistle blowing somewhere. A timer starting…or reaching its end.

Every life has a beginning, middle and end. Mine never seemed in that order. As memoirs go though, I have tried to tell it as it is…or at least how I saw it, how I played what was in front of me. It's a book of two halves, or rather two parallels…evocative whimsy and er, football. Pick a side.

As a meander through time there are highs and lows, a lot of heart, no little passion, humour and pathos. Oh, and nicknames and expletives as and where necessary. All part of the emotion and the drama. Like in the best of games.

As our clocks start running down, the memories find us. These are a few of mine.

REASONS

Best Of My Love
7 May 1983

Fear. It's a funny thing. Some take the lead in the face of it. Shitting yourself is also an option. Everyone has to own it at some stage though if they are ever going to master it.

The back of an ambulance is never going to be a fairy tale at the best of times. In the back of this one there was no cacophony of noise, no magic dust. Certainly no talking animals, singing birds or fairy godmothers. No triumph of good over evil, light over dark. Just a proverbial and lyrical 'sound of silence' and one of only two confined places I'd remember all my life. The longest, deepest, most tortuous road trip of my life took about five minutes. As road trips went, whilst I wish it had never happened, I wish I'd had a second more.

The 1980s had just started. We had not long moved to West Kensington, my brother off to the Army, my sister at sixth form college. The Eagles were a mere twelve but had just split up. Tottenham had turned a hundred and recently won the FA Cup. I was eighteen and university beckoned. All were the least of my concerns. My Saturday afternoons would normally have been roofing one in to the top of the net or making that last ditch slide tackle. On this late spring day I was on my way to Charing Cross Hospital, not that far from Fulham's football stadium. As an impressionable teenager trying to forge his path, that journey would make me grow up quicker than I should have, to tackle the lonely days and nights as surely as they would follow.

As scary rides go, by distance, it was mercifully short. Scary only in how frightened I could see my mother was despite her normal lovely demeanour. As hard lives go she had always taken charge of her own. In that moment she was desperate to say something, anything, afraid to do so. In her eyes, she had never looked more alone, despite my presence, despite me tenderly holding her hand. She was at rock bottom. I had her back.

We all have challenges in life. As kids. With jobs. With a family of our own. As the body ages the challenges become different but, whatever our age, statistically one in four of us has had, or will have, mental health problems. In two football squads of twenty-five players plus two managers, four officials and numerous back office staff on any pitch, statistically that's at least fifteen people. In a stadium of sixty thousand that's fifteen thousand. Everyone is fighting their own battles.

Today was the start of mine.

Together in the moment, there was no escape from our shared reality. The four of us united. The policewoman, the paramedic, my mum and me. Statistically then, one of us would experience mental health problems. I didn't know the policewoman or the medic so I couldn't prejudge them. I was never sure about me. Going to section her under the mental health act as I was though, I knew it was my mum.

Those five minutes were a maelstrom of emotions but, when the ambulance doors slowly opened, all I wanted was added time.

'I love you, Mum,' I whispered as we all slowly exited.

Mental health is multifaceted.

Mental illness is associated with changes in the brain's structure, function…and chemistry.

Paranoid schizophrenia is about managing the voices in your head. Whilst you learn to live each day as positively as possible, you never expect anything from it…except how your brain is going to test you; the goalposts can move all too readily.

What it does give you is creativity and strength, but also intellect, compassion and empathy. My mum had all those qualities in abundance; there is beauty in everything…you just have to be willing to look for it.

On 7 May, 1983, my mind was shot to pieces.

As days went, it was going to be the biggest game of my life to ever own it. I was helpless, isolated and had nowhere to run.

In this new reality, I desperately needed a friend.

SEASONS

You Are Not Alone
1969 - 1973

'Up the Mole!'

As three words and opening lines go in a timeless tale of mysticism, adventure, morality and camaraderie they were as dramatic as they come. Running on to my biggest stage to vanquish a horde of weasels, ferrets and stoats from the Wild Wood was where it all began. I was probably on stage for no more than a few minutes…five at most. As lines on a stage went, they wouldn't be the only ones I'd ever have to say (and not the most important either), but coming off the subs bench in the school play to seize and save the day became a metaphor for the next fifty years of saving.

Mostly myself.

I started Burnham County Infant School on Monday 8 September, 1969, my brother's birthday. My school report two years later became a strange precis for everything else that followed.

'Ian is rather shy, hardworking and responsible. He is quiet, imaginative, and conscientious. He enjoys his work and always does his best. Muscular co-ordination good.'

Not much to take away then (that I remember) from my formative school days, except that starring role and stirring call to arms in *The Wind in The Willows*. That and the black plastic National Health glasses I'd just got, which changed everything around that time including both my sight and perceptions.

It was the seasonal panto and roles were divvied up. At infant school everyone gets given a character, one they'll probably remember forever. That character's personality, their best trait, should never define you but more often than not does…like a first position in either football, rugby or hockey. Moles never really see the light of day and are generally noticeable only by the trails they leave. 'Moly', to his friends, was a humble, loyal, polite home-loving animal who, fed up with the spring-cleaning of his secluded home, ventured out into the outside world, which he looked to adapt to. As a character, it suited me.

Riverbank's anthropomorphised first team only had the four in it and, alongside Toad, Rat and Badger, Mole was extremely popular (as pantomime characters went). There aren't too many famous ones. Except perhaps Moly.

Somewhat appropriate then that I'd get the blind one (or half of him) as the role was to be shared, someone else getting the first half 'coming out' scenes and me getting all of the second half frenetic glory. It was my first substitute's performance (not the last), coming on after the interval to secure a result (pantomime style).

It was a packed audience (about a hundred and fifty). One of my, ahem, bigger crowds, but meant something to at least two of them…my mum and dad. All the training ground routines (well, rehearsals) meant nothing. All that was there on the night was the energy and emotion of the occasion…and instinct…which took over. Fifty years later and that one defining moment is as clear in my mind now as I never really saw it then. Time, for a second, for that precious memory, always stands still. I'd be back.

It was dramatic. It was intense. A very poor-sighted six year old boy, playing a very poor-sighted, timeless literary talpid. Wearing a mask helped, but very few acting chances came my way after, my spectacles (primarily) stopping me blazing any trail to Oscar glory.

I was always a trip hazard waiting to happen.

My early years were a blur, mostly remembered by an old photo or a pointed memory. Born in Bradford-on-Avon and then, care of my father's naval career, a lot of life on the road. A year in America (sailing out on RMS Queen Elizabeth) and some time at my granny's in Bierton, near Aylesbury, the selected highlights. The only legacy of my grandfather, a 1930s school head who I never met, was his Acme 'Thunderer'. The whistle was, I was told, used for many a football game…and for controlling the playground. Obey it or it was the belt, apparently. It did its job.

As the 1960s came to a close, we settled in to the small village surroundings of Burnham (our appropriately named house, Badger's Rest, straight out of a Kenneth Grahame novel). Britain was in freefall. Trade Union wars brought a state of emergency with general strikes, power cuts and no bin collections; all a desperate sign of the times. Talks on European integration produced much cynicism and dither. In the early 1970s the Prime Minister, Heath, was pouring money in to stop the rising prices and wages. Strange times indeed to be brought up in.

In a disco age of tank tops and flares everything was as dangerous as the terrible fashion. Poisonous paints and car fumes, houses filled with smoke from chimneys, pipes and fags, razor sharp ring pulls on coke cans, razor blades lying around. Noticeable (and therefore avoidable) dog shit on the ground everywhere (ash, importantly, in the dog food of the day turning it grey). Oh…and those lovely teddies with spike eyes. The list was endless. We did have *Rainbow* on TV though. Whilst the 'modern' world had moved on from Moly's parochial version of Edwardian England, how the country desperately needed a rainbow now.

Watneys Red Barrel, Double Diamond and Babycham kept the adults going. Bucket loads of sweets for a penny did much the same for us kids. Strange times maybe but, through the eyes of a young child, still idyllic. No seatbelts. No bike helmets. No worries.

For me though, as most, an adventure from dawn till dusk. Cereals had proper cool free stuff inside (small parts, choke hazard but still genius). Woolies had Pick 'n' Mix and Salt & Shake crisps (not for breakfast). We were outside all the time having messy water fights or playing in the street. Choppers and (space) hoppers were cool and excursions to the woods and their streams were adventures worthy of the kids in *Stand by Me*.

The Lido at Burnham Beeches and trips to the beach at West Wittering (never without my favourite marmite and gherkin sandwiches) were the top summer family day trips of choice. My brother and I slept in the attic conversion, nights ending with my dad reading from *Winnie the Pooh*.

Christmases, as I very fondly recalled, were also always memorable. The presents that actually came were inevitably simple yet full of the spirit of the season. As well as the huge filled stockings (satsumas, puzzles and Curly Wurlys) the Santa wish list always included a bigger bike that never quite made the day. For me though, those early '70s years were all about models and astronauts. The Captain Scarlet 'Angel Interceptor' Airfix model was second only to the ultimate prize, the plastic sweat-box that was the NASA 'space helmet' replica. I got one and for a brief period in time I was Major Tom.

For all the memories, if I had one lasting regret…that would have been to have looked after the class gerbils for a weekend. I was, sadly, never given them.

Shortly after my rodent oversight (something I'd never really get over) came a move to Long Close (Junior) School over in Slough…somewhere as I remembered it, near the huge Mars factory. Burnham Infants only ever had a hard court playing area at the front. Long Close came with grass. With the move came daily smells of the newly mown lawns and chocolate…and a first full school report.

Autumn 1971:

French…*fairly good, worked well after some initial diffidence in class oral work. Does not always participate fully in class work.*

English…*very neat and accurate. Intelligent and able and deserves his promotion.*

History…*remembers his facts and presents them neatly and accurately. Sometimes gets his facts muddled.*

Maths…*Ian is a very able little boy who works with enthusiasm. Coped in the higher class with his usual cheery manner. Deserves his excellent exam mark.*

Writing…*always neat and legible.*

Reading…*fluent.*

Geography…*neatly presented, very attentive.*

Art…*fairly good.*

Scripture…*very good, oral work improving.*

Games…*very fair, tries hard, plays keenly, steadily improving his game…should be useful when he is older.*

Exam result 90%, first position.

Cheery, neat, attentive, keen, tries hard, got facts muddled, should be useful when older. Lots to aspire to then. It had all started so well.

There was only one direction to go after that.

Ages six and seven are the 'sponge' years. Everything gets absorbed…not least from parents and how they related too. My father was away a lot in the Navy. My mother did the looking after and we had a lot of French and Spanish Au Pairs to support.

Postcards from some exotic destination were the norm in those naval days. Many sent from HMS Sirius (F40) of the West Indies and of Florida, including the Seven Mile Bridge (which got placed in the back of my young mind as some mystical place to maybe visit one day). When my dad was back, Saturdays were for sport: either to see Burnham Town play football down at The Dell (for me, primarily the crisps and bottled coke); or trips to watch him play hockey over at Maidenhead (although I'd mostly sit in our Austin 850 Mini and listen to the football).

Saturday afternoons inevitably ended, where possible, with Grandstand and Final Score…with the unforgettable Dickie Davies, the Teleprinter and the classified results. A hope with it that East Fife 4, Forfar 5 might one day turn up. Checking the Littlewoods Pools coupon was one of the associated events. The Pools were cheap to enter with the potential to win big…pick ten, eleven or twelve fixtures (out of twelve) to finish in a draw. Treble chances. Pools panels sitting in adverse conditions. Fabulous. Although we never won, it was all just part of our rich Saturday ritual, alongside the wrestling…some sweaty, make-believe world inhabited by the Big Daddys, Giant Haystacks and Kendo Nagasakis of this world. To any young kid this world of magic (and fakery) was pure escapism. We all bought in to it as the prelude to hiding behind the sofas when *Dr. Who* came on. *Match of the Day* with its theme music and 'Action Replays' restored a sense of calm and our Saturdays always finished with all being well in the world.

For the rest of the week our garden was my adventure playground with vegetable patches (and ants) to one side, a shed, swing and a treehouse to the other. It was also my make-believe Wembley. The shed was the goal at one end, the steps of the patio the other. The obligatory balls went over the wire fence (mostly regained by stealth at night by tunnelling underneath it). Footballers are either technical or not, instinctive or not; as a 'should be useful', I was neither. Dribbling around fallen apples in my wellies and slamming goals in to the side of the shed were my way of developing and accentuating better ball skills. I was just an eight year old living the romantic dream of completing a hat-trick in the dying seconds of a big cup final. My goal celebrations were both elaborate and epic and would have amused the neighbours (intentionally so in the case of young Lizzie, the original girl-next-door).

If football had become a regular part of my life then 18 March, 1972, was something of an epiphany. Leeds were playing Tottenham in the FA Cup quarters. I was glued to the crackling radio in the car park of Maidenhead Hockey Club during a hugely absorbing match between two teams of collection worthy players. Tottenham lost 2-1, but their cup exploits weren't over for the year. More was to follow.

In the summer of 1972 I was eight years old. It was the year I became a Spurs fan for life.

The big question.

Tottenham, why you?

Chivers Jelly and its word association with Spurs and England striker Martin Chivers, perhaps…or the fact that with a new school and an epiphany these things were now of far greater interest and social importance.

Possibly, and more likely, it was due to the Esso garage near Burnham Park which gave out many a promotional football 'collectable'. After Shell's 1970 World Cup 'coins', dear old Cyril (the petrol attendant) was more than happy to skim off handfuls of footy club 'foil' badges through the 1971-72 campaign. With it came two things: I was popular; and also gained a far greater interest in the detail of football itself (all the players at least). West Ham had some greats; Clyde Best was a legend. The Leeds players were names I'd heard a lot of, not least on the radio. Chelsea, Manchester United and Liverpool too. But it was Tottenham, who had just won the League Cup the previous season, that sparked most interest. Mullery and Peters were names hung over from the 1970 World Cup; Coates and my gelatinous friend Chivers new additions to the national set up. Spurs were on the rise and this current season, FA Cup notwithstanding, was turning in to a decent one. They had different qualities and personalities across the field that somehow made them even greater as a whole.

Every week going in to school they always had my back, armed as I was with all the necessary statistics to stand my own and combat any playground banter. As the end of the season loomed I knew them all inside out and was able to reel them off effortlessly. I knew the parts of their history that mattered: first (and only) non-league club to scoop the FA Cup; first domestic double; first British team to win a cup in Europe; Bill Nicholson and Jimmy Greaves.

And by May 1972 I knew they were 'the one'.

The '71-72 UEFA Cup Winners Cup was a two-legged affair, several weeks apart. For the first time in its history it involved two English teams, Wolverhampton Wanderers and Tottenham…underwhelming for some, memorable for others. Both sides were disappointed not to be matched with 'big' European teams. The players' wives had all been promised a Madrid or a Paris if they'd got there. In the end they got a trip to the Black Country.

As European finals go, cheap. At least they made it.

I knew the names of all the Wolves players (none of the wives), The Doog and all…even admired their (Esso) club badge. The Tottenham players however had invaded and taken over every part of my mind this season. I'd traipsed all around Europe with them (via the newspapers), shared some great memories and here we were, at the end of our first season together, in a final.

Five days after England's 1972 Euro quarter-final with Germany, Tottenham won the first leg at Wolves 2-1…two precious away goals, Chivers getting both. The second leg on 17 May was in front of a crowd of over fifty thousand. Mullery settled nerves by scoring early. Needing to score at least twice now, Wolves went for it and, despite being the better team on the night, fell short by one goal. Goalkeeper Pat Jennings was my (and everyone else's) hero.

I'd just watched the first of my top five Spurs games.

If Big Pat was the game saver, Hackwood Redstart of Empshott, a pure breed (Welsh) springer spaniel, was the game changer. Unusually good looking, his pedigree was subservient to any muddy puddle he came across. Like any Sam or Max he was just a dog, a real one. A very lovely one at that. His first night down in the kitchen on his own was a wailer. All night long. Thereafter, Robin became the glue that kept the family together, miles (and boarding schools) apart.

School reports offered little by way of a clue as to where the regular curriculum would take me. They did suggest the football boot makers had missed some tricks and practicing in wellies (my forte) was clearly the way forward.

Spring 1973:

Arithmetic…*keen and bright worker, always a high standard.*

English…*this hardworking boy consistently does his best.*

Geography…*doesn't contribute much in class, listens quite well.*

Art…*works well, but could do even better if he wasn't always the first to finish. He must slow down and learn to finish off work more carefully.*

History…*a disappointing result…some of his work has been very untidy this term.*

Games…*excellent, Ian is a natural games player who is destined to represent the school in the very near future. An excellent prospect, probably the most naturally gifted footballer in his class. He is certainly one of the best of his age that I have seen for a long time. He will be an outstanding Colts player next season.*

Housemaster…*continues to please us all and do well. A very thoughtful and deliberate boy who nonetheless has a very pleasant influence.*

Promising, eager, hardworking, hasty, listens…often quiet. History, particularly, run ragged by football. A clear pattern was emerging.

End of terms typically meant holidays in Wales, where my mother's family were all from. Brought up in the small mining community of Kenfig Hill, with its rows of terraced houses, she'd left school at fifteen to look after the rest of their large family. From then on, she educated herself and ended up becoming an operating theatre nurse.

Time passed way too quickly in Porthcawl (where all my aunts lived) and where the golden sandy beaches were both idyllic and stretched for miles. Paddling, rock pooling and rock climbing made me feel like a daredevil (slight as they really were). Equally endless sand dunes at Merthyr Mawr were out of some fantasy. The steel mills of Port Talbot on the way to Swansea and the further coasts of both South and West Wales acted by way of contrast and heritage. The land of my mother's was both stunning and beautiful.

There was a romance to Wales then. The sweat and the toil of the mines (troubled as the industry was at the time) was paralleled by the magnificent scenery. And rugby.

In the words of Max Boyce, 'I was there.'

Before another opportunity to do exactly that, came a last junior school report.

Summer 1974:

Latin…*more forthcoming in lessons this term. Quick to grasp basic concepts! Excellent and enthusiastic. I shall miss Ian very much.*

French…*commensurate progress made. He has done well despite absences.*

Maths…*good clear thinking mind, must learn to communicate his ideas more. Overcoming his shyness may help…basically good at maths…must learn to set his work out more neatly though.*

English…*results are exceedingly pleasing…I am truly sorry to be losing so promising and charming a boy.*

History…*steady worker with a sensible attitude to work.*

Geography…*he has been communicative this term. Can do well when he tries.*

Science…*poor, Ian has difficulty, but hard work should help.*

Art…*an artistic boy with a good sense of design.*

Music…*always works well, but with limited musical ability.*

Games…*I have the impression that Ian dislikes the game, which is a pity, as he is really rather good. Colts squad. Back. Ian, although small, plays hard. Needs more experience.*

Housemaster…*a good result from a pleasant and small boy.*

I don't remember any of the teachers…it's generally the ones that make you like the subject that you do remember, the bad ones you don't. As I progressed through the forms though, performances had slipped. Additional weight and complexity of material perhaps, or maybe just application.

Most likely, particularly in the case of football, a greater drop off in eye-sight and everyone else getting bigger.

By the time I had finished junior school I could recall all of the kings and queens of England (by royal houses and dates of birth, succession and death) as easily as I could the times tables. As well as all the football teams in the league, with pretty much all their players.

Childish things would have to go on hold for a bit. We were on the move once again…to naval married quarters on top of Portsdown Hill, on the outskirts of Portsmouth. We all needed new schools as a result, ones that would take full-time boarders. Up until that point it had been a lovely childhood. And up until that point, I never saw it slipping away.

The little stretch of green running along the front of the houses in Hoylake Road brought a magnificent view over Portsmouth and the Solent beyond. It also brought, for the summer at least, a new football and cricket pitch, a new set of kids to play with and something that completely threw me off my game.

I was ten years old when a girl first said, 'I love you.'

New Kid In Town
Autumn 1974

The Old Ride School, Bradford-on-Avon
Tuesday 17 September

Dear Mum and Dad, also Rob,

I have not had a very nice term, and I have got no friends, and I am very lonely. I miss you all. But if you haven't got the dates of my holidays would you please ask the headmaster for them for I would like to go home when the other boys do?

Today we played soccer and I scored the winning goal.

Would you please come and see me soon for I am very lonely and I miss you, especially Rob? In the evenings I am very hungry and I have got nothing to do.

Come and see me soon.

With love, Ian

Sunday 22 September

Dear Mum, Dad and Rob,

I still haven't got any friends and I miss you very much. I also missed Robin's birthday.

On Wednesdays and Saturdays we have half-holidays and we get an hour's break. On Sundays we get the whole afternoon off. We play soccer on Mondays, Tuesdays, Wednesdays, Fridays and Saturdays. I did not play on the Monday but I scored three goals in four matches.

I only want to write one letter a week so if someone writes I will tell you and could you write and tell them how I am? Which reminds me, Granny wrote me a postcard of the 'Discovery' from London, so could you write and tell her how I am?

I do hope you can hire a motor-caravan for the out-weekend. If you can, can you bring my purple pyjamas and my six pence? If you can hire one where will we go?

I do hope Rob enjoyed his birthday and his new bowl. I have not done any models yet but I am probably going to do HMS Fearless this afternoon. See you soon. Can you tell Daddy to get Spurs' results each week? Give Rob my best wishes.

With love, Ian

Sunday 29 September

Dear Mum and Dad and Rob,

I have still not got any friends and I am still quite lonely.

I'm in the Colts' squad of twenty-three players. So far this season I have played seven matches, won four, drawn two, lost one, and three have been rained off. I have now scored six goals in seven matches.

I only want to write one letter a week because I have only got a few envelopes left, but I will write to everyone on the out-weekend, and could you write to Granny because she wrote to me?

When you were coming back from work how did the windscreen shatter in to hundreds of pieces?

Have you hired the motor-caravan for the out-weekend next week yet? If you do get one could you bring some old clothes, my purple pyjamas, my Tic Tacs, my six pence, and a sharp knife, for I would like to do my models then, and some of the pieces need cutting out carefully?

See you soon.
Love, Ian

Sunday 13 October

Dear Mum, Dad and Rob,

Yesterday I filled in the timetable on my big pad. Today after tea I am going to do my model. One of the boys said he would help me make and paint it, for it is difficult. Today the weather is cold, and because my classroom has not got any central heating it is very cold.

Have you found a boat yet? When you go shopping on Wednesday could you see if you can find a boat? How did Spurs do on Saturday? Last Wednesday the Colts played Wycliffe and I was in the team, but we lost 1-0.

See you soon.
Love, Ian

Sunday 20 October

Dear Mum, Dad and Rob,

On Friday Auntie Mona sent me a letter so I <u>am</u> going to write to her at half-term. Why are we going in to Southampton on that Thursday?

Wasn't Rob naughty when he chewed up a pair of Daddy's black socks? I hope you sold the house. I heard from one of the boys that Spurs beat Arsenal 2-0. What are the navy blue trousers like?

On Wednesday when you come to fetch me can you bring my fifty pence that I had left over from the out-weekend?

I have not yet finished my Vosper M.T.B. model yet but I will finish it at half-term.

See you on Wednesday.

Love, Ian

Good Day In Hell
1974 - 1975

Names of teachers do escape you. Flynn was one of those that didn't.

Boarding at Long Close could only have been weekly, hence the need, with the house move, for somewhere with full boarding facilities. A recommendation was given by a future housemaster at Marlborough, where I had a forward place waiting.

The prospectus for The Old Ride in Bradford-on-Avon read like a hotel guide (even if the photographs looked like they were from the fifties). Recognised as 'efficient' by the Department of Education and Science, the fairly structured regime of the school had a scheme of merit plus points for good behaviour. Reaching a specified target got you a book award, in the top tier at the end of the year a cup. The blurb also pointed out…

…'*Uniform should consist of a handkerchief and comb at all times. Pupils are not allowed extra sweets or extra food. Please ensure they have pocket money.*'

On a positive side there were over six acres of grounds with five games pitches.

Flynn, the headmaster, gave an introduction to the place in his dark study. Cold, intense, foreboding. And then there was the trophy cabinet. I say trophy cabinet. Hard not to notice the wide array of canes on the wall that you could tell he was fiercely proud of. It looked like he treated them as he would some golf clubs, a different one dependant on the shot required…an arsenal of bamboo weapons, one or two of which looked more than capable of bringing down an elephant.

Flynn was an old style disciplinarian, a smiling assassin who ruled, quite simply, by fear.

I couldn't wait to start.

The summer before starting had been a joyous one. The sizable, open stretch of green outside the house became a playground for all the kids on the road. One Sunday, after a particularly long and enjoyable game of cricket, everyone retired to their respective homes for Sunday lunch. Shortly after which, there was a knock at our side door. It was the youngest girl of the group, seven years old I guessed. I had hardly spoken to her, if ever…just smiled and helped out with her fielding.

'I just called to say I love you,' she said quite randomly, lyrically and left-field. 'I have got to go back now for lunch with my gran. Bye.' And with that she disappeared.

I was left stunned for the rest of the afternoon. I never saw her again, as they moved the following week. 'The one that got away' had come and gone in the time it had taken to serve the spuds and Yorkshires. It was like the best of fairy tales, only without the jelly and ice cream by way of happy ending. I never knew her. I never forgot her.

In Bradford-on-Avon I was just another lonely boy in town. I vaguely recall our classroom. The average age for the nineteen boys in Form Four was nearly eleven. I was just over ten. I don't remember any of them.

Autumn 1974:

French…*excellent start, keen, neat, accurate, always among the top of his form. Emphasis must be placed on the spoken word, for his pronunciation is weak.*

Maths…*a good start to the term though he is very silent. Not much that he does not understand, but I am worried that if there was, he would be hesitant to ask about it.*

History…*he does not contribute much from an oral point of view but has produced some intelligent written work. Results from tests have been disappointing.*

English…*a very successful start for him…well-grounded in the subject with a very lively imagination, if inclined to muddle his facts (Bismarck shelling Hastings).*

Geography...*produced some very good work and beginning to overcome his reticence.*

Latin...*good progress. He takes in all that he is told but has got to the stage of being flippant and over-confident.*

Science...*he is covering a lot of ground and is making excellent progress. He writes an especially good description of his work, but during practical work sometimes seems to doubt the evidence of his own eyes.*

Art...*has produced some good work and his basic drawing has improved. Shows a lively mind plus an improvement with his use of colour.*

Colts...*it took him about a month to master some of the basic skills and also overcome his sight difficulties, and from then on he became a prominent member of the game with his strong running and sensible defensive play.*

Mark Flynn...*work has presented few problems. Socially the hurdle has been a harder one but after a slow start he has settled and is mixing more freely. He has been well grounded and has an active brain. He was a little fearful about the other aspects of school but has now established himself and is beginning to find friends. He has been a power on the football field.*

With models (of the Airfix kind) and the search for friends part and parcel of this school life, writing letters on Sunday mornings became the highlight of my week (good quality Basildon Bond paper and envelopes which stuck down well...and if not, a bit of Golden Gum Glue did the trick). Revitalising too, given a highly structured rest of the week. Days always started at 6:30 a.m. with the processional mile and a half run around the fields.

Human nature is about communication. Letters I sent were, if not prolific, at least a steady run of one a week. Except Sunday 6 October. Letters were always screened. Not just mine, everyone's. Just as well then that I didn't mention the weird undercurrent of and about the school.

Fear. There was a stench of it.

In this case it wasn't something humour was going to make light of. Some of the masters were just 'odd'. Boys were being sick in the corridors. Boys were wetting beds. Boys were disappearing for no obvious reason, particularly at night, coming back in tears. Sweets became an abnormal currency. They were homesick probably. If I had noticed, I didn't readily absorb it. Perhaps I'd put it down to my eyes playing tricks or being too busy playing football.

Why the missing letter though? Fallen through a crack? I'd probably never know.

Football became my lifebelt…and probably without realising it my saviour. Off the back of the '74 World Cup final between Holland and Germany (which had brought Ajax to prominence for the first time), football was all I cared about to stave off the emotional void.

Bill McLaren also helped magnificently in that regard.

The lounge room TV only had the basic channels but became a focal point of the Saturday afternoons during the (then) Five Nations. These were the halcyon days of Cliff Morgan's 'if the greatest writer of the written word had written that nobody would have believed him'…that and the legend of Llanelli at Stradey Park against the All Blacks. Games were massive and it was all we were ever allowed to watch. They resonated deeply. Over one hundred thousand fans packed in to Murrayfield for the game against Wales. Whether 'Hen Wlad Fy Nhadau' or the twilight years of the great Welsh players…Gareth Edwards, Phil Bennett, Merv The Swerve, Derek Quinnell, JPR, Gerald Davies…Wales had become synonymous with family and special holidays and their rugby the treat a lack of extra sweets couldn't fill. McLaren's tones were a light shining over the darkness. He had the voice and, as with Tom Baker's *Dr. Who*, when you heard it you knew all was well in the world.

If Tottenham had become the icing on a sporting cake, watching the back end of the golden age of Welsh rugby was the cherry on its top.

The term (for me at least) ended well despite the odd background noise.

Spring 1975:

French…*first-class term. Grammatically sound and beautifully presented. A thoroughly good all round performance.*

Maths…*a very good worker with an intelligent approach in presentation and good on paper, but he does find it difficult to put his answers in to words. He has seemed to understand all that we have done and is reliably accurate in written work, but is ever so silent!*

Geography…*another most useful term, full of sensible and intelligent endeavour. A joy to teach.*

English…*maintained a high standard, he finds new grammar easy to assimilate but remains a little shy in his attempts to use it orally. His progress has been excellent and he must be on his guard against complacency.*

Science…*classwork excellent…observed carefully and took very good notes. The examination however revealed a lack of experience. He must read questions not just once but over and over.*

Colts…*he has made a useful contribution to the Colts XI as a midfield player, showing both a considerable sense of position and determination. Still weak with his left foot.*

Mark Flynn…*an excellent performance, he has deployed all his talents to the full. Whilst still shy socially he may be becoming a little over-confident academically. It is good that success gives him faith in himself, but beyond a certain point this can lead to blunted perception and dulled curiosity.*

Football and rugby aside, the one 'event' I did remember was a blazing hot summer day, evening and night late in to the summer term. At one in the morning it must have been at least twenty-eight degrees. No-one could sleep. Some of the masters went around the dorms saying the swimming pool was open for use…and no need to bring your trunks. This left seventy-odd eight to eleven year old boys skinny dipping to their hearts content late into the wee hours. All 'supervised'. All very *Swallows and Amazons*…but way off being politically correct.

And, in hindsight, just plain weird. Properly so.

Summer 1975:

Geography….*I can only hope that he contributes to work as well at his next school as he has here. He can always be relied on to produce the goods, and has been a rewarding boy to teach.*

Science…*his classwork has been excellent and his experimental work has been well written up. The examination however was a little disappointing and he should make more effort to reason things out.*

History…*a first-class terms work, well done. His exam paper contained very knowledgeable answers. He is an excellent worker and I am so sorry that he is leaving us….first place.*

Latin…*diligent and careful and made rapid progress during the three terms he has been with us. I am really sorry he leaves us so soon as he is a rewarding pupil to teach, with an alert and enquiring mind. I wish him well.*

Colts…*over the term he has developed well. He has some good shots when he moves his feet and his fielding is now much surer than it used to be. Spectators, fieldsmen, batsmen and all umpires beware when he comes on to bowl.*

Mark Flynn…*an excellent term with which to conclude a sadly short career. He shows great promise for the future. Although he has not dealt with social problems with the same ease as class ones, he has gained confidence and self-reliance.*

Relied on to produce the goods, self-reliant, crap at cricket. Human nature is about survival. My time at The Old Ride lasted, mercifully it seemed, just one short year. Highlights (goals aside) being a tin cup for getting over one hundred 'plus' points and otherwise escaping the 'trophy room'. My singular blemish (for which, surprisingly, I only got minus five points) was for eating another poor kid's satsuma as he didn't like them and couldn't eat his. The 'rules' said he had to. Unfortunately I had left his extra peel on my plate. If I had ever spotted anything, it was that he always seemed to be scared and in trouble.

When the way over-the-top master's questioning came, I took the points deduction for the team for telling a huge porky on his behalf.

Lying would normally have come with a lot more pain. I was football golden boy and somehow escaped. The truth always comes out in the end. Without realising it, as history would reveal, it seems I'd had a very lucky escape.

Hotel California
1975 - 1979

In the mid-1970s I mostly remember my eyes. As Achilles Heels went, they were mine. Hazel with it. Trips to visit the opticians were plentiful, mostly to replace the black plastic NHS specs, which were always breaking…and mostly by way of a football. Araldite provided a quick fix, until they were beyond repair, and then onto the next set.

Marlborough had already been lined up and the choice of future schooling was mine. June 1975 brought a letter offering a place at Churcher's College, Petersfield. I'd been given an alternative and an 'interview' with the College's headmaster, Donald Ian Brooks (Dibble, by nickname). He seemed to like my slightly OCD knowledge of Enid Blyton books, but caught me out with his favourite trick question. Which way was the (possibly real) silver ornamental ship on his sideboard sailing (the trick being the flag at the top was set the wrong way round to the sails)? I would balls up that particular test, but Dibble's nautical conundrum was a million nautical miles removed from the torture chamber that had faced me on first visit to The Old Ride. Stick or twist? I hated getting things wrong and that failed puzzle both inspired and challenged me. That, the location and its relative proximity to 'home' (and possibly the 'holy grail' of all quests to find 'I love you girl') won over.

After the twilight zone of Bradford-on-Avon, where my relative vulnerability had been masked and camouflaged in sport, Petersfield became an opportunity to express myself for the next seven years.

The school transfer coincided with a move to a house in Alverstoke (over from Portsmouth Harbour), close to The White Hart pub. Just enough space for a garden kick about, but close enough also to Stokes Bay for a full on jumpers-for-goalposts. All I needed were pals to play with.

Our family had seemingly always been on the run. My Cambridge educated dad was a weapons engineer officer in the Navy and very structured. My mum, self-educated, was very creative and arty (across mixed mediums). I inherited both skill-sets and traits to a degree. And there the conflict in my head started. Routine versus creativity.

Autumn 1975:

English…*although inclined to be reticent in class, he presents written work of a conscientious standard and has a good imagination and memory.*

History…*top of the class. Considerable enthusiasm and ability. Excellent start and attitude.*

French…*advanced in comparison with most of class.*

Maths…*capable of some really excellent work.*

PE…*rugby and hockey looking most promising.*

Form master…*has obvious ability. Appears to be thoroughly 'at home' with school life in general.*

Housemaster…*emerging more of a character of late, he has settled down well! He will be an asset to the House in a quiet way. He has certainly 'gone ahead' in the required fashion this term, in the academic field. His games teeter on the edge of success too. A well settled and likeable member of the House.*

Headmaster…*this is a pleasure to read…one of the best first year reports I have seen.*

Like my other schools…ahead in the game early. This was a different type of place and a ray of light with it.

A lot of things remained constant in school life, like the red-blue eraser which never really rubbed out any ink (we all failed, miserably, on a lie that had its place right next to 'Santa Claus is real'). Other things however, like the novelty of hand-held calculators, were evolving. There was a much greater sense of freedom than before…the red phone box down the road made it easier to stay in touch with home. Set homework time in the evening gave way to a few free hours afterwards, mostly spent around the pool table in the Mount House games room with the radio on in the winter. It was the year of Bohemian Rhapsody and, as both novel and influential records went, it was the talking point.

The dormitories at Mount House were small (five to six people). Matron (ooh!) supervised evening washes. Large tuck boxes (no sweet sanctions!) were allowed as a matter of routine, giving rise to cat-and-mouse (with Chunky, our housemaster) during all the after-hours dorm feasts. All to the shimmering light of our stashed torches.

All the masters, Chunky included, typically came with nicknames reflecting their diverse personalities and traits (Chunky actually wasn't, but somehow it suited).

Bomber, always in a hurry, took religious education.

Mantis, all spindly fingers and stealth, took chemistry.

The school was certainly less Victorian and religious in outlook (more a four-star hotel than Bleak House) albeit morning assembly came with hymns and an address. Food was typical school food. Chocolate sponge and 'chocolate' custard (which never really tasted of chocolate) but a more appetising and probably safer option than its nuclear pink alternative.

The first year finished and rolled straight in to the long hot summer of '76 complete with water ban, standing pipes and all. It also meant football in the evenings with the local kids (by jumping the fences of the nearby school). Jumpers down for as long as the light held and next goal wins.

Autumn 1976:

Maths...*worked very well throughout term, but unfortunately he did not score so highly in the end-of-term test.*

Physics...*a year of excellent work, disappointing exam results.*

Geography...*good work this term, but still very quiet in class.*

Biology...*written work satisfactory, little effort in discussion.*

History...*rather a disappointing result after an excellent terms work. Revision appears incomplete.*

Form master...*most reliable character.*

Housemaster...*he remains conscientious and trustworthy, and he is even a little cleaner! He has emerged still more of a character this term and appears settled and at ease with his peers and has made friends here. He remains quiet and self-reliant, but is beginning to come out of himself much more and can always be relied on to behave sensibly and helpfully...it is unfortunate that he seems to have lost momentum this year. He has the ability to be near the head of the group in every subject. Neither has he been quite so active in House activities and games. He must redouble his efforts next year.*

Headmaster...*this should give him the confidence to join more fully in oral work...a good report to take home...augers well for the future.*

Christmases at the big house in Alverstoke were eagerly awaited. Of the new presents of choice, Action Men were always fairly robust as toys went. Subbuteo football players on the other hand were quite fragile, many an opposition player tactically knackered by a retaliatory knee to even up the numbers, where a prior 'incident' had occurred. All my players were kitted out in Tottenham strip and, care of my modelling bias, painted to look the part. Ralph Coates and Alan Gilzean saved me a bit of paint and were integral to my plastic pals' performances. My modelling passion nearly cost me a few fingers worth of nails to chew (biting them a habit, particularly in exam season). My first trip to hospital happened after I sliced my thumb knuckle open with the modelling knife (a Sherman tank I think it was). I wasn't cut out for stitches (which would keep coming).

Christmases always came to their sudden end after all the wind-up. Goodbyes at the end of the holidays, even just a weekend or half term break, were always the hardest. I was never good at them. Not for any reasons of school itself, boarding being fine once back in to its rhythm, it was just leaving Robin who, to each of us in the family, was just like a best friend.

Unlike its predecessor, this school had nothing by way of a menacing undertone. A couple of the weirder masters hung around the showers counting the boys in and out and their nicknames (something of a warning flag) reflected it. Other than that generally 'spiteful' stuff was more clear and obvious…whether cling film over the toilet or the removal of all that weird tracing paper that seemed to be dressed up as toilet 'tissue'.

As with any school, the kids could be broken down into the usual suspects…the scrappers, the shit stirrers, sporties, bullies, the bullied, swots and the rest.

'Clear and obvious' in the late seventies extended to the bullies. Our school had a few of them just as any other did, then or now. There was no massaging over of grades, no levelling the playing field of ability back then. Your grades reflected how crap you were and…if marks were poor, you had any other incapacity or weakness or were just a fish out of water…you typically got bullied. On retaliation, the shit kicked out of you as well. If you were luckier, just your head shoved down the toilet and flushed.

It was one big melting pot. Sink or swim.

I could have been one of those tailor-made for pastings. Short-sighted, little, my mum's bowl haircuts; and her dress sense of me often bordered slightly on the tactical side of error. Particularly with the strange navy blue flock sports shorts she'd got me, which were pretty unique and hard to describe. They were longer than most and the material was not unlike the softer bit of Velcro. More 1870s than 1970s. Just me…and fortunately Plug, who played prop for the rugby team, which meant no-one was going to judge me on them. The rugby short match-up and my own continued pursuit of all things sporty allowed me to fit, if not quite in 'first-team' sporty camp, at least in with 'the rest'…invisible and immune once more to what might have been.

The worst that happened (generally from the kids at the other school in the area) was a shout from across the street of, 'Oi, speccy twat!' As in any match, name calling didn't really faze me. I concentrated on my own game.

Schoolboys didn't hold all the cards when it came to 'relative' degrees of violence. Oggy's weapon of choice was his infamous blackboard duster (launched with some force from afar at any unsuspecting talker), his favourite slipper providing back up, if needed. Retaliation back at him was more subtle with the more daring covertly putting sugar in his petrol tank.

Spring 1977:

French…*he usually does better than this.*

Physics / Biology…*both capable of better.*

Latin…*learning work disappointing on occasions.*

PE…*satisfactory progress.*

Form master…*he is helpful and polite, an excellent form captain…he is quiet and helpful in form and has discharged his duties as captain creditably. He enters fully in to the life of the school in his hockey.*

Housemaster…*he is popular amongst his contemporaries and seems happy and settled.*

Headmaster…*below what he is capable of in some subjects.*

Drifting in to being a teenager, the summer of '77 was both a strange and hollow one. Tottenham had just got relegated from the First Division…and it hurt. It had been a painful season of poor results. We also moved house again…more naval quarters, still in Alverstoke, but closer to Stokes Bay and the beach. Whilst our houses had been many, being in and around the Portsmouth area came with some bonuses. Not least, endless trips to the dockyards…whether Sunday lunch in the officers' mess of whatever ship my father was on, or up close and personal views of all the ships that I'd spent many a year making models of (HMS Victory being the pick of the bunch). The latest house came with a bigger upside. The start of a fresh term brought a new pupil, Paul, transferring in from a different school…and it transpired he lived just around the corner.

Paul was a game changer. As was the summer of 1978.

The end of the football season had seen Spurs climb up from the Second Division back to the First, their highlight being the 9-0 drubbing of a poor Bristol Rovers. Life's new up curve didn't end there.

The last night of term had been a masters and parents 'cheese and wine' evening out on the lawns (which usually created the opportunity for some drinks 'mine-sweeping' afterwards). As it was, with the masters occupied, the dorm were just chatting away in the dark. Usual after lights-out stuff. The door opening should have been a signal for the sound of tumbleweed, broken only by our standard weary, 'Who turned the lights on?' routine (when, or if, one of the masters ever walked in).

It was the prefects who wandered into the room. On a dorm raid.

'You should all be very quiet,' they said before literally tipping every bed upside down, chucked pillows out of the window and flung mattresses everywhere. And then legged it with a parting, 'Masters are coming!'

Masters did come.

In the form of Mantis.

Everyone grabbed what was left of any bed, mattress, sheet and pillow and pretended to be asleep.

The door opened and the switch flicked…to the weary chorus of, 'Who turned the lights on?'

Mantis saw straight through the camouflage. And a very displaced dorm.

'You!' he screamed, wiry finger pointing in the direction of his first victim (the bed remnant closest to the door).

'Um, yes, Sir?'

'What's been happening here?'

'Don't know, Sir.'

'Go and wait outside my room and wait to be caned.'

'You, what's been happening here?' wiry finger back to the fore of bed leftover two.

'Um, er…stripping beds, Sir?'

'You can all go and wait outside my room and wait to be caned.'

And so it was. Off to the master's chambers we went to gather for the feast. About twenty of us all lined up in our best pyjamas, waiting for one of Mantis' cover drives. The queue included the younger brother of one of the prefects whose bed they had left alone…and who had miraculously remained asleep.

'Wake up, wake up.'

'Why?'

'You're going to be caned.' Ouch.

The following day we were all home and hosed for the summer holidays, one stripe to the better.

Paul and I rendezvoused at Stokes Bay to meet some of his other friends. They were out on 'The Dolphin' (a small, isolated concrete 'pier' about twenty metres out to sea that allowed you to championship dive into ten metres of sea when the tide was in, or ten metres of shitty sludge when the tide was out). We swam over and climbed up.

'Hey, everyone,' announced Paul. 'School's out. Anyone want to see our arses? We got caned last night. Ian…show him yours.'

And that was it.

My first introduction to Jon was to show him my arse.

The rest of the summer came and went, notable only for a World Cup in which Argentina beat the Netherlands 3-1, Tottenham managing to secure the signings of two of the best of them, Ardiles and Villa.

Change was afoot at school too…or at least decisions on what subjects to progress to O-level. Art had been a consistent throughout my time there. The highlights of my school artistic career: a Clint Eastwood cowboy themed bit of driftwood drawing; and a 'pen and ink' Great White Shark that Picasso would have been proud of (which made the school magazine).

The here and now though became the first battleground for my left and right brain face off. O-level choices to be made. In the end art regrettably lost, taking both Latin and geography with it. As a much more scientific path loomed, I knew I should have stayed true.

Autumn 1978:

English…*developing as a literary critic, quiet and conscientious, strengths lie in retentive knowledge rather than imaginative analysis.*

French…*the 'exchange' will provide just the right stimulus.*

PE…*a much better year's work. Has gained in confidence since making the hockey team.*

Form master…*an extremely pleasant and courteous member of the form, without being in any way forward. He appears to be a most well-balanced character in all respects.*

Housemaster…*in many ways he is an exemplary boy. Sound results indeed, but they are not excellent and I cannot help feeling that excellence could and should be his goal.*

Headmaster…*seems to be working well within his capacity.*

English lessons with Chunky were generally both fun and memorable. Interspaced with reading, writing and poetry classics (the only one I remember being Burns' 'My Love Is Like A Red, Red Rose') were the ten minute talks we each had to give. Mine were on models (of the Airfix kind) and *Reach for the Sky*, the Paul Brickhill biography of flying ace, Douglas Bader. In desperation I had picked it off Mum's bookshelves but found it a relatively easy read (the general story if not the detail), one which told the moving story of the legless fighter pilot.

Easter '79 brought the French exchange trip, providing a stimulus, not wholly related to my French studies. Staying with a family in Cognac, the two weeks included a road trip to Toulouse, across the Pyrenees and to Lourdes at Easter to see the candlelight procession. What that trip brought, for the first time, was an awareness of a bigger world and the majesty of it. Away trips were fun.

On the home front, houses came and went (again). A small terrace in the middle of Alverstoke Village and, more significantly, a thirty-two acre hill farm in Carmarthen. One retained accessibility to the beach and its green areas. The other came with an altogether different playing surface, just perfect for running.

Robin had matured to be his own self. And even more 'dog'. Berserk when postmen called, but otherwise warm, loyal, faithful, devoted. The best pet a kid could have. We'd often walk down to the beach to catch up with Jon cycling over from his place in Lee-on-Solent. On one eventful day, walking with Paul, Robin decided the jumpers of someone else's football game needed watering. As Paul had the lead, he took all the flack, one for the team and became an even better mate. Paul's influence at this stage was growing, not just for mucking about with whilst at school, but also with his circle of friends and the extra they brought to the table.

Each had a different skill-set…whether home-brewing, board game playing, generally loafing…or music.

My music repertoire hadn't evolved much at this point in time. Most of it from either cassette tapes of the radio charts or listening to my parents records…Boney M, Andy Williams, Barbara Streisand, Johnny Mathis, Herb Alpert and the Tijuana Brass. Those and the London musicals of the day…*Jesus Christ Superstar* and *A Chorus Line.* Hardly a distinguished mix for a teenager of the day. Enter Alun.

Alun was part of the Paul and Jon circle of friends (both Alun and Jon were at St John's, Southsea). Alun was more 'masters of rock' and had pretty much every classic vinyl in his record room…Black Sabbath, Yes, Rainbow, Led Zep, Deep Purple, Rush…as well as copious quantities of home brew. I'm not sure what I went round there for most over time…the musical appreciation or the ale…but being round there with 'the gang' was an education.

And a sense of belonging.

Back at school, vinyl was the colour of money…colour being the operative word. There existed a roaring trade in singles…all colours of the rainbow as picture discs went…a blue Blue Oyster Cult '(Don't Fear) The Reaper' here and white and brown Dr. Feelgood 'Milk And Alcohol' there, all adding to my new collection and interest. The 45s were small change though. LPs were where it was at.

The first LP I ever bought was *Eagles Live*.

I think it was the cover. A red travel case. Reflections of life on the road.

School reports as I headed towards O-levels consisted by now of a lot of 'fair and pleasing', 'good but I expected better' and 'signs of hasty revision'.

I had other interests. And not just vinyl.

Opportunities for playing sport had become endless.

Before arriving at Churcher's, I'd always lived for football. This was an autumn term rugby, spring term hockey school though. The playing of both games was new to me. Rugby came with my sight hindrances. Hockey at least allowed glasses and some degree of level playing field. In the '70s, health and safety concerns were never the uppermost of thought processes, particularly in hockey. And goalkeepers especially. Bamboo face masks, cricket pads and sometimes jumpers for chest guards made for a random and worrying set of 'protective' equipment. The weather was often never a show-stopper either. The blizzard and settling snow we once played in was memorable, if only for the hour after standing by the radiator in the library thawing out fingers.

I was never any good at gymnastics. The wooden horse box, straight out of *The Great Escape*, was a proper beast. It, the long benches, the wall racks and hanging ropes were all great for the endearingly fun, but spectacularly non health and safety, game of 'Pirates'. Not liking heights particularly, I was never the best of pirates. Five-a-side was my strong point (maintaining as much as I could my love of football) and the gym of a night became both my friend and a safe harbour. If numbers were short, I'd always make sure I was on the side with the fewest players. It was something I had become extremely good at (which I put lovingly down to those trusted old wellies) and I gave it my all. Almost (but not quite) to the point of obsession.

It was the one arena in which I was, temporarily, king.

The main school hall was (by day) all hymns (no arias), an occasional exam hall and cinema room at weekends. By evening, in the winter months, it was an extension of either the school fields or the gym (if otherwise engaged). Tennis ball five-a-side football became the norm, and honed the skills further. Scarcely an evening went by without dragging anyone I could find into a game of some description (often as not, just another attempt to recreate 'that' Glenn Hoddle volley against United).

The summer term came and the unfeasibly cold outdoor swimming pool found itself in play. Never really my scene again as, not being able to see without my glasses, meant in swimming races I inevitably zig-zagged from one rope to the other like a drunk walrus, generally swimming twice as far as anyone else.

Sports days too I was never usually in. There was always someone in my house (Nelson) who was faster at any race or who could throw further or jump higher. Occasionally I'd get onto the cross-country team, a legacy of those 6:30 a.m. runs and all the after-hours cardio.

The summer of 1980 brought the end of the first serious wave of exams. I had managed twelve O-levels…religious studies, history, maths, human biology and German all at A grade, the balance at B. Time for A-level choices, a fork in the path that would determine the direction of the rest of my life. In hindsight what had interested me most, I had (typically) always performed best in...history, biology and languages. Like poor art, they never made the cut.

Before going down the path of no return at school, that summer brought a number of other life defining events...

...mass excursions to cinemas for the new wave of 'big' movies: *Return of the Jedi* (queuing round the block) and *Life of Brian* (memorable as much for the film as its *Away from it All* travel monologue and pastiche of Venetian gondoliers). I was now tagged to and part of that wider circle of friends.

...Alun's O-level party and industrial scale introduction to beer. And girls. The latter a very brief and unsuccessful foray care of the former. Nonetheless, both were firmly on a small, bespectacled, teenage map going forward.

...my mum's hysterectomy; perhaps the catalyst for the start of her darkest days.

Take It To The Limit
1980 - 1982

Time shapes you.

For me, mates were a major step up and on from those lost and lonely Old Ride letters and days. Beer had become something of a rite of passage. Major hospital operations, nearly slicing off fingers excepted, were a new (and slightly worrisome) episode. And, some six or so years after 'I love you girl', they (girls) were back in the charts.

Another new year, our Lower Sixth, was momentous at the school for one very specific reason. Having solely been a boys' school for well over two hundred years, Churcher's was, for the first time, admitting girls. Our year became the test arena. Those first five (the 'Famous Five' as they were to be known) were an experiment on the school's behalf to go co-ed. The girls took it, and all the turned heads, in their stride.

With every other hound on their scents though, for me the first academic year of the new decade became merely an opportunity to embrace and develop just one thing.

Sport.

Up until now, it had all been pre-season training.

From here on in, it consumed me.

I was actually quite good…it was just that I couldn't see.

Contact lenses had come in to fashion and I had them. Unfortunately they were of the 'hard' variety which meant they were of no use to play rugby in, but not a problem for five-a-side football or hockey where, in both cases, I could still wear my glasses (now horribly ridiculous, being metal framed and, in the absence of lens technology, with thick lenses). I was a before my time Napoleon Dynamite.

In pretty much every case of sport at school, there will be that one oversized lad who just runs through everyone and who most of the play centres through. That wasn't me.

Not being able to see much on the field then, big or small, meant that my rugby had to be more instinctive, but gave me a superpower...one that reduced everything, including the big lad, to pretty much the same shape and size (a blur, basically). Everything that moved in relative proximity got tackled (grabbed, bundled or chopped depending on how good, or off, my judgement and radar was). Most of the time the tackles were perfect technique and big or small, hurt or not, I built a game on it.

Except for the one I didn't play.

The Second XV home game to Seaford College. Physics at 10 a.m. would never be anyone's preferred way to start a weekend, but back then we had Saturday morning lessons. This particular one I didn't make. Felt ill and went to the sick bay where I stayed in bed for the rest of the day. From the window adjacent I could see our game going off in the distance in the afternoon. The first game I'd either been late for or 'cried off' from. Having felt 'a little better' going in to the early evening, as it was an out-weekend, I then made a slow trip to Petersfield station and took the train to Portsmouth Harbour. All in some considerable agony. On being picked up by Mum at the Gosport Ferry, I fainted. One quick trip to hospital...and one appendix straight out.

Two weeks later I was back in school to be told that the games master had suggested I had pulled out of the game because I hadn't wanted to play it (they only had fourteen players after early injuries and lost).

I never forget the unjust sentiment and was never late to or missed a game ever after. Well...for forty years.

A-levels were now in play. I couldn't miss those.

Autumn 1980:

Chemistry...*usual consistent thorough manner, a pleasing exam result which promises well for the future.*

Physics...*has a marked, reserved attitude in class but achieves high standards in work. With attention to clarity and detail, an A grade is expected. Suffers from a lack of self-confidence to some degree but capable of B/A. Continuous revision required.*

Maths with Statistics…*he has benefitted from all last year's additional work and, but for his recent absence, would have done well in his exams. Made splendid progress and should gain grade A.*

Housemaster…*appears to have fully recovered from his recent illness and is well settled again. He has been a splendid help in the house and in the school drama. Grateful for his contribution to the Nelson House play.*

Headmaster…*the sort of work we would expect from him. I am pleased he is fit again and thank him for his help with the play. This reflects his high promise…he appears difficult but he has justified assurance academically and knows where he is going.*

Dibble was the complete opposite of Flynn and a breath of fresh air with it. Helpful whenever, he actually seemed to care. Exercising of discipline not his strong point, generally leaving that to his lieutenants, he was (in part) responsible for a certain empathy and calm…whilst the general school chaos ensued around him.

He also gave me another leg up. Being both the smallest and specciest, I was quite often overlooked (and by default 'available') after the 'who gets picked first' line-ups. Dibble set me on (what would be) a lifetime's journey of hockey, care of one game. He'd grabbed me on a free transfer the previous spring when not considered for the Under 16s, to fill in a Saturday gap for (his) hockey Second XI. I scored two corkers on my debut and remained happily with the Seconds until the end of my school days…Dad's hockey stick (I never seemed to have the 'street cred' kit), glasses and all notwithstanding.

I'd found somewhere where I didn't have to hide and as teachers went, I would always remember his name.

Scheduled sport aside, the other traditional 'activity' was the Combined Cadet Force. Split up into RAF (main event, pulling the glider), Navy (main event, canoes in the arctic swimming pool) and Army (mainly cleaning rifles), it was either one of those three or the Community Service. I was, proverbially, 'in the Army now' and…aside from stripping down the .303s…we had range shooting (couldn't hit any kind of barn door with my glasses, unless it was in hockey) and night exercise expeditions over at nearby Longmoor (couldn't readily see in the day, so nights were going to be fun). We once bumped in to some regulars who (based on insignia) might have been SAS and who were looking for some guy they had lost.

We have all been there. Well, not in the SAS…but, lost. Mine came on the week-long Army camp in Jerby, over on the Isle of Man. Not my coolest experience, managing the abseiling and somehow getting up and over Mount Snaefell in a freezing pea-souper, wearing little by way of proper protection other than my Harrington jacket. On the night exercise to finish I did manage to lose half a platoon…the half behind me (with me included). Mistaking the branch in front of me in the dark for a raised arm to signify 'stop', we waited twenty-odd minutes before it became clear it wasn't an arm, and we weren't with the rest of the troop anymore. But hey…if it was good enough for the SAS, then it was good enough for me.

As sports years went, 1981 was one of the greatest.

It started with my first trip to Cardiff Arms Park to watch the Schweppes rugby cup final between Bridgend and Cardiff. Cardiff won a poor game, but my memories were stoked by being with my uncle on the supporters' coaches out of Porthcawl. A first real rugby experience and a chance to see JPR Williams (having just retired from international rugby). The whole escapade turned out to be exactly how Max Boyce had described in song it would be.

It was the year of both *Gregory's Girl* and *Escape to Victory* which, depending on your point of view, were arguably the best and worst football movies ever.

Gregory could seemingly do no right in his quest for the object of all his school's football team's affection...Dee Hepburn's head-turning character 'Dorothy'. In the end, Clare Grogan's girl next door, 'Susan', turns out to be 'the one'. Gregory was me. Turning my head way too often for a 'Dorothy' designate and missing any 'Susan' similes.

Ossie Ardiles, stalwart of *Escape To Victory* on the other hand could do no wrong and Tottenham had made the one hundredth FA Cup final against Manchester City.

Come the afternoon of Saturday 9 May (my prep school cricketing exploits pretty much exempting me from those school duties) I was sat and settled in the prime seat in the college TV room. The only contrasting noise to Wembley (and commentators Brian Moore and Jack Charlton), that of dear Pip, one of our peers, revving his Capri in the car park below. Tottenham stalled on the big day and everyone recalls exactly what happened next. First, Ricky Villa's long and lonely walk back to the tunnel on being substituted as Tottenham barely kept themselves in the game, eventually squeezing a draw. And then the long wait until Wednesday for the replay. Evening prep complete, TV in the common room on and a mesmerising game unfolded. A cup final to stand alongside Wolves in 1972. Villa's redemption via his legendary, mesmeric dribble became one of Tottenham's most iconic moments and with it the cup was won. Aside from Mantis' big night out those three years before, this final, this evening, became the most memorable boarding school takeaway. Tottenham were always good for a special night out, even if they only came once a decade.

This one easily slipped in to my Spurs top five games.

Hard (as a Spurs fan) to beat, but that summer just kept on giving.

It was the year of Botham's Ashes, the third Test of which started on my birthday. With England looking all but out of it, Jon and I went to Lee-on-Solent beach for a long walk and to play games at the arcade. We returned to find Botham and Dilley had produced the fireworks to give England a very small chance. We left again the next day to go to the beach with the Australians cruising towards their opponents' meagre total. Bob Willis shamed both us and the Aussies whilst we'd been away. England, miraculously, had drawn level in the series…

…and with it Jon and I started a lifetime of missing the bigger moments whilst enjoying skimming stones and the little ones.

The last week of July saw Paul and I, sponsored by my school for 'educational reasons' (in our case 'famous' stone circles), cycling from Portsmouth to the farm in Wales. I'd blagged a good write-up to pay for the trip on the loose theme of the relative importance of 'rocks'. Jon came along as 'holiday' wingman.

For our first night, we camped at a site near Old Sarum, just outside of Salisbury. Our second day took us through Amesbury and on to Warminster for a deserved lunch. We found a cosy roadside pub that we reckoned we would (at seventeen) get food and cider (the real reason for our week long camping expedition). Beer (and cider) had started to become an important part of Saturday night boarding life. Pretend 'out passes' for the, ahem, cinema morphed in to a half in a pub garden (led by Pip amongst others, bought by the big lad). Pip was a complex character. Amiable at times, angry at others, but a great all-round sportsman to boot.

We had cider and a hearty ploughman's for lunch that cycling day, memorable for an innocuous event that shaped a lifetime's deep friendship still further. It was the cheddar that did it. Mine specifically, as a massive lump fell off my crusty loaf into Jon's pint. Quizzical looks as to what might happen next. Cue falling around with laughter. Simple (and stupid) in execution the Royal Oak pub had served us well.

Stones (various) photographed over the next few days we hit Cardiff on about day four, expecting a tortuous ride. The streets were empty though, being the day of the Royal

Wedding. Care of Charles and Di we made very good time to Porthcawl, where we set up the tent (two person, with three of us in it) in the Happy Valley campsite on what was Paul's birthday (all three of us had July birthdays, Jon being but a week older than me). My uncle met us that evening at The Breaksea and treated us to more cider than we were capable of handling. At seventeen, this was the first time we'd had a proper 'session', upgrading the sneaky boarding school corner of the pub garden ones. The journey back to the tent involved falling off bikes and a noisy (us) campsite.

Having succeeded in our main objectives (stones and cider) and waking up with heavy heads, the train completed our 'ride' from Cardiff to Carmarthen.

The Ashes moved onto the fourth Test. That game was petering out and rugby sevens were on another channel. In those days with just the three (and with no direct means of recording anything) a sporting clash became a big dilemma. Cricket lost the toss again only to find, on changing back half an hour later that Botham had ripped through the Australians again in our absence.

Lessons learned.

Never give up on anything. Or anyone.

The summer gave way to crisp autumn days and a last year of school. Rugby had, for now, become a playing passion and like in hockey I'd made the school Second XV. Always desperate for someone to watch me, Mum was ever there.

A final term of school rugby finished with moments I wouldn't forget whenever I finally hung up all my boots.

Best kick, best mate, best team, first team.

We played Portsmouth Grammar on the main pitch and an injury during the game to our kicker left us with no-one to take penalties. As part of my evening post-prep activities I'd often lined a few up, so stepped up to the mark. We (or I) had three opportunities. Without my glasses or contacts, proper shooting in the dark and not unlike my range firing.

One wide left, one wide right and the one right through the middle. It was windy, but I disproved the barn door theory.

Farlington Marshes, just outside Portsmouth, was a rare opportunity for Jon to 'watch' a game with me. Our school were playing his. I'd assumed he was late arriving (as the game kicked off) although there wouldn't have been much chance of me seeing him during the game as I was playing. It transpired he had turned up, they were short of a prop and he'd got drafted in at the eleventh hour to play. He'd also come up to me several times during the game and said, 'Hello!' but whilst I may well have tackled him, I had quite literally never seen him. We won, I'd set up the deciding try, but the fact we had managed to share a pitch together somehow added the pickle to our ploughman's cheese.

Our House had a good side that season…many of the first XV…and the Inter House tournament came down to Nelson and Drake. I'd got a centre berth (tackling prowess, rather than for size and impact). The game was close, if unspectacular. The one opportunity came from our twenty-five. Passed the ball I just ran and ran and ran. Diagonally up the pitch. Sheer pace was never my forte, but I managed the opposition twenty-five before being set upon by two players. Dinz, the only person who knew what I was doing (I didn't) had followed up and recycled for a try and a 10-4 win. One of the best rugby teams I'd played in.

The last game I remembered was my big chance. I was on the bench for the 1st XV. Pip, having a good game in the centres (and doing a great job of containing the strong pairing opposite him) got injured. Sent on to replace him I promptly missed the only tackle I ever remembered doing. I hadn't got used to the pace of the game, my outstretched arm way off my opposite man who went on to score the only (and winning try). I tackled anything that moved after that and looked a good fit…but the damage was done and the ribbing on Monday full-on. One missed tackle was all that anyone, including me, ever remembered.

A-levels loomed. Recalling anything academic wasn't a strong point.

Easter 1982:

Maths 67 A...*if he revises thoroughly and keeps his head he should gain an A or B.*

Chemistry 55 C/B...*attention must be given to the practical.*

Physics 52 C...*disappointing result from a chap who promised much more. Care needs to be taken and spent on a plan of revision.*

Form master...*concerned that he has not yet had an offer of a place at university.*

Housemaster...*always appears happy and well settled.*

Headmaster...*he will not be satisfied with these scores. There should be a university offer in the pipeline, but he should see me if he hears nothing.*

Tottenham pulled another FA Cup out of the bag to set up a last summer of sitting row by row in the gymnasium with the smell of freshly mown grass and the hum of a mower.

A-levels, with whatever the results would bring, were all but complete.

Our housemasters treated us to a full-on dinner at the West Meon Hut to celebrate a final boarding term. Treated like grown-ups as school days reached their conclusion, the beer and liqueurs flowed. Back at the room we shared, Paul and I tried climbing the scaffolding outside our dorm room later that night. Not the best of moves, given our relative disposition. Accidents inevitably happen and, being by now the complete teenager, the diced carrots spewed forth into the flat roof space below.

The next morning at breakfast was a heavy one. Feeling very green. And not helped by the pebbledash splatter on the skylight windows on the upper walls.

Turning eighteen just after the end of term heralded a new dawn of (legal) pub crawls. One of Jon's many talents was his ability to look mature enough to get mistaken for everyone else's dad…and consequently the best beer round getter-inner ever, no questions asked.

The birthday itself was spent on a pub crawl of Lee-on-Solent (The Wyvern, The Bun Penny and Belle Vue) and a cycle back over to Alverstoke and The Village Home. We ended up glamping in a shed at the bottom of the garden. It could have been a make-believe Wembley final goal at any other time but, in those early hours, all we really cared about was more beer. Our cups were overflowing.

Education should always be judged by what we remember after we've forgotten everything we were taught at school.

I don't recall the specific details of any lessons, save the odd blackboard duster, ten minute English presentations or the 'phosphorous' episode (where, and just for a change, it was a teacher who started the fire). I could therefore only judge my educative school days on the following…

…boarding school whilst generally 'okay' was still a lot of people trying to find an identity to call their own; some winning, some losing.

…solace in sport anywhere I could find it…be it rugby, hockey, football out on the playing fields or five-a-side in the gym (or with a tennis ball in the school hall).

…the goals and tries I scored.

…Tottenham, Wales and the Eagles.

School was out.

First album, beer session and 'I love you'.

And first signs of Mum's mental health struggles.

Pretty Maids All In A Row
July 1982 - June 1983

Being an (or The) Alchemist, it seems, was always going to sit way above my aspirational career prospects…and any paygrade.

My chemistry, they said, might not have been my own work. I think they were implying I cheated. Being either a (first choice) vet or a doctor wasn't going to happen…the latter most definitely not after a car crash of an interview at St Thomas' Hospital the year before.

Cheating way back then normally consisted of writing answers under your watch strap, one side of your rubber or carefully disguised notes amongst the blotting paper blobs. Hardly larceny on a grand scale. The simple fact that doing chemistry practical, reading small percentage increments and trying to see colour changes were beyond my eyesight didn't matter. You play what's in front of you…which for me, just as in rugby, was a lot of random guesswork.

My A-level mock results hadn't supported the necessary grades to get a place at Cambridge. But I went through the motions and the tours anyway. Perhaps because my father went there, it was something to hanker after. I didn't really know at the time. In the end the mocks didn't lie. Two Ds and a C post exam day weren't going to get me anywhere.

I was always told that if you didn't know your subject by the night before, then no amount of last minute cramming would make you ready for the coming day's exams. Playing football the evening before then wasn't really wasted time. The school concluded that, based on our school work, the results of mine and two others were significantly below any expectation and our papers were sent for a recheck. Not an arithmetical recount (the irony that my maths result might not have been correct because someone hadn't added it up properly)…just for some additional review comments.

In maths I…*'failed to begin Question 3 (inequalities) in a valid manner and made some mathematical errors in Question 4 (quadratic equations with complex roots) to name but a few. Two questions were near perfect solutions* (probably the first two, and most of the time I had spent in the exam, trying to be note perfect) *but little progress had been made on the straight line - circle question. This was clearly a candidate of above average ability. A tendency to work and then to think again was shown in some of the Section A questions…this may have caused a degree of panic so that insufficient time was allowed for later questions.'*

Peter Panic Pants heading in to those last five minutes. Sounds about right. Tripped over those complex roots.

In chemistry I'd…*'confused isotope with allotrope as well as an incorrect definition of standard electrode potential. And at times was unintelligible.'* As to 'the practical'? We knew what happened there…*'the table for results were clearly altered without enough care being taken. It seems that the original readings were amended. The observations were not very accurate and in several places alterations were made. The alterations sometimes resulted in the answer no longer making sense.'*

Back where we were then, basically saying 'I'd cheated'. Like, proper full on make-believe. Surprisingly astute from a person who neither knew me or wasn't there. With no knowledge of me, save some random scribbles, someone could see right through me. Not for the first and probably not for the last time.

And on that note, my school life passed, along with first career choices or, more left field, advertising.

It had all kicked-off so well. Top of the class in my first junior school term and slaloming downhill pretty much all the way from there. Possibly discipline and exam technique had got to me. Possibly also beer, music and sport.

A chink of light (of sorts) with an offer of a place at the University of Southampton doing a Business Economics and Statistics course, if the maths and chemistry D grades were upped to a B and a C.

With what paltry practical mark I had being held over, the written chemistry paper could be retaken on its own, after the summer.

Maths would follow in the next year.

A year off was coming.

I hoped faking chemistry wouldn't come back to haunt me in years to come.

The summer of 1982 brought my first paid job. Six weeks at the Royal Albert Hall in the month before, and during, Proms Season, selling tickets. All it entailed was sitting in a room at the top of the round of the Hall, picking up the phone every time it rang, taking details for bookings. All a manual process. But with the advantage of listening to live rehearsals all day for their coming performances. Easy to walk to, beautifully relaxing and as (work) places go one of the best. Once again, started at the top; only one way to go.

Having moved out of Alverstoke, the family home was now being split between some modern terraces in a new development in West Kensington and the Welsh farm. I found myself mobile in London for the first time and West Kensington (and the West End) proved to be a good night out for the Alverstoke crowd. Jon and Alun pitched up for a celebration weekend. Big trouble in Chinatown as things kicked off around us, hatchets (not ours) and all.

A huge awakening of sorts to the world outside.

Freedom came in many forms, with soft contact lenses being the biggest game changer of them all. It also came with a relative independence, the biggest opportunity being the August 1982 Charity Shield at Wembley. Not just at the traditional home of English footy but, for one day only, of Tottenham. The opponents for a first ever glimpse of The Lilywhites, Liverpool. Heroes come and go, but this was a Tottenham of 'legends'…Perryman, Hoddle, Ardiles, Villa, Crooks, Archibald and Hughton. Not bad for a first sight of my immortals and watching my beloved team coincided with a young Gary Mabbutt playing his debut Tottenham game. My dad told me he'd actually played with Mabbutt's dad back in his own Aylesbury days. Wembley wasn't too bad a place for either of us kids to start. His career would go on to be stellar. I'd always be watching on the sideline.

Chemistry gained the requisite C. Having put a case to the University that a full year out in the real business world rather than time out to improve my maths grade would be time better spent, they bought it. Maths retake waived left the rest of the year free to get on with life.

I had started some useful employment at a subsidiary of BP (where Dad, since retired from the Navy, now worked). These were the very early development days of commercial software for military applications. The end product of their prototype battlefield artillery system would be a proverbial brick (and some)…in reality totally impractical for everyday strategic use. Given the project's military application I had to sign the Official Secrets Act. All terribly exciting for me and all very James (not Basildon) Bond. The project sadly didn't need anyone in to fast cars, guns and arty shots of women. Just someone to make copious amounts of tea and photocopy a few trees. I'd found my level.

The company was located at Sanderson House, just up from Soho. The building was a one-time carpet showroom straight out of the sixties. And the hardest part of the job? Getting through that extra hour and a half to five o'clock on top of what used to be school chucking out time. The walk back to Embankment tube of an evening was always an interesting one, not least when the dark nights came in. Soho's reputation was still one of untamed and unashamed devilry, despite the sex industry's decline in the '80s. Out of the shadows would be some fur-coated lady smiling and whispering, 'Hello, darling.' If not, some random guy with a range of photos depicting the same ladies. 'Which one?' they'd ask. Easy to ignore, with a pick up in the pace of my walk, but a further education in the seedier side of life.

Photocopiers, tea making and a small wage packet aside, the project had other advantages, namely regular post-work outings. At that time, places like Le Beat Route in Greek Street were embracing an emerging (New Romantic) music scene. Best avoided. The Coach and Horses and De Hems Dutch Bar, proper boozers, became regular haunts.

The relative merits of Spandau Ballet and Duran Duran aside, my fledgling concert career was about to get lift-off. Bowie's 'Serious Moonlight Tour' evolved to Supertramp's goodbye event at Earls Court. Both classics of their time.

They were also the days of, ahem, Hoddle and Waddle and 'Diamond Lights'. Football down at BP's huge sports facilities in Sydenham were an added bonus. They provided regular Saturday fixtures and five-a-side tournaments were plentiful. Dad came and watched the one game that I recall him doing without Mum. I scored the single goal of a very dull game, severely injuring my ankle in the process. The following week's walk home after work was reduced to the slowest of hobbles. If not leaving me exposed (figuratively speaking) it still put me right in Berwick Street's full firing line. Frank McLintock, Arsenal legend and guest referee at one of our five-a-sides, did however manage what Soho's finest couldn't…booked me for a dangerous tackle.

I booked myself one Saturday after a game. Sydenham was about twenty minutes out of Charing Cross on those old six-seater 'contained' carriages. Beer made the twenty minute rail journey about fifteen minutes too long, there being no on-train exit from the carriage to any toilet. Every single physics lesson should have taught me that throwing something out of a moving half-hitch window tended to blow said objects back in. And when said objects were wee out of a plastic cup, subsequently having to wear it catches you up on life lessons very quickly.

Why do we grow up so fast?

We probably all pretty much go through our biggest life step change having left school. Big decisions to be made.

For some we took the obstacles on, however clearly we were able to see them, or however high or impossible they seemed. Sometimes the road isn't a clear one.

The year had started with the terrible news that Pip, our old chum, had committed suicide. In the Capri. It seemed unfathomable whilst at school that something would have been on his mind but clearly his mental state, whatever it was, had been carefully concealed. In hindsight, signs were there, but only in sporadic moments or little episodes. Our form master, years later, said he always wondered what else he or anyone could have done. There was little any of us could have, except to have seen and appreciated him when at his best, mostly on a sports field where he was a natural.

For Mum, the signs of her own mental struggles had been prevalent for quite a while. London and the smaller, more claustrophobic house couldn't hide her troubles any longer.

The sad morning of Saturday 7 May, 1983, was both my father's birthday and the day of the ambulance to Charing Cross Hospital to section my mother. There was (and is) no getting away from mental health. Directly or indirectly, it hits the people you have loved the most and lived a lot with. In Mum's case, that day the psychosis reached a peak.

Schooling away had given me the best of memories in the holidays, albeit fleetingly. She had always been there to listen to me. In the back of an ambulance I had no words.

In the weeks and months that followed, art became her therapy, both on her (mixed) ward in the hospital and once out. Colour therapy of sorts. I had given art up at school to save time for the raft of other O-levels and, watching my mum paint I knew it would always be the one (subject) that got away. It was the only creative thing I knew and could do (models aside).

Trying to stay both strong and silent took an immediate toll. The relative naivety that comes with being eighteen was about to lead to growing up fast. What happened in the weeks and months that followed for me became a fixed routine. Tea making by day, glasses from the Bacardi bottle by my bed by night. Evening runs on my made up circuit along the Thames through Hammersmith over to Barnes. Football on Saturday afternoons, a pub on the way home.

Repeat.

The tea making kept me sane. Writing 'Dear Jon' letters added to the restorative therapy and his tales of a hatred of ghee drenched Indian food aboard his merchant navy ship came back by way of return.

The bottle of Bacardi stared me out at most turns and became a battle of wills. The pub became an excuse. Partly to hide, but mostly to fawn over the Texan barmaid who looked the spitting image of Linda Blair in *The Exorcist* (a little older and without all the theatrical make-up and pea-spew).

The opportunity came one Saturday night. Ordinarily I would have drowned my sorrows and time warped myself back home. That night must have been following a good game of football. The offer of the post pub party with the entire bar crew (the head turning Miss Texas included) and various other pub patrons back at some flat nearby was too good an opportunity to miss.

It must have been one of my better games. The pub was a crazy mess, everyone there just about staggering to the party. Hollywood's finest look-alike was indeed there. Not that I would have known, and that she'd even have cared, with my very much shocker of a sozzled state. Another one that slipped away. Just about the only thing I remember is being sick and waking up later, propped against a lounge wall of the flat, after most guests had gone. The only other people there, a random assortment of properly passed out drunks and some couples crashed on the sofas. What also, one has to assume, was the party host (who more closely than not looked like a popular TV sitcom star of the day) wandering around naked, generally cleaning up. Awkward.

I left. And ran. And ran. And ran.

As rites of passage go, something of a car crash. All very humbling.

Drinking (bad). Honking (very bad).

If not out of control, not especially in control. My mind all over the place, I was a powder keg waiting to explode.

Running from all my problems was a race I wasn't going to win. At some point I was going to need to get chased by something (preferably not the past or from a horror movie) or…find something, or somebody, to chase.

Boys Of Summer
August 1983

I remember the oncoming driver. Mostly his eyes. One of those heart-in-mouth, squeaky bum occasions that happen. As pant-soiling moments go though I wasn't going to be tossing a coin to see who got to clean the seats.

If you are going to (try and) live in the fast lane you will need a car with the ability to at least take it on. Jon's old Escort Estate was all we had though on our end of school days (for me) road trip down to Falmouth.

Nobody on the road…except us. Or at least up until we tried to overtake a caravan which Jon's jalopy didn't really have the legs for. As it chugged and wheezed its way past, the car coming over the horizon on our new side of the road was approaching faster than something out of *Death Race 2000* (the Stallone one).

It had been a short but evolving friendship at that stage. Who knows who your best mate in life is going to be? And at what stage of it do you find them? Sometimes you meet a person and you just click. You're comfortable with them, like you have known them your whole life, and you don't have to pretend to be anything or anyone else.

He would still have been doing the cleaning though, had not all that time at the amusement arcade manoeuvring a *Defender* spaceship suddenly become time even better spent.

Jon was a very funny guy and he killed me a thousand times over with just his humour and its timing. This time though, he did nearly kill me…timing and some slide rule precision meant we were still paradise bound.

It was the summer of Wham! with Falmouth just as you might expect to find it in a heady, hot '80s. Freedom was, quite literally, in the air. And we had a week's pass on Jon's uncle Bernie's twenty-nine footer which was moored up in the estuary.

When you hear a great song…that great song doesn't try to be anything. It just is. And when you hear it for the first time you can remember where you were. Mostly, for us, The Laughing Pirate. And when it reached chucking out time, I'd persuade Jon to go to Shades Nightclub…mirrors, sticky floors, sweat and smoke. Not typically his scene, but 'Club Tropicana' belting out every night at least secured us another beer or two. Arguably not the greatest song ever, but the prospect of another beer in a bar down by the sea somehow cemented the time and the place…and for me offered some kind of respite. Some kind of switch-off. We would sit, listen and chat.

And then chat some more.

I'd have my day out in the disco sunshine another time.

Jon and I might as well have been Gregory and his mate Andy from the film, thumbing a lift to Caracas (where in the film, all the girls were supposed to be). The girls passed us by, the surf dudes having sewn the 'Dorothy' market up. The yacht, our biggest statement piece, never got used for anything other than a late night crash pad. Chilling on the beach and watching the world go by as good as we got.

Life, as in sport, throws people at you who you can rely on to cover your back.

That summer in Falmouth cemented Jon as one of life's proper line-backers. The only one to stop the tears.

On Saturday 3 September I walked from the house down to Craven Cottage to see Fulham against Portsmouth in a Division Two game…past Charing Cross Hospital, where I had last been three months before.

The start of that season marked the first rumblings of cash and bigger things. The Football League had accepted its first ever sponsorship deal and live league football was to be shown on television for the first time since the 1960s. Coverage of matches was due to start that October. At the top of the (new) Canon League, the big question going into the season was whether or not anyone could overhaul the dominant Liverpool team of the era.

Portsmouth, my second team if I were to ever have one, were on the up and the game was on *Match of The Day*. Up on the old standing terraces I did everything but blend in, wearing a bright green mac…not your typical football fan. Portsmouth were great value for their 2-0 win though, with Mark Hateley and Alan Biley scoring. Later that evening on the TV, there I was, standing out from the crowd.

It wouldn't be the last time.

Spurs had started the season badly. A loss and a draw in their first two games, compounded on this day by a further loss to West Ham. The end of this season was a very long way off.

It had been a long summer in a short, but intense, bit of life. The good moments, those Tropicana nights, had been special.

Mum returned to the farm, her art continuing to be loving therapy. With Jon setting fair to Warsash for his merchant navy posting, I headed along the road to Southampton. A much larger pool of people. And girls…a small pot of gold perhaps at the end of some improbably luminous rainbow.

Just before going though, Mum came back from Wales. Without Robin. He'd died, a victim of bastard ticks.

Desperado
1983 - 1986

'I'm All Out Of Love' was all I heard in the opening weeks of my first university term.

As Business Economics and Statistics wasn't going to open that many doors, as soon as I arrived at university I tried to mutate it to something slightly less, ahem, snooze inducing. There were no 'disco' degrees back then and all they gave me back by way of barter was the laugh-in that was Business Economics and Accounting. Like something out of the *Life of Brian* twenty shekels scene I'd haggled my way well and truly down a road to nowhere.

Beggars can't be choosers.

Nowhere, though, was Southampton. Away from home again, although this time without the rules. No 'lights out' (and faux 'who turned them on'), no mandatory homework sessions, no routine. And the introduction of girls. Well, more than five, anyway.

Time to shed what'd gone before and make a new start.

My first day in my new halls centred on getting the simple things in place.

Tennis girl scratching arse (tick). Farrah in that red dress (tick). Athena posters sorted and Blu-tacked to my walls.

A 'Dorothy' (straight out of *Gregory's Girl*) was the first person I came across. On the floor above, pretty much the room atop mine…and the guilty party when it came down to 'not changing the record'. To the pleasant, but endless, renditions of Air Supply the friends started coming…Fully, Rupes, Skells, Tory, Meht, Greeny, Bing. With them, a lot more 'hellos' at the Glen (Hall) bar and a quest to find the three or four extras necessary for a mates football team.

Whilst Wednesdays and Saturdays were the University organised club games, Sunday was 'bring your own team' intramural. Having secured the missing players to join ours, 'Public Bar Wanderers' became our team name of choice. The game each season against 'We're Crap' (Welsh, Brads, Lofts, Chowds plus other associated GeogSoccers) became the 'derby' match. Sunday morning hangover park football at its finest. And scene of my dining out 'special' goal…the throw in, first time volleyed pass to me on the edge of the area and a right foot volley by me to the top far corner. To this day no-one remembers it. Just me in my dreams then.

All the exercise and training from a pre-university year-off meant being able to drink and still stand (in the early weeks of that first term) came easy. 'Hollow Legs' became my moniker, standing me in good stead. The sport flowed. Wednesday, Saturday and Sunday (morning) football and Sunday afternoon hockey…topped up with football fitness training and numerous other games of squash and five-a-side during the week. Run, run and run. Repeat. Sport all day long, with the occasional break for lectures and lots of time for my new found friends. Physically, I found myself in rude health and in a (relatively) good place.

Cooking would take a little time to master. Meals were provided that year but there was still room for a snack. The egg I left to boil for three hours before exploding, its poor remains blasted to the ceiling, stench unbearable, suggested 'a chef' might be a career too far as well.

Evenings were generally spent at the Glen Bar and, if a Saturday, the Glen Disco (a packed refectory hall pumping out '80s classics). A ticketed affair, which sold out quickly, the trick, as always with student life, was to devise the best way of getting in (ordinarily via the toilet windows, a feat that one of those Victorian child chimney sweeps would have been proud of). Memorable greasy burgers and cheap cocktails completed the set-up. Those were strange music years. 'Wake Me Up Before You Go-Go' inter-spliced with 'Like A Virgin', 'Wild Boys', 'Alive And Kicking' and woah, 'Under The Boardwalk' (the Bruce Willis version). For the 'cool' kids, the Spandau Ballet 'New Romantic' wannabes, coupling up as quickly as possible the singular objective.

For me and the rest of the guys, it was more about the drinking and the dancing (yet more exercise) and a hopeful at best 'excuse me' for 'Careless Whisper' when the slowies came on. And then we would all pile back to my room (the closest) where my trusted *Eagles Live* LP would go on that tech gadget of choice, the Panasonic stereo stack system.

Side Three. Track Five. 'Desperado'.

Recorded October 21, 1976, at The Forum, four lovely minutes of it became our boys 'n' beers end of play encore.

'Your prison is walking through this world all alone.'

Apt for all us singles, but no-one really knew how much deeper it ran for me. Physically great, mentally distant.

'You better let somebody love you, before it's too late.'

Heading towards December, Dorothy One above gained a new neighbour. Dorothy Two was late to the party, having been staying with a family (including tarantula in a bowl on the dining table) pending any student accommodation ever arising, which it had done. She seemed nice and had at least morphed their upstairs musical repertoire onto 10cc and 'I'm Not In Love'.

The Engineers Christmas Ball, the huge go-to event of the student year, was looming and tickets were always hard to come by. So too, someone to go with. I took a chance and the challenge and invited Dorothy Two. A first proper 'date'.

Date night came and everything was going swimmingly well…until she had to make a pre-arranged phone call at the public phone booths across the foyer…after which she switched herself off. Most first term students were juggling the new found freedom of university and their held-over secondary school relationships. She was, unfortunately, no exception. The 'boyfriend' threatened to call it off, she had a rethink and left university for good soon after. I'd like to hope, this being my first ever 'proper' date, that this wasn't some kind of weird chemistry coming back to haunt me, more so just another 'it was just that the time was wrong' moment.

Onwards I went, stumbling my way through the most nauseatingly bland degree. The booze cruises to Le Havre helped. As also the 'greatest pub ever', The Frog & Frigate (all spit and sawdust, singalong with the guitarist Derek and dancing on tables). All aided and abetted by the legendary Glen Halls Beer Festivals. Jon swung by from Warsash on many an occasion to more than make up the numbers.

As the first year came to its close, one of Tottenham's better teams advanced to the final of the 1984 UEFA Cup Winners Cup. The opponents were Anderlecht of Belgium. Given Spurs' squad contained many of those 'legends' who had won the FA Cup twice in the two years to close off my school days, this was an added bonus. Not least as it was a student party night at one of the nightclubs down in the Polygon area of Southampton. They were interesting years for Spurs. Their recent ambitious project building a new West Stand from scratch had run massively over budget, without really delivering any tangible increase in seats. The works pushed the club in to (at the time) significant debt, forcing it to be sold, with the hope that it would then move in more commercial directions.

Wednesday 23 May, 1984, was a night for strong nerves. The first leg of the final had ended 1-1 in Belgium against the defending holders. Over forty-six thousand crammed into White Hart Lane for the second leg. Almost as many, seemingly, in the pub we chose to watch it. Tottenham had been depleted by both injury and suspension going into the second leg. Ardiles was on the bench struggling for fitness. Hoddle was injured and Perryman was suspended after a booking in the first leg. It was also the last game for one of Spurs' greatest managers...Keith Burkinshaw, The General.

Last one too for those long-suffering nails of mine.

It was an epic night with tension levels going through the notches during each passing minute. As the second half progressed the Belgians scored, leaving Tottenham more and more desperate for an equalizer. With six minutes to go the stand-in skipper Graham Roberts pricelessly scored. Extra-time beckoned. As did the first of many of my Spurs' related dilemmas. Stay and watch them go to the wire in a European final. Or make it to the dodgy nightclub to dance the night away.

Fully and I arrived just in time for last entries. We had opted for Madonna yet, as luck would have it, still got the subsequent penalties which the nightclub happened to be showing. Twenty-one year old keeper Parks was the hero, with Spurs winning 4-3 on the spot-kicks (against a strange backdrop of Lionel, Michael and Kylie). They claimed their third European trophy in fairy tale fashion and, despite the interjections of prime-time Madge (or as well as), the game became the third entry in to my Tottenham top five.

We played Side Three, Track Five well in to the night by way of encore. No particular reason…except it was always saved for the end of an evening or any special occasion.

My second year at university found me with four others (all geographers) camped out in the Derby Road 'Red Light' area of St Mary's, Southampton. A lot of students, a lot of Indian families…and a lot of prostitutes. Generally all co-existing without a lot of bother. Meals in the first year halls (boiled eggs excepted) having been in the main provided, co-cooking in this new year consisted largely of those usual student staples…pot noodles, Findus Crispy pancakes and a team effort Sunday roast. Failing any of that, spring rolls from the Chinese takeaway near The Old Farmhouse pub.

It was a happy house. A couple of strange dynamics, but otherwise content. Even down to me being the birthday kissogram for one of the girls...all in the best possible taste. Stupid things like that. Even with the Meatloaf concert at the Gaumont, where one of the bikers in the row in front of us set light to a biker's jacket on the row in front of him (fight! fight! fight!). We had each other's backs. Again, not least for our house party which was going swimmingly until one of the girls grabbed me to say there were some guys at the door looking to come in. As this was a student party, I couldn't work out why they hadn't just gone for that old 'mates of Dave' chestnut.

'Can I help you guys?'

Okay, so you're drug dealers straight out of some *Miami Vice* episode, but let's keep up a pretend brave front here.

'Yeah…where's it all at?' came the pastel pastiche reply.

'What? I mean, sorry, it's a student party, come in. Let me get you a drink, show you around.'

I showed them the '60s plastic pineapple that held loose change, mostly two pences. A cold, damp, fungus adorned bathroom. Farrah. Tennis girl. Industrial volumes of cheap booze (French). A whole pile of very, very drunk students.

They left. As quickly as they had arrived. Muttering the words 'tosser'…or something to that effect. I would make a good doorman yet.

Aside from finding myself in the firing line of feuding bikers and the local drugs gang, it was also the first time I'd seen someone struggle with a debilitating (physical) illness fight for as long as he could, until he couldn't anymore. A close friend of one of the girls from our house. Really nice guy. Acutely and very sadly aware of his own mortality at the age of twenty, he died of leukaemia not long after.

Football kept providing a release for all the things that never quite made sense. I played for the University thirds and we trained over at the Wellington Sports Centre along with Southampton FC. Quite often we would be coming in as Peter Shilton went out.

'Morning lads,' he would say. A top guy in the moment and, out on the training pitches, great to watch. Nice days kept coming back for more.

Easter holidays were spent over at the farm. Apart from seeing Mum (and her mum's own recipe Spag Bol), all I did was clear acres of gorse (beset as it was with those hordes of ticks), muck out pigs and run around the hills. Lighting fires to clear the brush became a norm, along with solitude and air through the head. The rest of the animals…horses, cows, dogs and sheep gave it a very parochial feel.

The train down was always a lovely journey. Particularly when reaching Swansea and onwards along the coast, past Llanelli and up the Carmarthen estuary…Ferryside on one side and Llanstephan, with its Disney castle on the hill, the other. The castle stood majestic on its headland with the Laugharne estuary and Dylan Thomas' Boathouse set off to its rear.

Magic (or at least 'magic' nights) came on our return for the last term of the second year with, of all things, snooker. Dennis Taylor played Steve Davis in the 'black ball' final of the World Snooker Championship. It was riveting, it was draining, it was exhausting. Our house, two guys and three girls, sat through every second of it, the small TV capturing history…

…with Taylor wearing my old school glasses.

The family maisonette in Kensington had, by now, been swapped for a smaller flat (still on the same estate).

My twenty-first birthday party was an all-day one there, notable for also being the day of Live Aid. As parties go, a perfect musical complement, the show stolen by Queen.

Jon was now posted at sea…one of his letters summing up the mood.

'I'm not really interested in relationships at the moment. When the right person comes along they will probably hit me right between the eyes.'

Followed up not very long after.

'We were in this pub, I went to the toilet and this really big, ugly bloke came in and, for no apparent reason, hit me right between the eyes.'

Much the same applied. My world was watching sweaty blokes, with cheap aftershave, daring mates to down pints of whatever (which, being the University footy club, could have been literally anything). I'd become quite hard on the inside. Going in to my third and final year I isolated myself a little further. Back in Glen Halls again I took a room in another block, rather than a ten person apartment with the rest of the Public Bar Wanderers.

Little things keep you going. Like familiar faces.

I'd often walk past one of my faculty friend's friend (a proper Gregory's 'Susan') on the way to and from the main campus. We always smiled but never said anything. Susan One became a routine over the year, our meet on the walk and any other brief, if chance, encounter always lovely.

There was also Susan Two, who I got to know through her joining our Sunday afternoon hockey team. Transpired she lived in my block on the floor below. I liked her. She was lovely. She was fun. We talked at length over a tea or a coffee in her room, but I was still holding back, perhaps to avoid being hurt somehow. I had my degree to finish…in what would hopefully be a final year of exams. And a huge pile of magazines stacked in the corner of my room…the material of which would put any would-be date off.

Farmers Weekly (the 'magazine of the soil' as it was once marketed) is one of those magazines, like *Horse and Hound*, that ordinarily had its own very dedicated readership. Not normally my 'thing' but, as most of its hard-core material formed the basis of my 'stimulating' thesis *Milk Quotas: A Producer's Nightmare*, the stash of 'dirty' mags had to stay.

Holding back didn't prevent me taking any excuse to run. The Southampton Half Marathon (and four not very exciting laps of the Common) gave me a creditable time of one hour twenty-four minutes…but also made me realise I actually didn't like running.

As dirty went, the University football first team were as bad as any lads' club of the day. Not in terms of talent, in which they were as good a team as I'd seen. Unfortunately just completely idiotic with it. Their idea of fun inevitably involved someone else's pride and fall, weeing into snow boots at Portsmouth Poly the least of their crimes. In the absence of social media, they got away with it. Nobody was safe, nobody questioned anything, nobody answered back.

My turn came when a (different) pot of piss was thrown all over the back of my dinner jacket at the end-of-season awards night, testing my patience as far as it would go. For the first time, I'd had enough. And I had my reasons. Time to own it. Having located the culprit and sounded him out, something had to give. Given he was the team's 'enforcer', probably me after a proper pulping. I stood my ground and played the 'hope someone holds me back so I can pretend I'm up for this' card. Which bizarrely worked. Whether the particular occasion or the team's Universities Cup final the following week, I managed to dodge another leathering, his apologies being offered up before their big day.

With that, the end of three relatively good years loomed. Extra stress and pressure to perform on those final exam days though and with it nervous-system overload. I needed help.

Help came in the form of a teddy. Or rather, quite a few of them (no spike eyes), picnicking on a beach.

Penygraig Farm
18 May 1986

Dear Ian,

If you can read this card you should have few problems with your exams…i.e. read the questions carefully.

After these exams your school days will be over (though not, one hopes, your thirst for knowledge) – you will be a man and have 'put away childish things.'

I can only hope you will be a man worthy of your parents – one who we can be proud of regardless of examination results – and that all your days will be as carefree as the picture on this card.

Whatever the future holds for you go forward and meet it, good or bad, knowing that we love you more than any words of mine can tell.
Good luck, Mum xx

More than words. Little would I know that in the years to follow, when she couldn't speak anymore, how important they would be.

Your World Now
1986 - 1989

Nudist beaches are very hard places to hide. The fact is you can't. There isn't much point in running either…you just draw attention to yourself for all the wrong reasons.

Having gained a 2:1 degree, there were a couple of last rites of university passage. The first involved pretty much burning down the Wanderers terraced flat during the 1986 Mexico World Cup. The 'Hand of God' they might end up being remembered for. For us it was, literally, one almighty cod. England were playing Morocco next. It was the most desolate of desolate England matches, the one that if you rolled every desolate game that England had ever played up into one, then this was the sum of all their dreary parts. We pretty much brought the house down, even when England couldn't. Fish and chips for afters, the chip pan was put on at half-time. England bored the pants off everyone for the next forty-five minutes and the chip pan was left to its own devices. The game ended. The fatty fire took longer to put out than England's participation in the tournament…but saved on paying for all the dart hole repairs.

Secondly, the epoch ending Graduation Ball. The notes for the night's program set the scene.

'A moot point of the Graduation Ball means the end of the best years of your life. This is the night to let your hair down (very difficult, and probably coolly undesired, if it is trendily cropped on top with shaved sides) before you go out to brave the pneumatic drills of a harsh world. Don't drink and drive. Use the taxis.'

That was, ahem, 'upbeat'. Better get pissed then (saving the well-meaning taxi advice for some stage later).

Liebfraumilch £5 a bottle. Niersteiner £5.50. Vin de Pays de Bouche £5. Cheap and very cheerful.

Melon cocktail; chicken, avocado mousse, mushroom vol-au-vent, Waldorf salad; profiteroles, Charlotte Russe.

Jools Holland, Buddy Curtis & The Grasshoppers and The Mint Juleps provided the entertainment.

And with all that, university was done.

All that remained was that obligatory summer road trip with the guys to the South of France, where we celebrated my twenty-second birthday on a camping week. A twenty-four hour bus journey down was met with canvas, flagons of wine, great beaches and top company. Our rep pointed out the tourist hotspots, including the largest nudist colony in Europe which flowed seamlessly straight off our beach. Double dares aplenty from her. As dares went, the nudist beach a shoe-in (or off). The supermarket a bit of a breeze. Its disco a non-starter.

Even for me.

Dreams (and holidays) never last and you have to make the most of life when you can. Summer was over and morphed in to real work and the South London years. A new satellite office in Croydon for one of the larger London accounting firms was where I found myself. A far cry from those early dreams of being either a doctor or a vet.

A tiny rented room in a small house, a short walk to the office, gave me lots of time in the evening…most of which was spent on the telephone listening to my mother, being a counselling service. Something, over time, I got very good at. Listening. An hour or two every night. You'd want your calls to your mother to be all about the day's events and what the future would bring. These were hard calls and I needed a friend more than ever. With Jon away, his letters became all the more relevant, awaited just for the romance of his tales on the high seas. I'd return the favour and the walk to the post-box became something of a routine.

Everything considered and bundled up (particularly the pressurised mix of work and exams) I wasn't able to think straight. Mental exhaustion, literally, struck. For escapism I found myself organising all of the office's socials, as well as the fledgling football team. Sunday morning became match day. Making sure everyone else had a good time valiantly jousted with the fact I was crumbling inside. There was an upside. A new set of friends…Rusty, South African Dave and Kiwi Reg.

Croydon had other positives…relatively easy access to Selhurst Park and Plough Lane. Spurs were doing their best to excite the imagination, having appointed Terry Venables as their new manager and bought in Gary Lineker and Paul Gascoigne. The club's commercial activities were extended further on 24 October, 1987, when Joe Bugner and Frank Bruno turned up for a heavyweight slugfest. A contrast of styles, one in their prime, the other over the hill. There was only ever going to be one winner. Two, given its success, if you included Barry Hearn in his first fight promotion.

Courting took my mind off things, bringing with it lots of greatest hit cassette tapes and associated insert message J-cards. A first serious relationship after a lot of fumblings, avoidance of the Dorothys and missed opportunities with the Susans; someone I'd met in my last term at university. Staying on for a year of teacher training as she was, meant a new source of correspondence and writing outlet…which became prolific. As also the long weekends away…Isle of Wight camping in Appuldurcombe (with adventure parking in Black Gang Chine) and rambles around the Carmarthen farm where my mother looked after all the animals in wind and rain, hand rearing them if necessary. The spectacular, rugged scenery from the heights of its hills and fields, those castle ruins at Llanstephan, Dylan Thomas' Boathouse and that sweeping estuary on a sunny day were all never more perfect places in a fond moment.

Sooner rather than later we were engaged to be married. With that, a first ever flat purchase over in Crystal Palace. The whole area was about to become a significant place on the road map of my life, whether through houses, hockey, football (playing or watching), work…and heady romance.

Doing unexpected things ran in her family. One of her elderly relatives wasn't that long for the world but did love telling his stink bomb story…letting them off in shopping centres and walking away smirking to himself. He thought it was funny. It actually kept him, if not young, alive and he seemed to take great pride in acting out his final years as if he was a kid. He made sense and stayed in my memory.

If I was to ever cut and run from being your archetypal accountant he would be one of my spirit guides. Maybe I'd already started, dinner jacket wee-gate and kissogramming small but tiny windows of what could be. Standing tall and daring to be different. My walls were always up, my mask always on…but if it slipped, from here on in, I'd ensure it was worth it. Less Henry the mild-mannered janitor, more Hong Kong Phooey; less Clark Kent, more Superman.

Back in the everyday and altogether real world, all of the rabid excitement of being a trainee accountant came with two sets of professional exams. All well and good but, with where I was at, I didn't have enough focus. And, as already proven, little or no exam technique. The first set of exams ruined a good engagement party and the Christmas run in.

I did manage to pass my first set of professional exams. Just. Marginal passes in all subjects…Financial Accounting (all about form over substance, apparently), Law, Elements of Taxation, Auditing and, lastly, unforgettably, Software Data Processing and Accounting Techniques. Never, ever going to be first pick on anyone's team sheet as exams go. All as dull as dishwater, but I was at least halfway there.

Saturday 6 August, 1988, was my (first) wedding. Mum was there, proud, choking on her tears, tears that could be heard through the service; all very emotional. That was my mother. A tremendous courage, depth, heart and soul and a deep, sensitive spirituality. A gift I'd like to think she gave me, being able to feel others' pain and having to rescue. To the extent of being a curse; or so I kept convincing myself. Then again, maybe I was just that one in four statistic too.

The honeymoon was just as you would expect Venice to be. Lovely…and full of Monty Pythonesque gondoliers.

The second set of professional exams were scheduled for early December. In November…five and a half years after the ambulance and her long battle to overcome her mental frailties…came the devastating news that Mum had throat cancer, the heart breaking diagnosis being a very short time to live. On 1 December I sent her back that teddy card she had sent nearly three years before, with a highlight over the 'thinking of you' bit. It reduced her to tears but became, as it had been mine, one of her most cherished possessions. All we could do, as time allowed, was provide the words, comfort, warmth and love to shine a light on whatever life she had left.

Cancer never has any upside. That December was a very hollow one and Christmas Day, whilst extremely quiet, was still lovingly treasured. The only ray of light, her fortitude and true personality shining. The physical illness kicked her mental one to touch. It wasn't the paranoid schizophrenia she had suffered with for some ten years or so that became her greatest battle, it was the cancer, a product of the '50s to '70s lifestyles. She was a better self again, albeit one with little time to express it as the days spiralled away. No more mental suffering, just the physical decay. Cancer treatment would inevitably involve both radiotherapy and surgery. In Mum's case, cutting out part of her tongue, making talking ultimately difficult.

Results for Professional Exam II came out in February 1989. I passed Management Accounting and Auditing, but failed Financial Accounting 2, Financial Management and Advanced Taxation…unfortunately meaning all the exams needed to be retaken in the summer. The retakes were the least of my interest.

Footballing life continued happily by way of light relief. Watching Arsenal pinch the league title on the last day of the season was entertaining, if only for the late, late 'it's up for grabs' drama. As a neutral, you can't beat a last seconds bit of pandemonium in a front room full of Liverpool and Arsenal supporters. For those Arsenal obsessives life was complete in the moment. Mine was just about to fall apart.

That league decider was on a Friday night and, as fate would have it, two days later we had an accountants' five-a-side tournament at Highbury Stadium…unfortunately now scheduled for the same time as Arsenal's open-top victory parade. Our team all turned up to be met at the stadium by packed crowds (waiting for the Arsenal bus and entourage). With their main gates being our only way into the ground, we were going to be very much part of the party. And with one of our guys often dining out on his similarity to Kevin Campbell (equivalent playing ability arguable), it meant we were mistaken for the advance party and feted all the way along. The irony of a Spurs fan Trojan horsing his way into the ground (having being cheered all the way) was another brief but welcome respite from the real world.

Marginal passes were obtained for all the exam retakes except Financial Accounting which was a marginal fail. It now meant just that one subject needed to be retaken. My 'nearly passed' status meant I was able to go on the firm's 'newly qualified' conference. I found myself joining a cast of thousands for two days of professional update and party that I hadn't technically got an invite for.

I wasn't in the party mood. Waiting in a ticket queue at Birmingham New Street station on the way up I eventually got served. Turning in haste to get my onward connection I was dumbstruck to see Susan One, who had been behind me all along, passengers in the night once more. I was, very briefly, back in time. A gaze, that same gorgeous smile and a lovely, 'Hello.' I felt a hug, for our first time ever, coming on. I looked at a clock as time and guards' whistles laughed me down, raised my arms by way of a poor apology, shook my head and ran, just catching my train.

Had my chance…open goal…muffed it. I wondered if I would ever see her again.

The conference had its moments but I took little away from it. Just some management training exercise…build an oil rig (capable of supporting a hardback book) using just straws and sewing pins. The winner…whoever completed the task for the least amount of virtual money (both straws and the pins costing). Everyone failed, except for that one person who went big, spent an imaginary fortune and built a construction worthy of being in the North Sea itself.

I would remember the lesson.

Time ticked inexorably towards the end of the decade. Another Christmas loomed. It was one of those years you want to forget, but know you can't.

Mum responded with fortitude. She stared death down and hauled herself through month after month, eventually moving from the farm to Morriston Hospital in Swansea.

Tuesday 12 December, Bishopsgate Hall, London, two until five o'clock should have been the date of my last ever exam. I was near breakdown and it was the last thing I was prepared for. My notification slip informed me where to be when. It also mentioned Tuesday 26 February. The results day. Pass and 'Accountancy' awaited. Fail and it would be look for another career.

Time moved fast and I did those three hours in a way I had never done any other. More of a gentle jog rather than a sprint, changing the habits of a lifetime, going against any and all type.

Methodically. Slowly.

But still badly.

Whatever the result, it would never change the fact that Mum's race was nearly run.

'Did you pass?' were her last whispered words to me.

Please Come Home For Christmas
December 1989

I used to love Christmas as a kid. The whole Santa thing. I can't remember when I stopped believing in him but, ever after, the whole seasonal affair never lost any of its sparkle and magic. Except maybe 1988 with its awful news.

There were eight days left to the big day one year later.

It had been a long week trying to close out an audit for a failing company, as well as getting stuck in the mud with that one bastard exam that had got both its legs out waiting to trip me up. The long home straight, a little recovery time and then the final journey to Carmarthen.

Mind exhausted, just not with it, tired, zoned out.

Lost in space.

Sunday 17 December was a date I wouldn't forget.

The last time I saw my mother in life.

The kind nurses at Morriston Hospital, Swansea were as lovely and as welcoming as always. My mother ever frailer, barely able to speak, let alone move. Almost nothing left of her, but a smile and a look. Sitting on the chair next to her bed, I held her fragile hand as she whispered her question.

'Yes,' I said, squeezing her hand, taking both a satsuma and another minus five for the team.

From the slightest squeeze by way of return I knew she could still grasp my attempt at honesty in the moment.

We sat for about five minutes, in silence, as the world hustled round and it was time to leave. I knew what would soon be coming. How I wished for one last dance, one last wish and one last letter but took solace in the fact she held on, post exams, to hear me out.

And then it was time for goodbye.

Silent but very real tears welled up as I whispered the only words I needed and wanted to say.

'I love you.'

Another frail squeeze of my hand with all of the ebbing energy she had left was enough to convince me that those three little words, and the absolute truth, ran deeper and were more important than the whitest of lies. I'd left it all out there and was glad I'd said what I did…so I never ever felt I'd fallen short.

Two days later my father called work in the early evening. I was near Gatwick, continuing with the long days and late-night audit investigation of a phone import company that was going down its own toilet. The journey up to the office in Croydon was as any other evening, stopping off there about seven to leave the files and pick up some more. The senior partner was the only one in, having taken the call, and was waiting for me.

'Your father called.'

I didn't need to make that next call, as I knew what it would mean. Having made it, I said goodnight to my boss and drove slowly home.

She had always been a fighter from, as much as I knew, a very young age. When diagnosed, she was only supposed to last months but fought out the whole of the following year. She had been desperate to die at home, rather than in a hospital, but unfortunately that's where she did, falling short of Christmas itself by six days.

Whatever the future holds for you go forward and meet it, good or bad, knowing that we love you more than any words of mine can tell.'

More than words.

Having to pass on bad news is always hard. At home, I waited for my brother, who was staying with me, to return from his late work shift.

'Mum died.'

A long hug and then silence as we both retreated to the quiet of the night.

In the morning, with a shrouded mind, I wished it had all just been a bad dream. Back to Carmarthen the next day and, in the evening after, a visit to see my mother's body in the chapel of rest.

It is hard to describe a dead body, one you've always associated with warmth and heart and love. The light had gone and a very generous, kind and loving soul very clearly departed. Being at boarding school, I may have known her for twenty-five years when she died but had, in reality, only seen her for about ten of those. Going in to those last few minutes, the last second, was surreal.

I kissed her forehead one last time.

Margam Crematorium is nestled in a plain four miles east of Port Talbot, separated from the sea on one side by vast steel mills. On the other, rolling Welsh hills. Unmistakably, the valleys and the green, green grass of home.

The cremation was held on Friday 23 December, four days after she died. The funeral convoy took an evocative, slow journey through South Wales. The day was cold and crisp, but beautiful. Horses adorned the adjacent fields on the way into the park.

In the chapel, the left side was largely Welsh, the other largely English. The singing was noticeably one-sided. It was impossible to hold back all the tears. So I did. Years of training. Straight line. Focus. Welsh hymns. No arias. My father talked eloquently about the season, little to know it would be a following December his mum would also pass.

'Abide With Me' was one of the songs to be sung.

For the Book of Remembrance I chose a bit of Byron, a resonant and evocative piece from one of Mum's favourite books, *The Oxford Dictionary of Quotations*.

'A mind at peace with all below.'

Outside a blessing on the plot where the ashes would be scattered…a plot close to the car park but one overlooking vibrant young trees and shrubs.

Life changes. Not on a sixpence…but on much bigger notes. Christmas Eve, 1989, was the very quietest of Silent

Nights. Christmas Day was the deepest and bleakest, Curly Wurlys noticeable by their absence. The farm was missing something. And not just all the seasonal cards. A heartbeat, a soul. All that remained were the memories to camouflage ourselves with going forward. Christmas died its own death after that. An undertow of loss and the stages of grief that would haunt me for many seasons to come.

There are some things in life that time can never mend. Subconsciously I knew 'I love you' would be the hardest thing to ever say again. I'd spent twenty-five years trying to run towards the light. I would spend the next twenty-five running away.

I Can't Tell You Why
1990 - 1995

There are, typically, five recognised stages of grief: denial; anger; bargaining; depression; and acceptance. That's the classical take on these matters.

In real time, it's not a competition. There is no limit to any of the stages and their order can get just the tiniest bit fucked up.

Angry tears, tightly masked, heralded a new decade.

I was locked up in my own world.

Little things, marginal gains, keep you going.

For me it had been exams, as much as I hated them and as much as it turned out I wasn't ever that good at them come the day. An exam for me was a bit like sport; the first five minutes to ease in to it and build up a head of steam, running around for most of the remainder, five minutes at the end in some sort of crazy panic to try and pull a half-decent result out of the bag. Exams had kept me going.

I played a game of football early in the New Year in the hope that it would give me a bit of a release. It never did. Some soulless park pitch somewhere on a Sunday morning. I wasn't really there. A bar football player would have been of more use. The pitch and the game lost in time.

As 1990 rolled, the marginal gains started.

Unexpectedly, and by some miracle, I had flopped over the line in my referred accounting exam. My perceived lie had become a smaller part of the bigger truth. And exams were thus complete. Done. Dusted. No more. And like the teddies on the card I was free from those chains that bind. In the depths of grief, I vowed never to take another test, another assessment, another exam.

At about the same time, our group secretary got ovarian cancer. She had looked after me when my chips had been properly down. There was only me in the office who knew, having seen her crying at her desk early one morning. My mother had taught me well without meaning to. The art of listening. Whilst finding time to do exactly that on all the early mornings before work days began, everyone thought we were having some kind of affair. Chances were they'd fire me…but I am not sure at the time I really cared. In the end the firm merged with a larger one and other people, many of whom were very good friends, went. Somehow I survived that cull…possibly because I just blended in again and was 'one of the rest'.

Mid 1990, the film *Ghost* was released. That it completed Patrick Swayze's holy trinity of films…*Dirty Dancing*, then *Roadhouse* and finally *Ghost* (something for everyone) wasn't the point. The point was a Whoopi Goldberg interview in which she expressed a simple view.

'People don't die unless you forget them.'

I never forgot the words, the sentiment or a new hope and altered reality. Never forgot the Swayze too. A bloke not afraid of dancing and living the dream until his all too early end. A bloke with all the best (movie) one-liners ever.

As Johnny… *'nobody puts Baby in the corner.'*

As Dalton… *'be nice, until it's time not to be nice.'*

As Sam… *'ditto.'*

Ghosts, Swayze and 'the lift' aside, in the moment it was still difficult to function and, as a result, the marriage broke down, reduced to a torn up scrapbook of dreams. I was in that horribly shitty denial phase; with it confusion, isolation and guilt.

I needed company. Boots, the kitten, was up to the job.

Anger followed denial…but was kept largely in check by running it out on the field of play. The other phases would take a lot longer.

Sunday morning hit-and-hope football on marsh pitches in the depths of the Accountant's Football League (Division Four) was about as far from 'could be useful' as you'd ever get. Highlights of most of our careers do come and go, but (as football went) our cup game against a team two leagues higher who had gone 2-0 up at half-time entered the arena. If the university 'volley' was 'best goal ever', this game took the best ever match award…a top corner goal direct from a free-kick way out and a proper winger's run and cross for a diving header from one of the team, my contributions. Big on the day for the 2-2 result (we lost the replay) it was the little things that mattered. Even when the little things come down to the lingering smell of dog shit on your forehead when you've headed a ball away on Wandsworth Common. Less of a park pitch (compared to say Regents or over by the sometimes flooded river near Ham), Wandsworth was more public, every time being an interesting 'experience'. Chasing balls down the road was incidental. It was a Rusty throw-in and I should have taken greater note of his smile and smirk, but always grateful for the everlasting memory. Some things are never forgotten and 'on me 'ed' became a memory shared over a beer for years to come.

Football, as always, kept me running…and not just in the London parks. Organising tours to play our affiliated offices abroad filled the off-season gaps. Games (or mini-tournaments) were Saturdays, with evening 'entertainment' and downtime Sundays.

Favourites remain. Dublin, staying in the hotel opposite the Guinness brewery, was (unsurprisingly) an all day and night Guinness drinking session (counted at sixteen pints) only to then resemble statues (not for the first time) on the pitch in a 7-0 loss the next day. The Rennes tournament held in the searing heat of early summer was punctuated fabulously between games with as much cheese and wine as could be eaten and drunk. No prefects and no Mantis.

Paris brought the infamous game over at the Bois de Boulogne in the fog. Rusty and I got two hours kip before turning up late in an alcohol fumed taxi for kick-off to find the team 2-0 down, and somehow conjuring up a 5-2 win.

Hamburg, Bologna, Prague and Edinburgh all had their moments. Amsterdam was like a European Cup adventure of its own, Madrid one of the loveliest places I'd been to.

On the tour to Guernsey I met a girl who needed to get away from the island and she came to stay for two years. A little lost as she was, she had a lifeline. And for a while life was 'normal', with Wembley (Bryan Adams, Extreme and Squeeze) being a hot day's highlight.

'More Than Words' resonated and two more Extreme concerts followed…one at The Apollo in Hammersmith.

The search for more places to run, more places to hide, became infinite. 1990 had been the year of Robin S. and 'Show me Love'. I had always used 'dancing' as a way of getting fit(ter), whether Glen Discos or Stringfellows (my guilty disco pleasure back in the day on the way back from Sydenham). Never the first to invade a dancefloor, I would be the person standing on the sideline waiting for the right moment (generally, the right song) to dip my toe in. Once the toe was in, the rest followed…and stayed. Robin S. and 'Show me Love' became my toe-dipper of choice.

Living in Crystal Palace at least allowed me a couple of easy Spurs away days, Palace and Wimbledon. And by 1991 Tottenham had conjured up another cup run to dig my mind out of the shit it was in. That year's FA Cup final was the Gazza final (or at least a small bit of it) injuring himself after a rash challenge in the heat of the moment and being stretchered off early. Paul Stewart scored one of the goals, catapulting himself in to Tottenham folklore in so doing. Of all the signed videos in WH Smith it's Stewart's I picked out and put on my bookshelf, next to the *Oxford Dictionary of Quotations*, a Douglas Bader signed *Reach for the Sky* and Dylan Thomas' *Under Milk Wood*.

Either this game or the Wembley semi-final prior to it, when Spurs beat Arsenal 3-1 (with Gazza scoring 'that' free kick) could have completed the Tottenham top five. Both would, in the end though, fall just short.

Jon and I were up on the balcony at the Punch and Judy in Covent Garden Piazza later that year, doing what we did best, drinking and chatting. We found ourselves, as always, watching the world go by next to, randomly, a recuperating Gazza and Paul Stewart. The toilets right at the top of that pub were small to say the least. Just the one urinal…which Jon found himself at when Gazza walked in. A naval joke about using the sink rolled into a long conversation in their confined space about all the pressures and intrusion of the papers. Even by then Gazza was aware of the price of fame and was discussing (with Jon) the impact it was having on his mental health. Jon returned to our beers having had a large 'thank you' from Gazza for just being…well, Jon. A lovely guy and always the man to reason out any problem.

Jon and I left for a pizza and Gazza went to Italy. The next season the Premier League started…with it the Alan Sugar years. None of which would disguise Spurs heading into a mid-table mediocrity. They were going through that sort of period where they might not have looked too out of place on Wandsworth Common, throw-ins and all.

Reg the Kiwi sadly died of skin cancer, way too young. A stalwart of our team (we all need that one who is happy to play in goal), we had his memorial game with its minutes silence over (fittingly) on the Bar Pitch at Crystal Palace.

At the same time I was invited to a Sportsman's Dinner, the day after Bobby Moore had died. Jack Charlton, one of his 1966 World Cup winning compatriots was giving the after dinner speech. The 1966 team all dined out often on the after-dinner circuit and to a man talked about 'the' side, and 'the' game, all told from their varying perspectives and vantage points. Charlton's speech was both as humble and as poignant as they come about both the World Cup final and Bobby Moore. They were a very tight group, closely knit, and as the clearly pained Charlton spoke, with a now changed narrative, you could sense a collective loss of their good friend. Our football team, Reg and all, would never be World Cup winners, but we celebrated most games as if we had been.

I was also lucky enough to hear Barry Hearn give some business lecture about how he'd made the big-time. A one-time accountant who liked to be different, who turned up at his offices whilst a junior, in a white suit and fedora, he'd do all his work audits up in the stands at Test matches (I'd clearly missed a massive trick). He had escaped the classical accountant's trail and branched out in to snooker. Whilst sitting in his snooker hall office he was fortunate enough to have two of the strangest fellows he'd not yet met walk in. Neither a stick-thin, ginger haired youth (Steve Davis), nor a muscular chap with a lisp (Chris Eubank) would have turned many heads elsewhere…but Hearn recognised both had something about them…a front and no little talent. He also knew that with Sky looking to take on and dominate the sports market there was a big shake-up to the TV norm coming…and with it opportunities. He took a gamble on both and the rest, for those stories, became history. When asked at the end what he put his own career and success down to, Hearn concluded 'bullshit and luck.'

Tottenham, meanwhile, hadn't got much of the latter. Ardiles, the most beautiful of ex-players, became one of a succession of new managers who came and went. You had to love him for who he was but Tottenham's performances were mirroring mine…stuttering and directionless.

Back in my own sporting world I settled for more Saturday fun to complement the Sunday morning football. And so hockey started up again, a local club (Tulse Hill) providing a warm shelter.

When not playing or watching sport, work happened.

Something about work…balance sheets, running large departments, didn't really suit me…as good, as supportive and as lovely as the people in my departments were. Life is simply about creating memories, the things you remember years later…and playing with numbers, rather than painting by them, didn't really cut it for me. Be like Barry, they said. Be different. Go rogue.

My first job on leaving the accounting practice was with the worldwide group ABB. Our small division was making ventures in to the oil and gas world (I at least knew how to build a pukka oil rig out of straws and pins). The actual job necessitated trips over to the tax offices and our divisional headquarters out in Norway. It is hard to describe the view flying over the magnificent fjords between Stavanger and Oslo in any descriptive terms other than both exhilarating and life affirming. That experience was topped and capped by the finance group taking the magnificent 1930s wooden yacht (of yesteryear Olympic ice-skater Sonja Henning) out for drinks and a meal one evening on the same waters. The same night we hit Oslo, going into a nightclub at two in the morning, coming out half an hour later with the 'lights' still on. Apparently it had got dark, very briefly, when we were inside. Life should be full of memories and occasions like this where the light never dims.

The little house in Crystal Palace was just Boots (now, a cat) and I. Until I came home after work to find him gone. The old lady next door gave me the update…he'd been run over out on the main road. I scraped the poor boy up and buried him in a small plot by the shed.

Things got lonely again, despite the football, hockey and more letters from Jon playing their distracting part.

It was at a party in the company of Jon and a couple of the football guys that I literally bumped into The Librarian. Librarian by job, extremely lovely by nature…one of those love at first sight moments that don't come around often. A different kind of lady. All heart. The summer progressed, as did a new relationship.

Jon and I had already arranged a catch up in Corfu to chew the cud and, as catch ups go, the best. We had got ourselves an apartment outside Kavos on a small stretch of beach, with its own beach bar. Going into the excesses of Kavos for one night reminded us that whilst thirty, we had thus far somehow successfully bypassed this 18-30 crowd (and, seeing the carnage, quite glad for it). Our holiday was quieter than usual but all the more special for it in our own no-one-else beach bar world. An opportunity to reappraise life and priorities. And in so doing, I lost THE shirt. Over a woman. Well, not over, just to. The best flower patterned shirt I'd ever had as well (guys are like that, they have that 'one' shirt…the 'one'). The girl who ran our little bar had put up with our ramblings for what must have seemed (for her) like a lifetime.

By now I was (probably) in the bargaining stage of grief, but as fair exchanges go…two for the (short) road, and on the house, in exchange for my prized shirt…we (all three of us) ended the holiday content.

Except me, missing my shirt, obviously.

Things were changing.

Having felt unwell out in New Zealand on secondment to their Navy, it transpired that Jon had developed diabetes and was now adjusting to having to leave the services.

He had gained a place at Portsmouth University to do Computer Sciences (I'd warn him off the snow boots).

I'd just got engaged to the lovely librarian. Jon had also met someone.

Both relationships escalated quickly.

Try And Love Again
1995 - 2000

The second Brixton riots were one of those 'I was there' moments. For all the wrong reasons. There I was standing, quite literally, on the front-line. I had come out of my shell. And was out of my mind.

It started off as a normal day. Home from work early, in enough time to pick up the car and drive to Brixton from Upper Norwood to pick up the fiancée, as always. Arriving outside the tube station exit and the next door 7-Eleven, it was hard not to notice the smoke coming out of it. A riot van turning up and parking right in the middle of the road suggested a 'normal' day was going to be anything but.

With the station shutting, the only thing to do was to drive back home. Back there, Ceefax revealed there to be a big incident brewing. With no means of communication, I had no idea whether she'd got caught up in everything or not. After a long wait, I decided the only thing to do was to drive back again. I did…only I couldn't get within a mile of the station for the crowds. As the dark started coming in, the only thing seemingly left to do was to park up in a side road and start walking.

Walking wasn't too bad at first. The longer it went on and the nearer I got towards the station though, the more difficult it became weaving through ever-increasing masses. The atmosphere was changing too from one of speculative interest at the back, bristling with intimidation towards the front.

And all of a sudden there I was. In a very tiny no man's land right in the middle of a riot, sandwiched between the opposing teams. In my suit and tie.

I quite clearly (to all but me) wasn't in Kansas anymore.

'Do you know if they'll be opening the station any time soon?' I asked the chap in his riot gear opposite.

The riot officer facing me was about as dumbstruck as he could be, just staring at me, utterly bewildered. The long scar down his face suggested he knew exactly why he was there and what normally happened next. I am pretty sure discussing the relative merits of station timetables and riot policing with the village idiot wasn't in his training manual.

Might be now though.

The gun shot about ten yards away gave a greater focus and perspective.

'I would leave now if I were you, matey. They've started firing shots.'

Accounting (particularly accounting exams) teaches you to make informed decisions and strategise a response based on all the facts in front of you, as quickly as possible. No qualifications were required to determine the next move.

Gesturing a hat tip and giving a nod, I turned and kept walking. And walking. Not quite the full jog, but something an Olympic racewalker would have been proud of.

Back home in Crystal Palace, I was surprised to see my new fiancée home. Turned out she had got off at the next stop after Brixton on her normal tube journey home and got a bus from there.

Little things bring you closer and this had been one of those. A move to Stoneleigh at the end of 1995 followed.

Given a succession of takeovers (and a lot of jockeying for position) surrounding the ABB company I worked for, it came as no surprise that the exit door came around sooner rather than later.

On then to Hertz, the UK headquarters of which were based in an old sixties building in Norbury. The building's only saving grace…being next to The Norbury Tavern, one of South London's less salubrious (or maybe even finest, depending on your memories) bar-nightclubs.

South London at the time (as I'd had a front seat view of) was a powder keg and my new workspace didn't escape attention. Early on in my tenure, the place was robbed. An industrial scale night-time operation through the roof, with computer on computer being lined up to then be manually conveyor belted up into the loft hatch, and then building to building onwards.

Unbeknownst to anyone, the boss and I were still there, camped in his office along the top floor corridor doing the annual budget (some new computers to add). Stepping out into the central lift atrium at 9 p.m. to make coffee, I found myself slap-bang in the middle of Grand Heist central. A surprise to both parties...and one of those time stands still moments where someone has to make the next move. You don't get many Mexican stand-offs in your life but this, as homages to Clint Eastwood went, was a real one.

'Oi!' I shouted…at which point three guys ran up the stairwell. I was pretty convinced I was in trouble now. As it was, their only concern seemed to be to get up the ladder and leg it. My boss duly arrived (mug with Earl Grey dregs his weapon of choice) to see the last leg disappearing into the roof space and off in to the night sky. Tea upgraded to much stiffer ones at The Norbury once all had been locked down. Overnight I had managed to change my status from Head Accountant to Head of Security.

A trip away with the fiancée to Switzerland provided a change of scenery. Interlaken is a very pretty and charming town both in and out of snow season. A railway trip along the valley towards the ski resorts of Wengen and Murren, facing each other from opposite sides of the mountain, was the highlight. We opted for a funicular up to Murren. The steep, granite cliffs of Wengen stared across at us from one side when we arrived. Snow-covered mountains created a magical backdrop to the other three. Something struck me about the place whilst we were there. I had no idea what. A sense, some feeling, that we had found ourselves there for a reason. I made a promise to myself to return some time, the right time, in the future.

Jon returned from his latest posting and we hit the West End for what would become our mythical 'Mugs' weekend. Neither recalled exactly how much was drunk, but thirteen pints stuck, the beauty as always being in the memory not the measure. No recovering Spurs players this time though.

In 1996 they were average. Arsenal were still dominant and mid-table mediocrity seemed to be Tottenham's norm. Like most other mid-table teams, they flattered to deceive; moments of sublime brilliance diluted with other moments of complete pudding. Another trip to Wembley for them might be a way off. The Eagles, back for a first tour since the early eighties, took their place; I made sure I got mine. 'Desperado' completed the set.

The following summer was my second wedding.

First, a stag day up in London to coincide with the third Lions rugby test match in Johannesburg. With many work, football, hockey, university and school friends by my side, it was going to get messy. I had tried to 'organise' things as best as possible to keep it all as controlled and PC-rated as could be. 'Cricket' was the drinking game for the day…get as many 'runs' as possible (one, two, four or six runs being awarded according to how dangerous my dare was) aiming to get through the whole day without losing ten wickets (a wicket being a 'dare' refusal).

It was all going well. Too well. Good game of rugby and the obligatory stripper (not organised by me) entering fully in to the spirit of things and gaining me back-to-back sixes for playing (naked) the double Sega Car Rally game in the pub. It was a stag do and all completely harmless. Pretty irreverent but all in the best possible taste, given the place was essentially full of just my friends. Until the four runs I was 'dared' to get the next round in. Not unique in itself, as I had just been comprehensively beaten on the Sega by one of only two ladies there, but neither of us had yet got our clothes back on. Six runs for the bar sortie, then surely! My referral was waived, my scorecard robbed of two vital runs.

Fifteen lagers, ten bitters and five Guinnesses the round to be ordered. Um, got it. Standing close to the bar, cheeks to the wind, was oddly liberating. The Australian barmaid couldn't contain a laugh at the absurdity of it all. Equally so everyone else. Trying to remember the round and advance my run tally was pretty much all that was on my mind.

The thing that struck me first was an almost immediate, eerie silence. It went very, very quiet. Very, very quickly.

I looked at the guys who were now looking past me in stunned silence at the main door. A sense of foreboding, I looked back at the barmaid who was now looking past me in stunned silence at the main door. I turned my head, very slowly towards the main door. And froze.

Fear is a funny thing.

About thirty feather-boa'd guys straight out of a YMCA tribute act had just breezed in, the saloon doors flapping like they do in all the best westerns when it is all about to kick-off. They looked at me in stunned silence, the smiles starting to creep onto their faces. The cowboy. The Indian. The policeman. A Clint Eastwood pastiche all to myself.

Mexican stand-off time. Again. The good, the bad and the Village People waiting for someone to make that next move. Fear is something you have to own. And now was a time for wearing my (non-existent) jersey with pride.

In organising teams, as I'd done many a time in the past, I had always been known for the detail by which I did my planning. As this game had played itself out, I realised my one tactical error for the day. Arrange your stag night right in the heart of central London by all means. Arrange it on Gay Pride weekend (without realising), no problem. None of those were the mistake. Not knowing the whereabouts of your clothes, when there are more than seventy people in various degrees of excitement around you, was.

I located them eventually. On the high chandelier.

As (management) training exercises went, the shooters and slammers could wait…as I set out to break the official world record for cooking up the most complex, but robust, pyramid of tables and chairs (straws and pins optional).

Jon finally got his 'Best Man' gig (having missed my first wedding whilst at sea) over by the river at Hampton Court. The photographer hadn't had such a perfect day for a long time…and knocked himself out on one of the low-hanging beams in his excitement. The weirdest thing about the day, lovely as it was? Susan Two, randomly flying through the hotel on her way to another wedding. Haunted by ghosts of non-girlfriends past, it seemed, I was always going to be.

After Hertz shut their Norbury operation (the UK offices, not the tavern), Sky TV over in Isleworth became both an interesting (and defining) place to work. My new role partly involved clearing up the fallout from a major accounting systems implementation, as well as looking after supplier, 'talent' and people payments. The job wasn't the big thing. The big things for me were the allure of both the sport and the movie studios they were building.

Sky was also close to Twickenham Rugby Stadium with both its museum and library. Fascinating old books about the birth of rugby going up to and in to World War One. Eclectic characters who appealed to my passions….sport, history and writing. A treasure trove, waiting to be mined. Which I did. After work, days off, reading about rugby war heroes who jumped off the page.

One in particular seemed to run through the middle of them all. Adrian Stoop, Harlequin. From there the research started and the writing flowed. The Six Nations trophy in front of me in the Stadium library most days provided the shiniest of focal points.

I was given the nod for a couple of memorabilia sales, one of which was the flat of a magazine hoarder. The flat, and the experience, were more intimidating than the front-line at Brixton or my YMCA tribute pals. Darkened rooms, the daylight blocked out by stacks of dusty magazines and papers, couldn't hide the ten years of stained tea-cup that politeness (and securing a sale) necessitated drinking from. The mince pie was an experience too, every mouthful slow and forced, unsure as I was of what the mince actually was.

The next year at Sky was a monstrously pivotal one for the company…correcting their central systems, bidding for Manchester United (Sky obviously, not me), morphing the output to digital as well as building in-house film studios. I had a chat with Barry Norman on a fire drill in the car park although it was unlikely he, or Sky, would be interested in the film script I was working on. I did ask him for his best advice though. Of greater interest was the email that went around late one Friday afternoon asking for 'extras'. They needed help up in the City on the coming Sunday for one of their new films in production. An opportunity too good to miss and an insight in to the film-making business.

Sunday turned out to be Man United against Liverpool and all the guys had disappeared off to a local bar to watch it. Just me and a first time actor called Simon Pegg (who had already bagged the ticket booth role). After a two hour wait a runner came to the tube foyer desperately seeking a guy to play a paramedic. Just me then.

'You…how tall are you?'

A leading question I thought, sitting down as I was on the turnstiles. In a field of one, hopefully not that difficult to avoid falling at the first. Don't push it, don't push it.

'Oooh…about…er…six foot one, maybe two.'

'Have you ever been a paramedic?'

'Many a time,' I mumble, only ever having been either a mole, or in an ambulance, once.

'Great…run down to the costume van and kit yourself up quickly.'

Another blag, another white lie and the green uniform was mine for the rest of the day.

The shoot may have been make-believe, but memories find you and these, briefly, took me back to eighteen again.

Tube Tales eventually came out with me (all five foot ten) on screen for all of about ten seconds, doing a poor man's Mick Channon 'windmill' goal celebration with the cordon warning tape. Sky, Simon Pegg and my movie careers had lift off. Sky's seasonal party that year became another trip down memory lane. Held at the power station in Battersea, The Power Station (with Simon Le Bon) played their set by it, Boney M played inside the main marquee. A weird but defining period in time. Life imitating art. And vice versa.

Jon's stag weekend brought tales from the riverbank back to life as well. Or at least the Norfolk Broads. Six of us. All close friends of Jon. Al, Paul and I from the early days and two more from other stages of his life. All of whom, as you might expect, with Jon at the core, blending in perfectly. Care of an 'in' at the local boatyard, we were able to hire a cruiser the week before the official start of the season. We had the Broads pretty much to ourselves. Beer and famous movie scenes from *Deliverance* and *Apocalypse Now* replayed for real. No cares. No worries. No phones. No ties. Card games. More beer.

Next up, the wedding at Britannia Royal Naval College.

The evening before consisted of a large gathering at The Dartmouth Arms. With it, a rendition by Alun of 'the swan joke' as only Al could. You had to be there.

The evening finished with a Best Man's speech that still needed to be written, or at least firmed up. Properly wasted I prepared my speech late in to the night.

We had split up, but my wife was with me. A sad time, a last time…probably a product of me going through a long depressive grief stage masked almost entirely by running and running. The walls I had surrounded myself with had left me lost in a time and space of my own, unable to hold on to a vow or promise. I never loved her more as I wrote into the early hours. A dignity, her kindness, her all round loveliness. Writing is cathartic, sharing it all the more so.

Come the big day, it was my biggest and proudest gig. The ceremony, conducted by the Reverend Caroline, was a gorgeous one. The dinner in the officers' mess hall a treat.

The dining hall was rich in both splendour and history. The oak panelled walls gave it a close, intimate feel. Crystal chandeliers, some original HMS Victory antiques (including cutlery) and oil paintings of Admirals of the Fleet through the ages added to its rich heritage.

I steeled myself and delivered the speech with a proud surety. And aplomb. Jon had effectively helped in writing it…or at least, unbeknownst to him, it was a compilation of all the glorious adventures from many a 'Dear Ian' letter. Cheesy in parts, choice words in others, rich in sentiment and feeling. Most of it centred on Jon being the go-to guy if you ever needed a friend. Not just me…anyone. All the choice events were in there: being so mature, he must have had a beard by the time he was five; favourite (mugs) bar, The Polar Bear off Leicester Square (the irony of its name not lost given all his ocean adventures and trips to the ice); finally getting that smack right between the eyes when least expecting it; and how, despite not being the sportiest, he'd got the gold medallist, Siobhan, to be his wife as well.

With that and other anecdotes…speech done.

'Phew,' I said to the naval officer next to me 'I need a wee now.'

He pointed to my lapel microphone and indicated it was still on.

It was a beautiful day. The happy couple had something that's hard to find and keep believing in. Magic.

Six in the evening on a freezing Saturday night on the Bar Pitch at Crystal Palace was never going to be the best place to get an eye haemorrhage. It all seemed quite innocuous. A blip on the eye and the small trickle of green (during the hockey match) didn't readily seem much to concern myself with. Over the weekend it became apparent it wasn't going to shift. A quick visit to the optician on Monday afternoon prompted an immediate trip to Moorfields Eye Hospital.

As I waited for what seemed like donkey's years on, of all things, Bonfire Night, I watched a very young girl being gently walked in, very afraid, as it was clear she couldn't see at all. Realism struck about where I currently found myself. It transpires the 'green' on my eye was really 'red' care of a broken blood vessel just under my optic nerve. Not much that could be done with it, given its relative proximity. In the moment I had a degree of perspective on lots of things, life in particular.

The dilating drops they used to enlarge my pupils (easier for the specialists to see what had been going on) left me pretty much without vision for the next four hours or so, glasses or no glasses. After escaping, I found myself slowly stumbling around the City of London, a blind man trying to find a way back home. A tramp stopped me and instead of asking me for money said, 'Cheer up, mate.' As I walked twenty metres further, the irony sunk in. I turned back to him and gave him a tenner.

'Thank you mate,' he said. 'Thought you'd beat me up.'

Loneliness, like seasons, comes and goes.

This 5 November, my new friend aside, it had pitched a rather large tent in my front garden.

The blood spot dissolved, but unfortunately blood isn't the best friend of photoreceptors in your eyes…taking a lot of them out with it, which left me partially sighted on the left. Peripheral vision was retained, but with a large grey blob in the middle. Fortunately I'd always played on the left, so as hockey went, at least I'd have most of a pitch to see clearly. Table tennis and squash remained awkward, however.

Protecting my good eye should have been paramount.

On Saturday 14 August, 1999, I was able to (just about) see Tottenham for a first time at White Hart Lane against Everton. The big date a first for me, but also three weeks off the centenary of Tottenham's first ever game at White Hart Lane. My programme for the day was full of stats, not least the head-to-head upfront between Les Ferdinand and my old doppelganging mate, Kevin Campbell. Les was the mags centrefold for the day…his favourite TV personality Sally James. And why not? The first record he bought was The Jackson 5. And who doesn't need a Jackson 5 love-in? His three 'reasons to be cheerful' were his family's health, football and life itself. Tottenham and Les indulged me and 34,535 others with a 3-2 victory and the experience was a mini life-list tick off.

It had been an interesting year for North London. Ten years on from my invasion of Highbury, Arsenal had gone public with a need to move in order to evolve. Tottenham, ironically, under Arsenal's ex-manager George Graham had just won the League Cup. It was all change.

For me that meant a new chapter, Sky having come to another tame end. Head of Finance at Pret A Manger next up. Enjoyable, but exhausting.

The good thing about Pret (in those days) was throwing everyone in the deep end. Whatever your title, you'd be in a shop for your first two weeks learning the trade. I always was the worst sandwich maker in the universe (er, marmite and gherkin excepted), even before having to repetitively make multiples, under pressure. The shop manager, to his credit, realised pretty early on that he'd got a reputation to protect and moved me to the barista area. Even worse. All formulaic. Doing things fast and furiously by numbers had never worked. So he put me on the tills, counting the cash. I had found my calling. A step up at least from making tea.

The manager was a Spaniard called Fernando. And he became a best mate in all the corporate jiggery-pokery of Pret's (as was Sky's and Hertz' before that) growth strategy and pains. It helped that (with a twist of fate) he had played rugby in Spain and Jane, his wife to be, was from Cardiff. He loved everything Welsh (rugby top of the list) and, with the 1999 Rugby World Cup, as luck had it largely in Wales, we found a good trajectory right from the off.

That trajectory included tickets to the New Zealand and France semi-final at Twickenham, the greatest game I had seen…right from the Haka down to the closing seconds.

If Pret did one thing right, it looked after all of its staff, which included the sizeable outing to run the Nike 'Dam to Dam' over in Holland. I'd visited Amsterdam before for a football tour. The usual…very messy late nights. This time round however it was the perfect visit. The half marathon was delayed due to the upfront in-line skaters tripping each other as they hit the bottom of the tunnel going under the canal (proper carnage). Once underway, the 'race' became a beautiful meander through all the villages outside the main city…bunting, trombones, accordions and water (and beer) stations aplenty…then a long run for home with thousands of happy clappers to carry us over the line. Amsterdam was now sat up beside Paris as one of those timeless cities full of memories.

My friendship with Fernando far outlasted the time I'd stay with Pret. Not before I had heard the immortal words, 'Please form an orderly queue with the women and kids at the front. And you sir, do you mind going at the end?'

'So…what you're saying is we are pretty much fucked, and I'm playing with the orchestra?'

New York Minute
2000 - 2004

Taking thirty middle managers on a 'management training exercise' to the summit of Mont Blanc in avalanche season was always going to be a fustercluck.

As it was, the avalanches dipped some toes in first and the trip reverted to more of a training day out towards the glaciers by the Mer de Glace…to see who might be up for another substitute exercise the next day. Scaling the sheer cliff face of the mountain instead, certainly not the better option. If my poor sight had always been my Achilles heel, a fear of heights was inevitably going to rule me out of the rock climbing. The glaciers were still both intimidating (for me at least) and exhilarating. The iron ladders bolted to the sides of the cliff to get on to one of the glaciers equally so. A mind battle (and triumph) of will over fear.

The next day the other twenty-nine edged slowly onto the precarious looking Aiguille du Midi Arête, inched their way (slowly) onto the Glacier du Tacul and disappeared off in search of an overnight cabin ready for an early start the next day, tackle and harness in tow.

I wandered back through the Aiguille canteen viewing station and then readied to get the cable car back down.

The cable car is in two parts. The vertical part that takes you back down to the Plan de l'Aiguille and the horizontal part that stretches way across the valley and back down to Chamonix. The vertical cable was the easy bit. I failed to get on the horizontal section by one person. As it set off, I awaited its sister car's five minute return. No sign. And no sounds of any machinery turning.

An hour later and the steamed up original car returned, having been manually winched back in. Air windows at the top were open and hands were waving out. Once back in the station, its doors opened and a tearful set of passengers exited. It seemed the cable car had got stuck, hanging over the valley, swinging in the wind, its sad occupants wholly unamused. Even more so, as the weather had suddenly and horribly closed in.

We were now all in a freezing pea-souper.

The vertical car kept bringing more tourists down from the Aiguille. Another hour and nearly two hundred people were stuck on the very small escarpment. A log jam in zero visibility. To add further to the degree of disorientation the noises suggested a helicopter was buzzing. First distant and someway below. Next somewhere close. With it came the immortal words…'orderly queue' and all that jazz. I wasn't on a front-line in suit and tie with chaos, intimidation and simmering violence all around me. This time I was halfway up the highest point in Europe with absolutely nowhere to run.

It seemed that as I was attired vaguely appropriately for where we were all at (a creek, up it, no paddle), the station manager suggested I should go last…a better chance in the hypothermia stakes should it arise. Having cleared with her that in the event of anyone dying there today, there was a very good chance it would be us at the end (with me most probable), my new chums and I congratulated ourselves on our good fortune. I bequeathed my gloves to the poor lady in front and the rump of us awaited our fate.

The helicopter was using its front beam to work its way up the side of the mountain all the others were presumably climbing the next day, avoiding the overhanging cables as it went. It then flopped over onto the precipice. Four people went in. And off. Ten minutes later it was back.

Maths would probably have served me well here. Two hundred people, four at a time. About fifty trips then. Ten minutes each. It's five o' clock. Easy exam question. All be over by midnight. One way or the other.

Trips came and went for what seemed like hours…until just as one helicopter left, a second buzzing noise replaced it. Now there were two navigating the soup, cables and all. Darkness fell early and sirens wailed (not just in my head).

'Don't worry, 'e is ze best pilot in ze 'ole of France,' my new bestie, the station manager, helpfully informed me.

'Just my luck then I'll get the other one, who by default isn't.'

When all's against you what can you do? The cable car operator (given an absence of any operating cable cars) was watching *Who Wants to Be a Millionaire*. In French. On a tiny TV. And why not? Peering in to her small cabin window I offered up my best guesses. One in four. What chances?

Eventually the queue reached its last four and, still alive as we were, off we went, down through the heady clouds. It's a strange feeling falling. In the dark. In a short space of time, rather than over years.

Just for good measure, someone farted. Badly.

Everyone assumed it to be me. I took a deep breath and one for the team, even though it wasn't.

The helicopter dropped too and for a minute all senses were scrambled. Then, all of a sudden, we exited the thick clouds to the leftovers of what had been a warm summer day. The somewhat hallucinatory, bizarre but exhilarating episode was shaped even more so, in my head at least, by a dual share in the virtual million euros we had majestically (and very loudly) garnered a while back. Such had been my awesome French recall when pretty much all the frites were down.

On return to England from lofty peaks, I left Pret pretty much the same way I'd left all the other roles; I just wasn't suited to huge corporate workspaces, with all their internal politics and scrabbles to get to the top of some very greasy poles. Head held high, walking around the offices, shaking hands and signing out with a big leaving do was about the last thing I did in the nineties.

With that the century was all but over, save time for the first shoots of a new relationship...with a Belgian.

The non-existent millennium bug ushered in the noughties. Fireworks over Waterloo Bridge heralded the new century and just maybe a new dawn.

Same old story. In the absence of corporate focus, sport became all the more consuming taking over the week and exhausting all my mental faculties in the run-up to weekend games. Starting Monday, weeks became a growing pressure to look ahead to, focus (and then deliver) on an hour and a half on Saturdays and Sundays. Repeat the next week. Park football had almost run its course, but hockey was still a constant. Goals flowed (my personal highlight a cup semi-final goal on the Palace Bar Pitch which the umpires said would have graced a national league game).

Again, no-one remembered it.

Our umpire of choice was Hugh, the dad of captain Big Tom. An ex-Wimbledon entrant back in the day Hugh was the best, his honesty and unbiased attitude made him liked by team and opponent alike. His time-keeping always spot on. In the last minute of a game (Bar Pitch again), running out from a defensive short corner, I nicked the ball from their striker's stick and ran the length of the pitch. With the goalkeeper drawn to the edge of the 'D', I deftly slotted the ball between his legs and, as I fell to the ground, watched it roll forward, up to and into the goal for what would have been the winner. Time had sadly run its course and Hugh, unfortunately, had counted it and the seconds down and blown for the end of the game, just before the ball crossed the line…thereby scrubbing from history (by that one extra second) my 'greatest goal ever scored' story.

The football boots were sadly the first to go. By now I couldn't afford any more traumas to the eyes. One spiteful off the ball elbow from a weasel of an 'opponent' saw to it. The two, Hugh and Weasel, made for the best and worst of park (and pond) life. Not long after my hockey boots went the same way, back and sciatic problems making it hard to continue. Sport had looked after me for thirty-odd years.

More free time though to advance the new relationship the added bonus. Heralding from Belgium, meant a feast of fine wines, chocolate and beer from her step-father, a one-time police chief in the locality, still getting his dues.

Further opportunity for travel came with a late summer wedding of a hockey mate in Chicago, the first part of an extended holiday to America. Wedding all lovely, Chicago fine. The second part a trip to New York and all the must-see sights, including the World Trade Centre and its Twin Towers. Tuesday 21 August was as any morning and a nine o'clock lift up to the top floor of one of the towers was an extremely quick experience. The lift doors opened out to a glass expanse, miles up into the sky. It gently swayed in the breeze. My heights issue, once again, got the better of me. That nauseating feeling of 'what if something happened' wafted over me and I took the next lift back down.

Exactly three weeks later, the morning of 11 September, 2001, was (to start with), as any other ordinary day. At nine o'clock the world changed. I was helping to move out of the old marital home that day, the last item to be moved a small television, which remained switched on as the events in New York unfolded. Pretty much everything collapsed, generally and specifically.

The suburbs of south-west London gave way to Farnham, and an idyllic (albeit rundown) cottage atop Beavers Hill on the western side of town, just up from The Jolly Sailor. The sort of special place you knew to be 'the one'. The previous owners, seventy-odd years of marriage later, had loved the place; so much so, the old lady had died there. The old boy was desperate to see it go to welcoming hands rather than a queue of developers. Being a Major in the Army, showing off the pictures and medals on the wall of his father at the Battle of Jutland, to my father, was a deal-maker.

ENIC completed their own deal to take over Spurs and its slow rebuild from a loss-making enterprise began.

Changes everywhere, not least (sympathetically) to the house. A refurb, modernisation and extension plan for the house commenced, care of an old builder friend of my dad. Unfortunately a one man band…and very slow. Staying at my father's guest house (while he went through treatment for prostate cancer) was never going to be the shortest or easiest of rides.

A year later the cottage was eventually finished. Inside, in keeping with what had been there before, an open-plan downstairs now centred around a three-sixty fireplace. The garden was restored with a fruit and rambling rose pergola outside the dining room. Its various corners had their own defining features…arbours, sheds, shrubs, thousands more roses and other plants.

The Major came back for one final visit and left smiling with a tear in his eye. He died a short while later, reunited with the one he'd loved…and happy, I'd like to think.

The house and garden unloaded a rich vein of creativity and an opportunity, in such idyllic surroundings, to extend my tentative rugby film script. Always one to hit and hope, I blindly posted finished copies off to various (film studio) locations. Unsurprisingly, all the rejection letters came, my absolute favourite from Disney. Being 'thumbs-downed' by Mickey Mouse (who at least had the good grace to appear on the letter) was as good as it gets. Not my first rejection, and wouldn't be my last, but worth the frame I put it in. In the end, and with a significant amount of research already carried out, a more sensible logic dictated turning the script in to a biography of one of rugby's more iconic yesteryear players.

I shared Adrian Stoop's adventures over many a session with his ninety year old son Michael…and with it a lot of Michael's own adventures. Whilst there was starting to be a financial need for me to go back in to full-time work after a sabbatical year off, researching the Stoops' boy's own lives became much the same for me. Work took a back seat.

Adrian Stoop was the England captain for the first ever international at Twickenham. In both deed and legacy, also the person who brought the Harlequins to life. Responsible for saving Douglas Bader's life, that story was a chunk of *Reach for the Sky* I had never picked up. Decorated in World War One, his life was still a relatively quiet one compared to Michael. It was Michael, at Rugby School, who stole and hid the commemorative plaque his father had done much to accentuate. Michael also stole Rommel's famous car (of 'Colditz' board game and Airfix model fame) taking it for a joy-ride…and trashing it in the process. He did everything but win the Victoria Cross in World War Two and, in later life, played chess to a very high competitive standard.

He was also the card-playing best mate of Lord Lucan.

The more I revealed about Michael's father, that in part gave him closure on aspects of his own life, the more he realised I was very good at doing what I was…digging. On more than one occasion he played a mental game of chess with me, feeding me nuggets of other seemingly unrelated information to see where, and how far, I would take them. First, his stories about the wider family's big art collections including the *Femme en chemise,* an early and very formative Picasso painting…the mysterious, young model of which (Madeleine), who'd then been airbrushed out of art history. Michael laughingly mentioned that *Femme*, one of Picasso's most unsung (and deliberately swerved around paintings), had hung for many a year (when he was a kid) in the toilet. Having realised that he'd attracted my interest on that one, he stopped just short of telling me, or at least as far as his memory would recall, who the girl who had set Picasso off on his dramatic artistic odyssey was.

He then moved his chess pieces to more personal and unknown secrets about the Lucan case. Interesting as they were, why me? The one day I touched a raw nerve on the case, he terminated the session. Our subsequent meetings reverted back wholly to his father as if nothing had been said or gone before. I liked Michael…we challenged each other. Not to a game of chess but with life's riddles.

Work eventually caught back up with me. Specifically four one day (each) a week consulting roles to tide things over. The first, at a garden fertiliser company, involved taking on HMRC over transfer pricing. Everything that I had tried to avoid being trained for.

Michael's tales of daring-do were far more interesting.

The second, and of far greater interest, was a small B2B marketing agency stuck in the sticks of Odiham. 'Birddog' had upgraded its offices from an aged horse stable over in Andover having made a small chunk of change on the back of the telecom privatisations, at the turn of the millennium. Swiftly following the dotcom crash, the company had now reverted back to being a small outfit in a two-horse town, ticking along, wondering what to do next. A chance for me to get in to advertising (destiny!), through the back door. The dull 'Henry the mild-mannered janitor' persona of the day job would always be there, but a new opportunity for coming up with inventive campaign one-liners was huge. Somehow the company had survived the crash, largely by walking away from trouble before it had started…and by understanding the value of its own time and having a life. In the competitive world of B2B marketing, Birddog were the original underdog. Not unlike the members of 'Average Joes' in *Dodgeball*. We'd get on fine.

The third of the quartet was at an engineering company. They designed and manufactured clutches for warships and power stations but now needed someone to come in, hold the fort and sort out a bit of an accounting mess (which I was actually quite good at). On my first day walking around the factory floor I saw a picture of HMS Sirius, my father's old ship, on the wall. This place felt right too.

The final role I found myself doing was at the hotel that my dad had a share in; someone needed to be the licensee, something I'd never have imagined myself either doing or being when contemplating the relative merits of a Business Economics and Accounting degree. Becoming 'a guv'nor' required two small things: being certified fit and proper by a judge after proving a decent understanding of what was required…and by taking an EXAM! Bollocks.

The irony that the only exam I'd ever aced (fifty out of fifty…and one hundred percent) involved alcohol was not lost…and so I ended up a licensee. Not really a calling, just another series of misadventures, the best of which involved Carl, the (blind) blind-awareness consultant and a priceless bunch of lawyers and accountants. The whoop (actually the collective term for a bunch of baboons, but wholly apt in this case) were on a jolly playing up to their secretaries over dinner. Carl was a good man. The whoop were staggeringly awful and wouldn't have looked out of place on a stage full of six year olds playing the Toad Hall antagonists.

There were five of them…ruining a packed dining room with their very boorish behaviour, trying to impress as they were the young ladies they had with them (and who looked like, fairly certainly, not their wives). Interrupted from my later conversation with Carl, to the sound of one of them holding court with the whole restaurant, one of the hotel's staff took me off to one side. Full marks in exams, I finally realised, only got you so far. Practical experience, wherever you may be, counts for a whole lot more.

'Take him to one side. Pull his pants down.'

'What…in a restaurant?'

'No, I mean make it look like you're his friend, get him out of position and turn him inside and out.'

'Got ya. Thanks.'

Apparently Foghorn's starter wasn't right. Which was odd, as I told him, because I was sitting next to their table eating my dinner, a blind man over on the other side of the restaurant eating his. Neither of us had seen anything.

'Ah,' said a disorientated Foghorn, trousers slipping.

At this point one of his chumlies sauntered over. I say sauntered. More of a penguin waddle. It didn't help that he had the most ill-fitting and lop-sided toupee I'd ever seen.

'My hare was off!' bellowed Wiggy.

I struggled to keep a straight face unsure as to whether he had indeed had the hare, or simply the schadenfreude of the situation.

'The wine was pretty sub-standard too. We demand an extremely large discount!'

A muted Foghorn, readjusting his belt, knew what was coming next.

'I was sitting next to you and, quite apart from insulting the waitresses at every opportunity, you never complained about anything...completely the opposite in fact, as noted by the number of bottles on your table.'

'Ah,' came a pompous reply. 'And who exactly are you? We are three solicitors and two accountants and are quite happy to sue you.'

The very audible, deliberate (and predictable) arrogance was unbelievable.

I felt a real 'Up the Mole' or a *Miami Vice* or a *Roadhouse* Dalton moment coming on...be nice until it's time not to be nice.

'I'll repeat my point. I'm not sure what you are looking to sue for. And for the record I'm Finance Director of the hotel.'

It was the weirdest situation imaginable.

'Ah, then we are talking to the right person.'

'Indeed you are. I'm also the licensee.'

'Riiight. So what happens next?'

In the (relative) heat of a sticky moment next goal won.

'You all get to leave.'

'When?'

'Now. Forget all the desserts you haven't had yet. And forget the bill.'

'But...'

117

'No buts. All of you. Now.'

'We are all staying along the road. We'll be coming back to discuss this tomorrow.'

'Game over tonight though, so if you'd like to leave.'

'Hurrrummmph.'

'One more thing.'

'What's that?'

'You're barred.'

Moly was back and masks (and gloves) were off. As the party trouped out, dining normality was restored to a quiet ripple of applause. I resisted pulling my shirt over my head and running around the room doing a windmill.

Back to Carl, and a decent human being.

It transpired Carl had lost his sight at school, aged about fifteen, some twenty-five odd years before, following a bad tackle in a game of rugby. He had been wholly paralysed and unable to do anything for over two weeks but all of his faculties had come back…except his sight. He hadn't been anywhere near, or had anything to do with rugby since. He was fascinated by my rugby film script and asked if it could be somehow transferred onto cassette tape by the Reading Services for the Blind. I sent him it but heard nothing from him until, six months later, the simplest of letters arrived in the post. Carl had dictated a one page Basildon Bonder to his wife to write. The letter was lovely to receive and the sentiment contained within a joyous affirmation. The book wouldn't be a best seller but had a currency all of its own.

Birmingham

Dear Ian,

In forwarding these cassettes containing the Adrian Stoop script, I suggest you do pursue your efforts in getting this material put onto film as I found it damn good!

Certainly during the past week I have relived my own brief rugby career, albeit in the apparently far more skilled boots of Stoop and Poulton etc. The daydreaming was, however, pleasant. My only regret is that I wished for it to be much longer so that my enjoyment could be prolonged.

Thank you for the opportunity of reading the material.
Regards,
Carl

Carl mentioned (another time) that he had sat down in his familiar armchair over a couple of evenings, with a glass of his favourite whisky, listening to the rugby story play out. I realised then that the 'film' script wouldn't ever be seen by thousands, not least Mickey, but had at least been heard by one. I realised, on listening to him, that he had been able to achieve closure on the part of his life he hadn't been able to shake off. And that was all that counted. Disney has its time and place…just one person taking immense personal value from something I had written was more than reason and satisfaction enough for having written it.

Multi-tasking four roles whilst trying to finish off Stoop (the book) to my publishing deadline left me time-poor. In the absence of physical activity, sporting crumbs elsewhere had to suffice. Tottenham weren't helping, succumbing to transition, a shadow of the soon to be Arsenal 'Invincibles'.

The 2003 London Marathon was special. Not anything I was ever going to enter (as much as I'd been running most of my life, I always hated running) but getting to the finish line six days late was important to me. It had been twelve long years since Michael Watson's infamous boxing tear up at White Hart Lane against Chris Eubank. Lasting seven rounds, it had been a glue-to screen. As middleweights they were extremely slick and dangerous. Short, sharp counter-punching. Career ending too, with Watson having to give up with brain damage. Told he would never walk again.

Six days, two hours, twenty-seven minutes, seventeen seconds was the time it took him, boxing's forgotten man, to slowly shuffle his feet to the finish line and close off his own personal journey. I'm sure me seeing him over the line didn't add much to his own private crusade but, by way of humbling and motivation, it did mine. A triumph of heart, courage, strength of spirit and that will to never be beaten. I'd seen some of the great sporting events in my time. This, and his own personal closure, was up there.

A return to America, this time Miami and the Florida Keys. The Westin Beach was one of those hotels that stay in your mind, kicking off the start of the Everglades. A busy hotel but the opportunity to get life, and a strained relationship, back on track. Paddling a canoe out on the water, pace of life slowed down. A road trip along the Seven Mile Bridge to Key West brought it all back.

Moving forward, a joint fortieth birthday with Jon in the gardens of the house at Beavers was one of those brilliantly hot summer days…family, friends and cricket. Everything gloriously old school English and summery about it.

Jolly hockey sticks too. The hockey pitch at one of the Farnham schools was always lit up during a week for what looked like training. The draw of the pitch I kept passing was too much and, at the start of the next season after lap upon lap of running the fields to get fit, I was back playing. A thrown together team of newbies, misfits and kids that needed organising. In sports, particularly hockey, but also park pitch football, I'd always found myself not necessarily the most technically gifted, but the one who stitched things together, on and off the pitch. This team was no different, needing a bridge over (if not troubled) muddy waters. My Channon goal celebration was gone (no-one knew who he was) but as a collective we were good, winning the league.

2004 was turning out well.

At the beginning of December, Stoop's biography was finally published. It had been a quick, focused turnaround from handing it over to the publishers, their editing, final draft and a cover. The only problem, *Adrian Stoop: Father of the Harlequins*, the title of the book that the committee had decided on. I was given twenty-four hours to come up with a new one. One chapter had referred to '...*those halcyon days, seeing the immortal Harlequins.*'

Immortal Harlequin it became.

I was walking through the aisles of the Tesco Superstore in Sunbury early in the month, hoping for Rugby World to have been published (it was late that week). And there it was. I eagerly grabbed a copy and went straight to the back pages, to the book review section. And there I was, with an unexpected five star rating. The stars, lovely as they were, weren't the bit that resonated. It was the book review next door that resounded more. Bill McLaren's. The voice, the anchor, of the first time I'd been sent away. The man who had first introduced me to sport's power to resonate, heal and bring people together, whatever the circumstance. Just about made my year to be in such beloved company.

It wasn't until after the book had been published that I finally had the chance to read it through properly. It took the turning of the first page to fall off my proverbial chair. As part of the dedications I'd put in a long poetic quote to capture the book's essence. I had picked it especially for all the friends I had known from my playing days. Lines from a stanza out of Byron's *Prologue to The Siege of Corinth*.

Line five (of nine)... '*A mind at peace with all below.*'

My dedication had unknowingly contained the same line that I had used for my mother's memorial.

Quite often fear hooks itself onto the unknown, to what might be in front of you, to what you might have to face. Funerals, heights, ambulances, exams, eye surgery, a trophy cabinet full of bamboo.

When you produce something, you always hope for the best. The day *Immortal* was published, Charlotte was born. The first time I'd been back in a hospital since Mum died. When she arrived and drew in air for the first time, she had no idea whether she was coming or going. As I held her in my arms, her lips quivered and I started breathing too.

Simon Pegg, my movie debutant in crime, had progressed to *Shaun of the Dead*. I was still renting videos from a local Blockbuster. I wasn't too concerned, great film as it turned out. Tiring as this December had become, Christmas 2004 was different. Marginal gains were becoming magical (and big) ones.

My daughter was just two weeks old but this Christmas was about more than just presents. It was the first time in fifteen years I had woken up to a totally different Yuletide tale. Woken up several times actually, in sharing the feeding duties.

It took those early days of infancy to acquaint myself, a little while to adjust but, slowly, like the right relationships, the bond that formed was both instant and deep. Based on trust, based on interaction, based on understanding and the ever deepening love that came with it.

She gurgled to herself and waved her little hands round. She started to cling to me. Unable to concentrate at work, she consumed my thoughts. She took charge of my life.

The magic might be back. Santa might be real again.

The New Year came with welcome distractions. A letter from Carl being one of them.

Birmingham
Dear Ian,

Finally I am able to write in gratitude. This being for forwarding the completed copy of Immortal Harlequin *and also I can now give my congratulatory comments on the book which are, I believe, that you have created a thoroughly enjoyable read.*

My connection with you and your first born is that my sister gave birth to her, what she refers to as her one and only child, some twelve weeks ago, this baby she also named Charlotte.

With your permission I would like to contact the Royal National Institute of the Blind in order to make the book available to their members (on cassette).

Regards

Carl

A kind letter also from dear old Chunky, now a headmaster elsewhere, congratulated me on the book (he'd taught me well)…and was very astute in his reading, picking up the Picasso Easter eggs I'd written into it.

Harlequins were relegated at the climax of the season to National Division One. I had hoped my book wasn't a bad omen…but in the end it came down to the last kick of the last game. A penalty for three points. No more, no less. Go over and stay up or miss and go down. The penalty shaved the posts, the wrong side.

And that was it. Down they went.

Down went my book too, albeit in a different way. The club, despite the on-field problems, was investing in itself, which meant replacing the old West Stand that I had spent a lovely summer writing *Immortal* in. When finished, a time capsule went under one of the corners and in it, amongst other items, went the book. Propping up walls, instead of building them, a new story to dine out on.

A few days in Paris with Fernando and Jane and Jane's parents for a sparkling Wales rugby match against France countered it. It was a night-time game and very cold. Wales were down, if not quite out by half-time. Straight after half-time, with two very quick tries, Wales were miraculously in front. I'd been in a monstrous queue for the toilettes. They delivered the Grand Slam over the rest of the Six Nations season when I wasn't. Timing is everything and, similar to the time capsule, something to be treasured.

Jon visited for a catch up to talk about things in general, mostly kids, Siobhan having given birth to Jules two years before. The Plough along West Street, fleetingly renamed

The Scream (and reinvented as a student dive bar) had the Champions League final on between Liverpool and Milan. It was busy and, being both full of students and a football night, loud. It quietened when Liverpool went 3-0 down at half-time. We downed a few and chatted a lot but, with the football pretty much over, we decided to call it a night. 3-0 comebacks in major football finals are pure fantasy. As we finished up, the second half began. Steven Gerrard grabbed a goal, if not a round. Stay, we said.

Istanbul turned into the most famous of nights for both football and for Liverpool. Both of us as well in a 'we were there' way…one of our great school nights. Never give up on a good thing…and, if it is 3-0 at half-time in a massive Champions League game, hang in there.

Not just because the beer's student prices.

Before anyone had blinked December pitched up again. Charlotte had her first birthday and it was as it should be. One of her presents, a copy of Wales' Grand Slam DVD (for photo opportunistic reasons, obviously). For her first proper Christmas (over in Belgium) she'd worked out what boxes with wrapping paper on were. She picked the biggest and slid it across the floor to centre stage. Inside was Pooh Bear's ride-on, aeroplane shaped flying machine thing. The greatest gift ever. I wished I'd had one. Action Men? Pah.

The meaning of Christmas was no longer at a stocking's bottom. Christmas, wrapped up in presents and a thousand tiny traditions had never been quite the same since that last goodbye…but it had now become a combination of hope, memories and expectation, keeping those lost in our hearts whilst cherishing those that were still there. Nearly half a lifetime ago the lights...and the magic...had gone out. The love for a little girl was bringing it all back.

I watched her grow in to an awesome world of nappies and nurseries. She moved from gurgles to single words, to three word sentences (mostly containing 'one', 'more' and 'please') and she was such a joy to behold.

I'd never forget how she used to waddle over to me, as if to demonstrate any and all of her new awareness. It was the things she did, the rate she learned, teaching me how to smile again. To forget the past. And, if I had always been entranced by her crawling, she now stood tall. On her own. She trusted me implicitly knowing I'd catch her if she fell. She laughed and cried in equal measures…a labour of love that was teaching me how to love, baby step by baby step.

As a little gardener she blossomed, always a bucket and spade to hand to help outside.

She was making a better person out of me. Possibly the one I'd always been, but never really knew existed. Perhaps one that had, without realising it, been lying to himself all along. As she grew up, she was showing me another side I had never let out…the caring and devoted one.

With one of those, 'I love you this much!' and sweep of hands that often took out anything in their way, I was sold.

She was very good at all the important things that only a young kid can see and say. Her little life was like a piece of drawing paper on which everything she did left lasting, and illuminating, impressions. The colours, the tones. Her paint box, her brushes. Never far from my head. In waking or in sleeping hours.

Morning, noon, evening. Work, rest, play.

She loved life, if sometimes confused and scared by it. In the midst of a rush I once badly cut myself shaving and let out the loudest 'f' word ever. I hadn't realised she had been by the bathroom door. Her face crumpled, because it was the first time she had heard me 'go loud' (I rarely ever did, except to emphasise something) and she presumably thought she had done something wrong. I felt horrible all day and was so glad to hug her extra tight during bedtime stories later that evening.

The moments kept coming and I kept counting them.

The time I removed the bars from her cot and showed her the new 'grown-up' bed was one.

She kept jumping up and down on it with unrestrained joy. For a second time in her life she knew she was as free as a bird (much to her amusement I played 'Freebird' later). Everyone was growing up.

And then her first rainbow.

Normally some random scribble on her pad of carefully crafted crayoning. That day it rained and the sun came out. I grabbed the opportunity with both hands because I knew there must be a bit of magic in the air somewhere. I got her to chase me round the house in the imaginary quest to find an imaginary rainbow. She found me. I asked her to look as I opened the half-hatch stable door and there it was. She put a hand in front of her mouth in shock and admiration and awe. Imagination had become reality.

For good effect I played 'Over The Rainbow' too.

All the dreams you dare to dream, they really do come true. According to the original (movie) Dorothy.

'Daddy, come at once! I have a question.'

A call to arms by she-who-must-be-run-around-for left me short of time with an added orange juice carpet stain to boot. She'd captivated me right from when I first set those battered eyes on her. She knew little of love but she exuded it in its purest form. She made me talk gibberish. Often.

The question related to colours but it also came with the simplest of presents…a tiny canvas.

'That's you, Daddy!'

My daughter's best impression of me, the character she saw. Lovingly created. Lovingly received. Unbeknownst to her, not unlike where I was normally at…a bit random and all over the place but beautiful in its execution.

Watching her drawing pictures of me made everything clearer. No need to order my thoughts anymore. No need, in the here and now, to make sense of it all.

To finish the days I read Pooh Bear's tales to her just as my father had, once upon a time, to me.

Then it was our favourite bit, after the stories, with the last activity, colouring in. Mostly felt-tipping by numbers which she loved, her speciality being funny faces. Priceless moments…saddened only by the thought that my mother (whose easel, time worn pastels, crusty oil paint tubes and watercolours still lay in the corner of the conservatory) had never got to see it.

And so to sleep. Ladies prerogative. This little one, like all, wanted (after the excitement of colouring in) to be held until she drifted off. The tunes she played in my head were both lyrical and lovely…melodies that hadn't been played before.

Harlequins were also catching up with themselves. With a more than useful squad they were, expectedly, keeping up their promotion bid, post relegation. That wasn't their big epiphany though. It was the interaction with the fans that made the season…both theirs and their oppositions. Best reflected in a game against London Irish. One of the Irish fans had asked for a tribute to a young lad who had died in the week previous from leukaemia. The parents hoped that the crowd would enter into the spirit of their rugby game coming, making it a piratical one, because the lad had loved his pirates. They did. It became a season to cherish because it went beyond sport…if not to heal, at least to commence the journey, the 'process'. Something I knew only too well.

Tottenham, meantime, had a conveyor belt of managers walking the gangplank. Hoddle, Pleat, Santini, Jol, Ramos. Through it all, they'd still got the Lane. And a cup final.

Whilst I was lucky enough to catch the League Cup final from the smallest of Moroccan hotel 'sports' bar TVs (tiny sports bar and tiny TV), Tottenham's highlights reel of the period wasn't a big one. 'Lasagne-gate' ended up being it, when they closed down Arsenal for the Champions League fourth qualifying spot; having stayed overnight in Canary Wharf they were struck down by a mysterious food related illness on the season's last and most pivotal game. Shit. Or more aptly, the shits. Arsenal took a place at the top table.

I learned, somewhat appropriately, given all the ails that had befallen Tottenham, that 'sick as a parrot' was a phrase whose origins belonged to them. Something about a ship's parrot being adopted by them on the boat back from a tour to South America in 1909. After World War One, football needed a reboot. An expanded first division from twenty to twenty-two clubs was proposed and adopted with the first two in the pre-war second division guaranteed to go up. To make it 'interesting', someone needed to get relegated with a third team brought up. Spurs had occupied the relegation positions in the last season before the Great War. By vote, Tottenham were relegated at the expense of Arsenal who had actually finished way off the pace in fifth in the second division pre-war! The vote was held on 10 March 1919, the original St. Totteringham's Day. The parrot died the same day…and a colloquialism was born.

Time passes though, time moves on and distractions came randomly, thick and fast.

An alumni reunion weekend at Southampton University meant getting Public Bar Wanderers back together. Various celebration parties were being held, but for us it meant one night more at the old Frog & Frigate, where Derek was no longer the guitarist. He had bought the place. Outside they had undergone huge dock regenerations at Ocean Village, but The Frog still commanded its own little place beneath the arches. Inside, time had stood still. Having reminisced with Meht about the ones that had got away many decades before, the saloon doors opened and my face froze again. Susan One (Birmingham station Susan One) walked in to the party. The same hello and same smile. And, finally, that hug. Then she was gone, another event calling.

I never saw her again.

The next night a mad lady locked me in an attic.

It was another of those weird tales you can't make up. A reunion party at the Students' Union Bar the night after the Frog. Nearing close, the boys took their long stroll back to the Glen accommodation. One for the road, for old time's sake with some other old friends, for me. The taxis outside reminded me of the Graduation Ball. Do not forget to use them, the menu had said. Having lost the will and ability to walk far, the taxi seemed the logical option. Unsurprisingly there was a queue. Help came, surprisingly, with an offer of a lift from someone going the same way. Great!

I took her kind offer without knowing what was about to evolve. The volleyball in the passenger seat footwell was funny though.

'Hey, it's Wilson,' I said jokingly.

'Yes, it is. How did you know? He's my best friend.'

Gulp.

I talked around what, despite my tired state, I suddenly realised wasn't a joke. I steered the conversation onto films (I should never get myself started on films).

What a great film *Castaway* was. Tom Hanks. Brilliant.

Before I knew it, I was about fifteen minutes into a five minute journey…that wasn't going anywhere near where I was supposed to. I was either going to have to execute that moving-vehicle-open-door-falling-out number that worked so well in any other movie…

…or wait for the next stop.

Whenever.

We ended up near Shirley (don't call me Shirley)! At her place. She invited me in and said she would call for a cab.

'Sit down. Talk to Sam and Pete, Dave, Bob and Frank,' she said. And then disappeared (not literally).

There was me, two goldfish, a table, a TV and a sofa in the room.

She could have been the original (Oz) Dorothy for all I cared. Even in my state though, I knew (yet again) we most definitely weren't in Kansas anymore.

She returned with a couple of very large gins (no tonic) and said something to Bob (the TV) and Frank (the sofa).

'Called a taxi,' she said. 'At least three hours.'

'Right.' I check. She's right.

'You can have the spare room.'

'Fab, I'll be away pretty early, don't worry.'

'Follow me, then.'

I followed her. Upstairs. Slightly quizzical as she pulled down the loft ladder and disappeared up it.

'Come on, up you come.'

We have all seen those horror films where sticking your head into a dark attic hole maybe isn't the best thing to do.

So I did, expecting horror fade-in music on my way.

Once up, it was dark (it was an attic).

'Are you ready?' she asked.

I was properly done for now. What was the worst that could happen?

I heard the light switch.

My eyes took in what was no longer an attic. All I could do was gasp, hold my breath and live this dream.

In front of me, all around me, was a midnight, moonlit desert island scene complete with thousands of tiny stars. She may have been off her proverbial trolley but there was absolutely no doubting she was one hell of a brilliant artist.

'Goodnight,' she said, going back down, leaving me to a dreamscape, a camp bed and a pillow. The trap-door shut.

I was utterly in awe of my nocturnal surroundings. And anticipating the meagre diet of bread and water for months to come.

Next morning a coffee and a cab stood waiting.

Ruby slippers not required.

Some people and places are always timeless. The marketing world though was about to undergo seismic shifts with the advent of all things digital…and with it all things 'social'.

Social media had tentacles in all aspects of work, rest and play. Simple connection sites like Friends Reunited had morphed like bats out of hell to the much bigger beasts of LinkedIn and Facebook. We were all about to be exposed to the consequences of our own brainless actions...those in the public eye (like footballers) but the rest of us mortals too. The world was changing at a pace. All of which meant the Birddog offices weren't going to seize many more days out in Odiham and the shires. It had to adapt and evolve. London, and streets paved with gold, was the logical next step. I had dropped the consultancy role and Dad's hotel had long been sold, so it was Birddog and Sunbury, spread over the week, to keep me mildly entertained on the work front. As 2007 kept jogging slowly on, what could possibly go wrong?

The Rugby World Cup was held in Paris in September. My last time there had ended up a first-class weekend with good friends watching Wales. This time it was Rusty and South African Dave and some tickets for South Africa and England in the pool stages. We made it to the game after an expensive night before in Harry's Bar (tour rule number one: never lose the 'must buy the next round' forfeit game when single whiskies were approaching eighty euros each). England unfortunately went AWOL in their game, losing by something of a cricket score.

That evening was a strange one. No mad ladies, just us having to chaperone a couple of late teen Australian sisters downtown the problem this time around. The promise to their aunt to get them back to their hotel later on that night was, as promises go, always going to be a rash one. Having turned the pub (opposite Harry's Bar) in to full on Aussie 'no rules' until four in the morning, neither of the twosome had any idea where their hotel was located. Just a random landmark or two.

A promise is always a promise in my book. Even if that escalates to that next stage of a promise, 'a challenge'. I had a mental map of Paris and the job of escorting them back to 'a' hotel, 'possibly' about half an hour away.

By a process of deduction, way longer than half an hour (and a good rapport with the cab driver) we found it. Seven o'clock in the morning and the driver finally got me back to my hotel. Not quite a million euros clocked up on this adventure, but not too far short.

Paris would always be a lovely place for memories.

So too, Eagles concerts. 22 March, 2008, was the first time at the O2 for me…and it was very warm inside. As we got close to a 'Desperado' final encore, I was fully in the moment. And also aware of the single lady next to me…we had chatted at length about our mutual love (of Eagles). I woke up, roughly halfway through our big climax having, ahem, fallen asleep on her shoulder. No disrespect to the Eagles…just a long year. Close in the here and now, but no cigar. Next time, maybe.

Charlotte had her time whether it be designing carnival tee-shirts, World Book Day costumes or a trip to the theatre in London to see *Dirty Dancing*. She was, as always, lovingly transfixed by 'the lift'. Equally, and as memorably, she was still doing her painting which was as gloriously free-form and characterful as even the best Picasso.

'I like painting,' she said randomly one day. 'It is in my blood.' She could always bring me to tears with something like that, straight off the bat…but…I didn't do crying.

Picasso had a reasonable amount to answer for so far in my life…I blamed it on Michael (Stoop).

My favourite quote of his (Picasso) had always been, 'It took me four years to paint like Raphael, but a lifetime to paint like a child.' Who was I to argue on that one, seeing my daughter's prodigious and resonant output?

Before long I was back on the footprints of Madeleine, Picasso's mysterious and elusive model and muse. Having enjoyed researching and writing about Adrian Stoop, my thoughts turned to writing again. Having written a 'chaps' book, as I enjoyed challenges I thought that writing a ladies book, romantic fiction, would be it. I needed a story…and an exhausting search for the young lady in *Femme en chemise* became it.

My first mistake was to explain my pre-formed thought process to a taxi bus full of extremely drunk women after a hockey club do. Shot down in flames (repeatedly) about my ability to conjure up anything that could ever be considered passable romance and the greatest love story ever. Worst journey ever. Bar one.

The second one, if not a mistake, certainly found me in the wrong place at the wrong time…the curious spot being an afternoon workshop, 'Writing Romantic Fiction', at the Guildford Book Festival. Surprisingly, no blokes (guessing they'd hopped in my taxi after I'd hopped out). On settling in, the first question to everyone from the course guide, a leading Mills & Boon writer was, 'Who had actually written a book before?'

Hands up. Gulp. Just me, then.

I explained about my rugby biography.

'If you think that allows you to write romantic fiction, you might as well leave now,' came the rather unexpected reply (weird, as Mills & Boon had just published a series of rugby themed 'love' stories). It was like having the rejection letter before I had even conjured up a story.

'Do you think she likes me?' I asked the lady alongside me, realising I'd already been cast as the antagonist in this odd love-in. I kept quiet and took my notes for the rest of the day in fear of a blackboard duster heading towards me.

'Fuck you, romantic stories,' seemed to be the message (a big CAPITAL LETTER one) coming straight down my side of the road.

I should probably have given up the ghost then, it being the second time I had been asked, 'How very dare I?' And that's what it became to me; a dare, a challenge, a promise.

Sometimes in trying to find the answer to something, it is better to start at the end and work back.

How would I describe *Les Demoiselles d'Avignon*?

A large oil canvas. Brutish. Five nudes (in the South of France, been there, got the tee-shirt, didn't get to wear it), their eyes large and quiet, like masks. Hiding. Or hidden.

In the foreground, a bowl of fruit.

Masks, hiding and bowls of fruit.

Been there, got that tee-shirt too.

Les Demoiselles d'Avignon, *The Brothel of Avignon* and *The Young Ladies of Avignon* were some of the titles given to the Picasso painting that had revolutionised art. No-one knew what drove the great Spaniard to paint it…whether it really was a brothel in Avignon, or as always with Picasso, much more going on underneath the layers. Clearly the artist had been in two minds. Not unlike the painting…fractured and emotional. Me too.

My interest in the painting, painting being in my blood aside, had stemmed from Michael Stoop's stories about the other Picasso, *Femme en chemise*. The woman in that picture, known forever as 'Madeleine' was the artist's 'one that got away'. He had never let go of her and kept her in his heart, mind…and attic. For years she had stuck in my mind too, alongside Michael's peculiar riddles. Blue in both tone and expression, the picture represented a past that had caused him some emotional turmoil, followed as it was by several paintings depicting maternity and the very same lady.

She'd been airbrushed out of art history and become a terrific and beguiling mystery.

I realised that some of the best times I'd had, ones that had given me most kicks, were in the years up to Charlotte being born, doing the research for *Immortal Harlequin*. With a little time on my hands, thoughts of what drove the artist to either painting (and what the connection between them was) gave me a hobby and research to pursue once more. Brick road journeys that give you your focus back.

Les Demoiselles d'Avignon was overwhelming. Maybe even unfinished. Why? How to narrow things down? Where to start? What was Madeleine's secret? And why had Michael Stoop dropped her (and me) in it and then shut the door? Too many questions. Small sections of dusty, old memoirs from some of Picasso's contemporaries gave clues.

'To find the answer you need to find five English girls.'

Jaime Sabartes had dangled a big carrot.

A challenge. I liked challenges.

The answer to the century old mystery, a buried secret, what really drove that great Spanish artist's tortured mind and revolutionised art history…seemingly lay in England.

Why was I now chasing a ghost down blind alleys, dead ends, dusty attics even? *Femme en chemise* lived at the Tate Modern, a Stoop family donation. She had those eyes that followed you all round the room. All my research, random connections and conspiracy theories about her made me follow a trail to Brookwood Cemetery.

It was Halloween, All Saints' Eve.

The railway out of Waterloo used to be the Necropolis Line, with third-class carriages for the dead or anyone that couldn't afford either classes one or two. I was in second and trying to see Brookwood clearly wasn't easy. Eyes and the mist. I had been through it many a time before on the journey back from Birddog; it looked familiar but it was a different place in a fog.

The cemetery itself was a haunting one. Monks used to sleep in the old mortuary of an asylum that had once stood nearby. Now there were a whole load of them that lived in the cemetery. There used to be a nudist colony there at one stage too (not this time, thanks).

The vast acreage of the place had, back in its day, been a Victorian Valhalla. Giant sequoia, rhododendrons, cypress, laurel, wellingtonians, silver birches, copper beech, azaleas and cowslip. Fascinating, never-ending pathways leading to crumbling mausoleums and graves.

Whispers echoed in the wind.

How did I find myself there...at a crossroads...heather, tripping over (complex) roots and rabbit-holes, blankets of fog, freezing clearings and trees swallowing up the graves? I was surrounded by fungus, decay and death but a wintery tale away from growth and life.

Half-blind, amongst corpses, looking for just one. On a mission to validate something of little or no consequence. Stumbling around, trying to read gravestones and centuries old type. Tracing with my fingers on old, cold lichen.

Why her? A long dead lady who might (or might not) be the lady in the painting. It certainly wasn't the day job.

Hidden deep among masses of ferns, I found her grave (fashioned once upon a time, seemingly, as a bed of roses). A moving epitaph, penned by her spiritualist husband, who had joined her twenty years later spoke volumes.

'Life's melody remains unbroken.'

As signs go it was unexpected, poignant and (reflecting on the day over a pint at The White Hart, nearby) gave me back my appetite for a fight. Romance never dies. With my head back in the writing game, my novel wouldn't either.

'You'll be sleeping in the spare room. Your computer and all your books and boxes are there. Take a few months to sort things out and then it will be better if you move out.'

As signs went, that was crystal clear.

Nine years of a relationship, over in the time it took to say, 'I don't love you anymore.' I hadn't seen that coming.

Looking around the family home, lovingly revived over the years, I picked out all the bits that had given me most pleasure: the panorama of the sweeping garden, stuck as it was in winter's bleakness; the open fireplace; my daughter's toys; and her little painting table that she had often retired to in conjuring up another mini masterpiece.

Everything in its correct place, except my head. It was a mess, as I felt various shades of tired, empty and raw.

All of a sudden the dark clouds started appearing again. I wanted to go back in time. At least to the 1980s, the best time of my life, and never come back. Those student years, listening to late-night FM in my room, with my drawings and dreams, and not a fucking care in the world.

Endless, carefree, crazy days.

I needed all the adventures again.

Those make-believe desert islands. Carving initials in to trees. Happy days of swinging between them. Being able to fly (often falling, but at least trying).

Here I was now. Losing my grip. Unravelling again.

I couldn't keep doing this…the same old dances in the same old shoes.

Christmas 2008 was a difficult one. There was solace to be had in an early shopping trip to London with Charlotte.

Hamleys was its usual nightmare before Christmas, even in early December. I had promised Charlotte we would be going to 'the big toy shop' though and, as always, I liked to keep a promise. Half an hour to queue to get in, stretching all the way back round to Liberty. After what seemed like an eternity later, it took two seconds once inside for Santa Bear to go on the 'this one, this one' list. More than worth another smile. And another elbow from someone breezing past.

Turning to see who had banged into me, I momentarily caught the eyes of a young woman, who got out a fleeting apology before she was immediately swallowed up into the massed throngs ahead. She was quite nice, I thought. And realised that not only was this unlikely to be the time and place to woo the Christmas stockings off someone, teddy bears were very much the order of the day. Concentrate on the job in front of me.

As I surveyed the carnage around me…a lot of headless people going about their affairs with their kids, bouncing into each other like pinball machines…the slightest hint of enjoyment struck me. The last place I'd expected to be was the one I was getting most kicks from. And that was it. I'd been looking for the whole enchilada in the wrong places. Books, timeless mysteries, salvation, love. Especially, love. I'd tried too hard, never knowing when it would catch up with me, never being at or in the right time or place when it did. For all I knew it could be just around the corner.

Just around the corner, a stuffed, robotic penguin being thrust into my hands brought me back to the moment.

'Please, Daddy, please. Love you, hands round the back and back again.'

Everything exists in limited quantities, except the never-ending story of a very seasonal cuddly toy in the arms of a four year old. One toy bird to the better, our next stop the Promised Land that was Oxford Street's Disney Store. The large Pluto was met with a quick rendition of, 'How Much Is That Doggie In The Window?'

Hard not to smile as Disney rode to the rescue again.

We walked back through Soho. The streets I had known so well in my late teens were now (thankfully) empty, save an old lady trying to palm something off on me (hopefully not the same old picture cards…or a poisoned apple). Just a sprig of heather, fortunately. I had been ambushed again, a befuddled mind still stranded somewhere between 'once upon a time' and 'happy ever after'.

'For luck,' said the old lady, pressing a bunch on to my daughter's lapel.

I wasn't convinced I needed the dried out remnant of a season gone by to remind me that luck was the one thing I was down on most.

'Please, Daddy, please.'

A pound coin lighter, we headed off.

On my own again, I'd take all the breaks I could get.

After The Thrill Is Gone
Winter 2008 - Spring 2009

'That's an 'A', Daddy.'

As first lines go, it was the one I had always feared not being able to read most. The eye chart at the opticians.

Forty-five years of age, the weird irony of my four year old daughter teaching me how to say letters I'd so lovingly taught her, but could now neither shape nor recognise, was never going to be lost on me.

Education should be judged by how it's played back.

Ophthalmic specialists were something I'd got used to over the years. I had lost count of the number of tests I'd had. This particular specialist I'd got used to, too. Pleasant, friendly, professional. We had shared the deterioration in vision as time had passed, but precious little else. I knew her name...Emily, I think...but that was all. We would have a date every six months or so and she would tell me what had got worse. I knew her voice mostly and as dates went, she was costly.

'Could I see the clown?' she asked most times as she lit up the screen ahead of me.

No. But I had my four year old with me this time who was finding it funny. No. I couldn't see the clown. But that day I was feeling like one. Generally and specifically.

As Emily's instruments played tricks with my eyes, my mind continued to distort my thoughts. Just like my vision, everything inside my head was a floating confusion, a series of jagged pictures. An inability to separate light from dark, a palette of colours blending into each other. All, without my glasses or contact lenses, I had to guide me. Had the last ten years of my life, like all the shapes in front of my battered eyes, been just an illusion, content as I had been, to watch the world, I thought, turn slowly round, with the occasional bit of Tottenham (alright, a lot!) to quicken my pulse? I had missed the world's halting progress, as it had slammed into the buffers. At speed. One minute I'd been gliding along, the next flat on my back, nursing a scrambled head. Thoughts going round in circles, everything felt so unreal. I was real. Or at least I was when I'd looked in the mirror that morning. Through the fog of raw emotion, the reflection of my true self hadn't been anywhere in sight.

'I'm going to put the dilating drops in now,' said Emily. 'They'll take a good few hours to wear off before you'll be able to see with your glasses on.'

I sat and waited, chatting away with Charlotte. 2004 had been one of the best years. The year she was born, the year I had grown up a little…and realised that after a few failed relationships, where I had endeavoured to try and love, and a succession of passable financial jobs (before the current stability), where I had learned nothing of any great value, I didn't really know what I wanted out of life, save seeing my daughter grow up happy. 'Seeing' being the operative word.

'I don't love you anymore,' was both a wake-up call and the moment life and love changed in an instant. It had only been half a week but this day was the day it all hit home. I couldn't see but everything was in sharp focus. I was tired. Tired of wanting to be someone. For anyone. Always being blinded by the everyday beauty of the world, of the people I'd met, but always subservient to the pain and emptiness inside. I had closed myself down emotionally. And not just the past ten years. I had been trying my best to dodge the painful parts of my life for too long.

It was the slightest brush of her hair I sensed first as she peered deep into my eyes. Watching her, watching me. The dilating drops might have opened my pupils wide but, as opticians went, she had always been very easy on them. No need to have caught her eyes across some bar. Hers were, then, all mine separated only by a microscope and assorted other optical weapons of choice. She pressed herself a little closer. Examining, probing, her face almost touching mine.

Her soft hair caressed mine, as she gently moved side to side, creating this strange sensory experience. The warm air from her nostrils, as she exhaled, drifted over my skin. In the darkest of rooms, she found herself utterly in the realm of my senses. I sat transfixed, but felt a lightness of being. I could see her light. She could see right through me.

My random, rambling but rather pleasant thoughts were interrupted by her professional suggestion.

'I think we should take another retinal picture,' she said with a disguised concern.

Probably just another hole in my eyeball needing sewing up. The last time had hurt; my sight had been saved back then but would never quite be back to normal. Somehow, though, the prospect of any further physical pain just didn't seem to register, given the way I was currently feeling. The incremental deterioration in my sight, the inability to define faces clearly, read well and see platform signs had mirrored that of my relationship. Slowly drifted away from me.

I held Charlotte tight as she led me by the hand. As my mum had also held me tight on my early opticians trips for those black, plastic NHS specs. Same age, faded memories. I was glad she was there. The optician too. Both, lifebelts to cling on to with no clear and obvious sight of dry land on the horizon. A dawning realisation I was once again in a troubled and confusing place.

Charlotte provided a focal point of sorts. That morning she looked up at me from the bed, curled my lips up and said, 'Smile, Daddy,' and I knew. The more time I gave her, the more time I would keep my own troubles away. There was, however, a limit to how long I could hole up in the spare room. My frustrations compounded themselves. At some time I knew I'd have to move out of the cottage...no more seeing Charlotte on a regular basis. No more watching her grow daily. It was going to be experiences, on a part-time basis, rather than every day occurrences.

Work helped, although the train journeys up to London were monotonous and car journeys to Sunbury difficult, so much so that I started taking the train there too. A chance if nothing else to read the papers and catch up on the news of the day and latest trends. Social media seemed to garner most of the press.

It was hard not to see all the articles on and for 'online' dating. A relatively new concept it was something that had never entered my mind until that moment in time. As the train passed through Brookwood, the sky brighter than the last time, my eyes opened up to the opportunity of making something happen.

My mind raced away with itself, wondering how I'd go about it. No idea what weapons I had in my armoury, what weapons I'd actually need in a whole new world of online possibilities. A profile or a persona? Would anyone believe it? Did I have time? First date watching me play hockey? I remembered how time consuming all the writing, emailing and listening had been in the past. What was I looking for? What was I ready for? What would I find? My impressions of romance and of love had been washed and diluted in so many colours of experience. Not for me, then.

Online dating wasn't a concept I bought.

So I did.

'Dogs love you because you are handsome, funny and kind and like you kissing and stroking them.'

Some of Charlotte's truisms were brilliant…this, one of her best. All that was needed for a dating profile, if written through the eyes of a child.

Capturing a personality in a few words and putting it in a box was never going to be easy. No point in asking my friends…they were guys. Writing prologues to love stories not their thing, great as they were for filling in the gaps.

I had late nights, lots of them, trying to understand the mechanics of it all. And learnt the rules…give just enough away, don't criticise, be nice until its time not to be.

I had later nights reading profiles.

I tried to steer away from all the guys…something weird (on a dating site) about getting the low-downs and tactical formations of the oppo. The other gladiators, surprisingly, or unsurprisingly, followed a paint by numbers formulae.

'Into abseiling, scuba diving, motor-biking, parachuting, mountaineering and Ironman.'

Not really my bag. No football or hockey or running.

'Someone who doesn't want to make love to thousands of women, just thousands of different ways to one.' How many times did I read that? That 'one', whoever she was, was surely going to be a lucky lady. Or not. Romance was, ahem, alive if not kicking.

The most consistent thing seemed to be an awful lot of Dangerous (quite Desperate) Dans out there. Their typical profile was full on daring-do and monstrous achievement. There was a small army of middle-aged guys going through their own middle-aged crises. That'll be me then. Without the 'Dangerous' bit.

Conversely, a raft of female online dating profiles stared up at me from my computer. Hundreds of them, all trying to entice and allure in their own ways, both in pictures and in their words. A massive jigsaw puzzle of not-my-types, beguiling loveliness, laced occasionally with way too good to be true fantasy. It was like being in a toy shop leading up to Christmas.

'Are you what I have been looking for?' Mmmmn. No.

'Love and marriage?' A coffee and chat possibly a better place to start.

'Boo.' Run!

'What does a lady have to do to make you laugh?' Good question. No idea.

'Not a gym bunny, nor a bunny boiler.' Hair definitely off though.

'Dynamic sex kitten looking for lust online.' Sound of chap falling off chair.

'I am not just looking for a sexual relationship - if that's all I was after I could get that anywhere. I am looking for the whole package. The physical chemistry; the intellectual chemistry; the passionate chemistry; the sexual chemistry.' Gulp. The 'c' word. Four times over. Shit. Run, again!

'Uniforms. I adore uniforms.' Oh dear, dear. I had tried being a doctor but failed the first interview at St Thomas' Hospital aged just seventeen. I'd no idea what I was doing there. Head (for a change) in the wrong place at the time. Ballsed up all the questions. I had been a paramedic once too...stepped in as an extra on that film shoot, not knowing that it'd mean ending up in an ambulance again (although paramedic and ambulance do quite often go hand in hand). The hardest 'job' I had ever done. So, sorry, no...not into uniforms.

'Ah, thank God, you found me. Perfect timing. Destiny, the sofa, a bottle of wine and a DVD had us in mind.' Or not.

'We will both love dancing, travelling, cinema, music, fitness, healthy lifestyles and find joy and fun in the simple things. Whether coffee in a lovely café, holding hands and strolling by the seashore, or simply cuddled up on the sofa with that bottle of wine and one of our favourite DVD's.' We've been here before.

'This weekend I have nothing planned and I never do well without any plans. I have too much time on my hands and that gives me time to dwell. I am thirty-five years old and looking for my soulmate. It would be lovely to cuddle up on the sofa with…' Oh, please.

Despite the apparent fondness amongst the ladies (all lovely at heart, I'm sure) for their sofas, bottles of wine and DVDs, their real tangible gauge of 'the one' always seemed to be universal…height. Tall, dark and handsome featured large, more often than not followed by 'at least six foot'. The big lad at school would have been very happy in this playground. Whilst I had never been him, trampling all in my stride I, ahem, did technically have six foot two in my armoury (in a movie, now DVD). What's an extra inch or two (or three) between friends?

The more profiles I read, the more I realised that whilst writing profiles was an entirely new sport, there was a very cheap art to online dating. A sport I'd rather not be playing and a sketchbook I'd rather not be filling in.

I had to start somewhere. Badly critiquing everyone else was a very defensive strategy.

Where to begin though? An empty online dating script box required me to paint a picture, in not SO many words (I had never been one to use a couple of words when a few hundred would do) of who I was, where I was at and what I was looking for in my ideal match.

Brought up on Viz and Dave Allen this could get messy. *Can you describe yourself?*

'Old school gentleman, new romantic.' The 1980s were so last year.

'As fit as a butcher's dog.' Once upon a long time ago, maybe.

'Never going to be an oil painting, but there's still life.' Mmmmmn. Stale cheese might be a little too hard to palate in a faux Michelin starred field.

Perhaps better the truth.

'Fit, fabulous, forties, successful, happy, on top of the world.' Never further away from it.

Oh, bollocks to this.

'Six foot two.'

Winging it with a lovely bottle of wine (sofa and DVDs excluded) had always been the fail-safe plan of attack. Now was no reason to change the habits of a lifetime.

White wine. Tick. Big bottle of. Tick.

A few of my favourite things...

...sun, sea, sand? Tick.

...snow and mountains? Tick. Dangerous Dan territory though, perhaps best avoided at all costs.

…fish suppers on some warm sea-terrace as day turns effortlessly to night? Tick.

Other things (maybe) worth mentioning…

…tendency to be over-analytical? Leave that out.

…body of a forty-eight year old, hair of a seventy-eight year old, eyes of a hundred-and-eight year old? Something for everyone, nothing for anyone. Review that one later.

…great at both shuttle runs and running defensive short corners? This was a dating site, not a sports bio.

It was hard.

Take me back to the days before computers, when letter writing was an art in itself, where flirting was subtler. In a world of online jousting I was a hapless, horseless novice.

Before computers and fractured sentencing, letters had taught me the finer art of capturing a moment. Writing had always come happily ever after. I had never had to capture myself or anyone else (in a closed, intimidating space) for a minute in time though.

A check of my birth sign characteristics might help.

Cancer…

…sympathetic, patient, emotional staying power, shows vulnerability, needs to feel something with strength before truest feelings emerge.

…not easily summed up on first acquaintance, it takes a long time to get to know them, a tough outer shell makes it difficult for someone to penetrate, protecting against them giving away too much too soon.

…when in love, Cancers are supportive, compassionate, dedicated and tender. They not only adore affection…they are generous with it in return. They are in love forever, no other sign equals the intensity, they hold on to loved ones with a tenacious grip and the objects of their affection have a cherished place in the heart long after a relationship ends.

…worst tendency to be smothering.

It was like rereading one of those old school reports. An awful lot of truth but very hard to translate in to a rabble-rousing 'come and get me' speech though. Six foot two was still looking favourite for top spot on the rostrum.

Who or what was I looking for?

Ah! Easy question at last! Someone who liked watching and playing (field) sport 24-7. Someone who liked football, acted interested in it, didn't schedule other events for the big game, wore the jersey with pride and avoided having any discussions at pivotal points in the game.

Someone who could be all the other players in my five-a-side team. Forward, playmaker, defender and keeper.

Fist pump. Nailed it.

Billy Joel and 'River of Dreams' came on the radio, kept things real and took me back (almost) to the 1980s.

'I'm searching for something, something so undefined, something that can only be seen, by the eyes of the blind.'

What, like a mermaid that could dance…or something? Not that real then. Thanks Billy, sounded good, but didn't narrow things down and I couldn't see the fans flocking.

Hang on…actually Billy, for all your scenes from Italian restaurants and bottles of red and bottles of white (items of furniture and digital video discs optional) there was some truth in that…someone who would leave me wanting more. Someone who could give the greatest of presents. Not the ones where you know what you are going to get and just rip their wrappers off with a lusty anticipation…the ones where you've no idea what is inside and you slowly unravel the packaging with tender love. Something unexpected.

I missed all the intimacy, passion and mental joustyness that came with being in tune with someone. All of which I craved. I missed making someone's dull day a brighter one, someone's routine day a brilliant one, someone's rainy day sitting on a sill staring out of the window in to er, a shared rainy day sitting on a sill staring out of the window.

Actually, that read well. Thanks Billy. Nearly there.

As filling in dating profiles went though, that was about four pages when only four paragraphs were required.

I couldn't even colour in a box, let alone think outside one. Editing clearly necessary to make me sound more (or less) ordinary. As tiredness descended, the kaleidoscope of words and female forms running rampant across my mind became as blurred as the ones before my eyes.

Falling slowly asleep in bed, my subconscious took up the baton. Vivacious? Petite? Athletic? Mere words without the proper woman to frame them around. Something else had to be present, over and above the ability to look hot in Olivia Newton-John pastel shades and spandex (okay, even if it was an '80s photo). Heart and soul, emotional depth, affection, sensitivity, warmth and passion. Someone who laughed. One with whom doing things was both effortless and left me breathless. Someone who appreciated the value of time, who wanted to evolve a relationship, rather than take it right back to the Stone Age. Someone who retained a certain mystery above and beyond the chase.

Glass half full (Bacardi, on the side table) and bed half empty was as succinct as I was going to get. As plans C to Z span round and round, night turned to day.

Wham! and 'Last Christmas' on a clock radio woke me up to yet another day on the festive run in; a casual reminder of the happier ones that had gone before. Nothing that had gone through my mind in the small hours had stuck.

I reviewed everything I'd written on my profile to date, passed it off as waffle and scrubbed pretty much all of it.

Being full of it was one thing, initiating action another.

I scribbled five more, paid the subscription and, in a fit of pique, pressed 'Activate'.

I had no idea what to expect or where it would all end up. If supporting Tottenham was a mirror of life, then it would probably mean some sublime moments, some great seasons, a lot of graft but an awful lot of face-palming and mediocrity. And a trophy every ten years or so.

It was a stampede.

That never came.

The gazelle, a couple of wild horses, the odd cow and a dear deer. Tumbleweed settled on the keyboard, my inbox a ghost town. Was I invisible, or were people (like Emily) able to see through me? An available online population had looked right into those battered eyes and voted with their feet. Mickey smiled down at me from the framed letter on my wall. I clearly needed a few lessons.

'Deep. And crisp. And even'…definitely going to need a little more if it was going to stand the test of introductory line time. It was a good place to start though.

All I needed now was a middle and an end.

'Hair of silver, buns of steel and heart of gold is me in a chemistry lesson'…hmm, my missing middle piece? Crikey. I had no idea where I was going now…probably the other side of the moon in my 1970's plastic NASA space helmet for all I knew. Going off-piste in a space shuttle was one thing. Finding someone out of this world another.

'Looking to share a magic carpet ride adventure'…aha! My somewhat fairy tale end. More upbeat than 'Desperado' at least.

Halfway through my supposed first active week, doing something was better than doing nothing.

It was a dating maze. Not unlike the Littlewoods Pools that were the highlight of my '70s Saturday afternoons. Try and predict those scoring draws from across four divisions with a little bit of current 'form' and a few statistics thrown in. As a family back then we had never won much. Scoring big now might also be a pipe dream.

I sent a few emails still none the wiser as to the etiquette or formalities of online dating. Or how to land the jackpot.

The silence spoke volumes. I sent a few more. No idea what I was doing right or wrong. Batting above my natural place in the order? Dangerous Dan cornered the market? Too cheesy? I varied it. Went random and rogue…a bit of Apollinaire, a bit of maudlin French to raise the bar…only to fall flat when testing it out on probably the only maudlin French girl on the dating site. No-one had any time for me.

Back to the silence. And yet another fruitless day. Going around in ever-decreasing circles, someone else to try and impress, be that one-in-a-million for. I sat waiting for the time to pass. Nobody made one.

Slowly they came.

I'd already learned that I couldn't hit a barn door with a .303 rifle. The only musket I did have in my armoury was I at least gave good email, a legacy of a lifetime of letters. All I had to do was draw someone in. As to finding the love of my life? If it happened, it happened.

I responded to a few messages. I'd always been good at listening, gently caressing the pain, fear and frustration out of people. But boy was I having to listen now. Life would appear to have thrown quite a lot at many. They wrote, in the main (in my direction at least), with a little hope fuelled by anger, bitterness and loneliness. I empathised.

Come the new year, the dates started…some unusual, some uncomfortable, some lovely. The breakfast one. The lunchtime one. The evening one. No-one was entirely who they made themselves out to be. All running somewhere and nowhere. Some rude, some pleasant but all very much playing their own numbers games. Doing their own maths. Each date a five minute ease-in to get up with the pace of the game and then a five minute scramble toward the end (sliding scale of time in between) to land a return fixture.

Two things became very apparent from my exhaustive review of the potentials and maybes. Firstly, an awful lot of people loved cuddling up on a sofa with a bottle of plan B and a DVD. That was always going to be a very clear and present danger. Secondly, that chemistry was the required (seemingly only) spark to ignite any and all relationships.

Hello chemistry, my old friend. A big enough flame and a half decent result was something I was singularly failing to generate now as well.

The online dating game smacked of desperation (never more so than with me in it). There were no rules and a lot of idiocy (me again). A massive melting pot of personalities and baggage (er, ditto). Here I was leading a fruitless charge like the poor bloke at the front of the Light Brigade. On a donkey. With three legs.

Everyone was looking for something real in a land of illusion. If I'd learned anything by now in this first season of a form over substance competition...

...I always found myself in a queue behind someone with a greater hunger for a quicker fix.

...never, ever get engaged in an email conversation with anyone going by the handle of 'Raven'. First email normal. The follow-on a whole thought process and sermon (from Raven) that deviancy was the way to go in the dating world (husband included). Be afraid. Very afraid. Keep running.

...the Village Hotel is an odd place to bring someone trying to shed a lot of baggage to meet your hockey team as part of an end-of-season dinner dance. To be fair, the team were great. Perfect gentlemen (else I wouldn't have invited her). Very welcoming, very easy. As the music and evening morphed, she relaxed.

'Thank you for dancing me through chemistry,' she said at the end.

Finally!

I'd passed a practical exam! Tequilas all round.

She wasn't finished.

The whole dating game was becoming another cathartic process, not unlike all the sports I had thrown myself in to over many a season; distracting myself with other people's problems, running around making sure everybody else got the result they were looking for.

Time (and energy) that would perhaps have been better utilised in working on my own game.

The other thing she taught me, just prior to finding the great love of her life (the following day), was that showing vulnerability, not confidence, was a very attractive quality. She gave me something to work on and with.

I'd stepped out of my comfort zone, trained hard, lost a lot of weight (too much) and started to look thin. By now I could answer all the questions for a dating profile in just the one word. I knew who I was and where I was at in life.

Lost.

It was a fantasy world and no one was enchanting me. My heart was in the right place. My head and the woman of my dreams weren't. The last thing I wanted, or needed, was a deep, spiritual, emotional affair.

Seabreeze changed all that.

In the mass of dating profiles, she popped up. One in four million. She didn't have a photo. Her email was short and to the point. Why Seabreeze? And why her, then?

It was that time of year again; looking out of my study window I saw the withered stems, once flowers of beauty, yearning for warmth, the new year, a new season and the opportunity to come back for more, full of life. Beyond the flower borders in a lost, far corner of the wintery garden sat the seated arbour. Bought to be a feature, it was meant to have been the real heart of the garden. For now it stood untendered and unloved. Weeds surrounded it. Its fortunes seemingly a reflection of my own.

A single cerise rose, out of season, the only focal point. Graceful. Tender. Fragile. Hauntingly beautiful. Alone.

Not a far cry from her profile photo which captured my imagination when it came in.

Maybe that was it. The little she'd offered up came with hope. Aside from a mutual liking of rugby and the Eagles though, something else didn't seem quite right. This could be an adventure for all the wrong reasons.

The 'first date' when it came was unusual. Running for the train again to get there on time, hating to miss the start of any game, the world and my life were back to their rush. All I knew was…she was different. And I had no idea why.

I had no idea how it was all going to play out and I was, strangely, nervous. Maybe it was because I was listening to what someone (chemistry dance lady) was saying just for a change, making myself more vulnerable.

Should I mention my eyes? Brown, obviously. She'd see that straight up…but I was wearing my -10.5 (soft) contact lenses. Should I tell her that inside they were right royally buggered. Haemorrhages and sewn up holes, all legacies of sporting triumphs and disasters, blurred yet further by their deterioration into middling age. Uncertain in the dark and in the evenings, often appearing rude at times as I struggled to recognise faces. Shit. What if I couldn't recognise her? I was working myself up. Again.

What about mentioning the saddest day of my life. That I'd said 'I love you' to lots of people since my mother died but never been big enough to believe it myself.

Snap out of it, man! Get your head in the game!

There was something more about this one at stake.

For the first time in a long while I had got my game face on (whatever that meant in the context of a date). And the big match, when it came, played out like the best of them. Initial meet and then getting to know the opposition over a short and a half.

Her questions were actually quite good…and on point.

Favourite piece of music? Easy one, to have kicked it all off. 'Desperado', that's why we were there wasn't it?

Three essential items? Oooh, seeing how I react under pressure. Um, one, a picture of my daughter just after she was born, the moment I realised I needed to be a different person. Two, er, probably *Immortal Harlequin*, just to be able to pour over it time and time and time again to finally find all those schoolboy errors I'd made. And the er, third, um, wasn't sure…I'd come back to her on that.

The last time I broke someone's heart, a bone, the law, a promise? Double oooh. Okay, in order…my second wife (which haunted me for a while after), never, possibly being naked in a bar (steward's enquiry), never.

Good energy during that first forty-five meant I didn't get substituted for the second half…which played out at a bijou fish restaurant up near Oxford Street. So far, so good (except for the life-size replica Dalek staring me out from the office windows opposite).

With no '70s sofa to hide behind, the revelation when it came (just as dinner was arriving), whilst not exterminating me, still proverbially knocked me off my chair. Traumatic circumstances had left her a little reclusive and some five years later, here she was investing all her faith and trust in me. Gulp. The sense of 'adventure' suddenly became one laced with all sorts of uncertainties. The moment became a stick or twist (i.e. run, fast) one. I was never a quitter and, as Charlotte lovingly once said to me, if someone gives me something (particularly time, in adversity) then they should get as much as I could give back in trust and in good faith. Everything was relative though and, quite frankly, neither of us was in good shape. Stick it was.

The 'date' rolled in to extra time at 'The Ice Bar' and the early hours via 'The Roadhouse' (no Patrick Swayze).

Walking back over my running fields in the early hours of morning to Beavers was a magic carpet ride of its own. As often as I'd run, I'd never seen them quite like this. The frost that had come down early shimmered in the silvery light of the majestic full moon. The trees were silhouetted against a mystical, icy Narnia all of my own. A crisp, cold, night air invigorated my senses and reminded me of all the magic that nature can bring in support of a mood or the moment. Here I was, on my familiar sporting turf, feeling strangely out of place and slightly disorientated. Alone in a weird crystal vision as time floated on the frozen air. The path to the cottage just up ahead, the cottage that had been lovingly crafted, inside and out, was clear. Behind its doors a sleepless night getting to grips with this new equation.

Still cohabiting, I hesitated before entering. Turning to catch what I could of my little fantasy world and athletics track that I had just walked up, in the cold light of the full moon night, things looked different. Altered perspectives, differing shades and darker shadows.

The quiet of the house suggested everyone was in bed. I went to mine, stepping over a pile of Picasso research as I did. Time was an all too precious commodity and today's had gone too quickly.

I knew that stepping into her world would take courage. Equally, I might never see her again. She was the sum of all my fears. Someone who if I went after, I would be utterly lost. I still wanted a rematch.

Looking in the mirror, for the first time in a long while, I saw a slightly different person…one with the faintest hint of a smile.

In bed, thoughts about the day I'd just experienced kept coming and I felt slightly confused. Had I just woken from a dream? Sometimes a face, like a haunting melody, stays in your head all night…and by the turn of another day it has gone. I hoped she would still be there in the morning but what role she might have to play in the rest of my life I had no idea.

I could still walk (or run) away.

I should have. If only for the sake of my mates' sanities.

The month following the 'date' there had been little or no word. Saddling up the horse again, a Harlequins fans' black tie dinner seemed the perfect venue for a second attempt. No-one wants to go to a ball on their own. Bit of a hit and hope…but she agreed.

Halfway through the evening…and meal…no sign.

Finally an appearance and a delightful evening to follow. The reason for lateness it was later revealed, untimely news about the health of her mother, who died six weeks later.

No word over those weeks, until the days after, when a text came in, saying she had been walking the beaches of Southern Ireland, listening to a particular piece of haunting Celtic sounding music (*Buddha-Bar,* Nicos, 'Secret Love').

Ireland poignantly beat Wales that weekend to win their first Grand Slam since 1948, the year her mother was born. Wales could have won, a Stephen Jones last penalty kick of the game just dipping on the wind under the crossbar.

Then, once more, she was gone and I'd have to wait for another crack in time.

March and April came and went, lost in thought as I was. If chance ever found us right and I got to see her again, I'd introduce her to the rambling roses. I'd saved them a long while ago and they had responded in kind to become the majestic centrepiece of the garden. Once a year, for just a week, they all opened to concentrate the most powerful, sensuous, romantic aroma around one space…the pergola that was rapidly becoming the heart of my creative, floral masterpiece.

By night, if warm, it was a little heaven on earth.

That May was extremely hot and an out of the blue text signalled a third meet, at Beavers, which I had for the first long weekend on my own. With it another attempt at trying to piece together the parts of her jigsaw, lost in grief as she was.

Moules et frites and Sancerre settled things down nicely (a considered and concerted attempt to break the Spag Bol mould). What happened next became a pivotal piece in the garden's journey. The long neglected arbour. It was a beast of heavy wood but somehow we carried, shoved, cajoled and forced it from one side of the three hundred and sixty degree garden over to the other. From a lonely, remote and unloved place in the past, it had now found the sun and an open terrace facing the rose pergola.

It belonged again.

The weekend finished with a return to Harlequins for a Cosmopolitan and Dove Men Care sponsored attempt on a Guinness World record…the highest number of guys in one place in just their underpants. All for a worthy cause, a Prostate Cancer Charity. Side by side a Harlequins second rower in just budgie smugglers put a lot in to perspective.

Going from Business Economics and Accounting to the centre pages of Cosmo in just my underpants was a strange hop…but a conversation starter for years to come.

I knew what would come next.

The disappearing act.

July 2009 was fairly pivotal in my general meander through life. I had been on my own many a time before, in between relationships, general phases of life. Now I found myself in some kind of strange limbo, unable to separate a feeling of isolation from being able to move myself forward.

I needed a breather.

One of the few places I knew that had any kind of draw, some kind of pull of its own, was Paris. The last two times, rugby orientated and in the company of great friends, had been spectacular. The City of Lights had always been good to me.

Paris it was then. Six days to wander, to relax and chill. To live with myself and my new found circumstances. For the first time in my life I was away on my own and it was a chance to get to know me better. Practise French (poorly). Do some people-watching and escape on the magic carpet, resolving to fatten myself up on a diet of croissants, frites, foie gras, white wine; any and everything that Paris, with all of its allure and charm, had to seduce me with during my stay.

I had no idea what I'd find there.

I stepped out of the Gare du Nord straight into a pile of dog shit. Which was supposed to be lucky. That moment it just didn't feel it.

Summer in Montmartre was gorgeous. Away from the touristy bits, a very peaceful meander through time.

The hotel, the same one on the Rue Ravingnan as back in 2007. Room 411, high up, with its double French doors opening to the south east and west of Paris, a panorama to savour over the rooftops from the film *Amelie*.

The quaint façade of the Bateau Lavoir, Picasso's early lodgings, sat next door and with it a climb up the hill to the square, at the very heart of Montmartre. Time to switch off and fully absorb myself in Picasso's world…Le Lapin Agile (both an historic music inn, his playground, pick-up joint and inspiration). Kept looking seedy and tawdry, I liked it.

Time stood still for the week. The ageless cafes on the square became my home, La Mere Catherine mostly. The world passed. The artists set up, drew the tourists and left as sunset came and their evenings eventually finished.

Seabreeze kept me awake at nights…I still had no idea why. I knew she got me, read me like a good book, seeing way more going on between my lines than anyone else had. No-one had ever Trojan horsed my walls before and it was a little disconcerting. Why was she taking me on this one-way trip into the unknown? Why her?

She'd kept revealing little bits of herself, but only ever what she wanted me to see and then she hid herself again. I broke away. She kept coming back for more.

On the last day of my 'holiday', as the hot summer rain gently fell, I relaxed in La Mere Catherine and wrote her a letter. A proper letter with my Waterman, ink and Basildon bond (A5). Once started, I couldn't stop. Page rolled into page, minutes rolled into hours. A real restorative process. From Paris with love.

A month or two later, deep in to the summer, I'd almost passed on the lack of any reply. Rhodes with Charlotte was a good break, but a final fleeting, family one…a crossover of a few days for old time's sake. The memory of the year before with a starring act on stage for their talent night all too resonant…the rendition of 'Baa Baa Black Sheep' was perfect (Charlotte, not me).

On Halloween, the text came in.

She'd been reading my letter. Again. At the top of a hotel in Marrakesh, as the muezzin called to prayer…and for the first time since she'd been walking along that Irish beach, was listening to that haunting Celtic piece. As music went it seemed to join us in our infrequent and random dealings.

She visited for what should have been an evening catch up in December at a pub but in that moment it snowed, heavily, and we were very much locked in. Snow, with its calming wintery effect, seemed to work for us. Deep. And crisp. And even. Piece by piece I was catching up with the shifting sands (or snow drifts) of her time.

Heading into the new year, trying to keep a respectable distance from her, whilst she tried to avoid and deal with her own shit, was killing me. I spent more months standing back from her, letting her deal with all the issues that had made her unhappy.

I was fighting myself though. I'd left broken hearts too many times….let a lot of lovely people down, fallen by the wayside, controlled as I had been by a selfishness and my own singular actions. I was hopelessly lost in this situation however…it was now or never.

I hoped she would forgive me if I made a proper mess of suddenly and randomly making an effort to try and see her once more.

Daz, my latest hockey team-mate and road-trip buddy, soaked it up on numerous trips to our away hockey games.

Murren was that place, high up in the Swiss Alps, that had so mesmerised and haunted me the last time I had visited, some ten years before. Time was running out for Seabreeze and me but, testing fate again, I suggested a ski trip, exactly a year on from her mum's death. Something would happen I said. Something…but I had no idea what. Something that would remind her that her mum was still around.

It was that kind of deeply, haunting place.

Lost as she was, she came.

The weekend was a short one…a long way to go on a whim. Barely time to get there, put the skis on, get up the mountain and come down.

Get some skis and boots we did. Go up we did. Come straight back down we did, as mine didn't fit and I needed to change them. Bigger boots procured we stopped by the side of the ice rink for a coffee.

And then it happened.

The opposite side of the valley, those oppressive granite walls; mountains that formed a perfect white canvas on the other three sides. In the middle an ice-rink, perfectly placed in another weird, almost imaginary, Narnia-like scene again. Even more hallucinogenic than my silvery running fields. A young female skated to the centre of the now empty rink to practise her routines. A tiny dancer, a few warm-up moves and, once poised, she awaited her music.

The first chords were instantly recognisable.

'Secret Love', the hauntingly beautiful Irish beach and Marrakesh tune. I let out a tear. Seabreeze shared hers.

No-one really spoke that afternoon and evening, both lost in stunned thoughts until it was time to leave.

Kept forever on the edges of her world, I found myself stumbling and fumbling in the dark. Not knowing who she was, where she was at, what she was doing…but somehow still jogging along, still moving forward.

'Make sure you look after Charlotte. She's your guiding light.' Words, again, I would never forget; this time the best advice I'd been given. A piece was still missing though.

Before I could stock check the whole crazy affair, for a final time, like the best of fairy godmothers, she was gone.

The past few years had shown that hoping someone might turn up on my doorstep one Sunday lunch and just say 'I love you' was pure Disney. The only person I had time for a relationship with was Charlotte. How she challenged me. Not to a game of chess. Obviously.

She challenged me nonetheless. To be better. To open myself up to all the possibilities of being a child once again to find something buried within that had been locked away. How clearly I now saw the road ahead.

The best thing about the strange times in your life is you get to see the true colours of everyone and everything.

My grey little world started to colour itself in. Waterloo Bridge had always been a regular feature and part of that.

June 2010 was different from other big beer nights, neon landscapes and walks back through the fields. Walking over the bridge after a fair few drinks, its colour palette seemed more vivid than before. This particular walk was to be the last of its kind. Having taken a leap of faith and secured a small cottage in the (very) sleepy backwater of Ash Vale, a couple of stops up the line from Farnham, the time came to leave Beavers for good.

The last night was hot. Not unlike the May weekend the arbour had been moved. My roses were out, as were most of the other flowers. Roses that had ripped me to shreds as I had painted the walls of the cottage one final time.

Now they sat calm and still.

Peaceful. Romantic. Enchanting.

In the early hours, in one of those drunken states you wake up wondering what ever happened, I remember every minute. I stumbled around, lovingly kissing the flowers. All of them. Each one, each kiss one of those lovingly endless ones that take the breath away. Minutes lasted hours. There were no favourites, each one special. I took in their odours, each one equally lovely in the moment and the moonlight.

I could only hope the neighbours weren't watching.

Part of the plan…the Charlotte plan…was to try and stay one year ahead of where she was at and what she might be thinking. Hard for me, on a part-time basis going forward, with little practical experience to draw on. Or so I thought.

Ash Vale presented a child's paradise. Another cottage, only this one a little smaller, one of two Hansel and Gretel chocolate box conversions that once formed part of an old Victorian glue factory. The two little homes shared a path, splitting right and left at each other's front gate, communal gardens at the back spilling out right onto the towpath of the Basingstoke Canal, opposite The Swan.

Swans and ducks all over, walks in the woods, the cat and the schnauzers in the cottage next door. For me…the

Army ranges. Acres of muddy puddles, undulating terrain, hills and off-road tracks to run around. Not unlike the farm and the Farnham fields. The concrete target pits at the end gave an extra dimension.

Christmas 2010 was set to be a lonely one. Alternative weekends and Christmas Days meant I was set for a quiet time in the cottage. Which suited me…in so far as I could just get on with research and writing.

As it turned out Kevin and Kevin, who owned the sister cottage, invited me round for dinner with a couple of their male cabin crew friends. Laced with wine, more than a few double entendres, offers of more sausage, followed by the Queen's Speech, it turned out to be an unusual, unexpected and very good one.

Kevin and Kevin and their pets looked after the both of us as we settled down to our new life. I needed something (low maintenance) for Charlotte to look forward to. Dogs Trust Max (a dog) became an online sponsored chum and Kevin and Kevin (goldfish) became a new family addition.

Sympathetically updating the cottage and gardens took time. As did the five mile school run.

Work was balanced and, with the arrival of 2011, snow brought with it more delights. The eight foot snow Scooby that I had conjured up at Beavers to mesmerise a four year old was going to take some beating, but our snow dogs and frog princes came close. How much I loved watching the large snowflakes just falling and the trees and arbour slowly being covered in lashings of gentle loveliness. A frozen canal bought a winter wonderland feel to everything. We'd found ourselves in a good place.

Easter became the first little holiday on our own. Blind as I had been, Charlotte was guiding my life in a whole new direction. A very special one at that for which Euro Disney was a great place to start. Reality or not, the magic carpet was fuelled up and very much pointing the right way.

Paris was what it always had been, a dreamlike place. A fantasy. Where everything is nothing that you expect. This time, though, stepping cautiously out of the station, no dog shit. In this new present all I could do was hand back time to serendipity.

Staying down in the Pigalle, close to the Moulin Rouge for a night, before moving to the theme park, I saw things with open eyes. A clearer surround. A brilliant horizon. A different one. The way to the hotel cemented everything as Charlotte tried to bounce a pink Stade Francais rugby ball over all the cobbles. Unconditional love all around.

Sharing the Rue des Saules and the Sacre Coeur, sharing Paris, was a dream come true. Captured memories. Bottled time. Even watching the Paris Marathon, and a blind man running it, was a spectacle.

Up into Montmartre, La Mere Catherine and the artists' square were their immortal selves but came with a six year old's plea for a portrait. Taking a chance on an older lady artist who used pastels seemed to be the right choice. Not least when she fell backwards off her chair, if only for the lasting memory. As the sun beat down on a timeless square and all the tourists came flocking, Charlotte became a study of youth, innocence and concentration. Beautiful with it.

Quick and easy. Fifteen minutes later and a near perfect reflection. Something I'd seen my mother do all those years before. It made our, and the artist's, day.

We took a night-time taxi tour around the Eiffel Tower. Something Charlotte knew about, something she had been taught in school. Only this time giant lights flashed on and off every hour…an out of season Christmas tree, before its time, but mightily impressive with it.

The Disney Square was a spectacle of colour. Now I felt like a child. Or at least had found the child inside. Hidden away for so long. And the hidden bits that had hurt for so long evaporated. By taking myself back in time I'd moved myself forward. And grown-up immeasurably as a result.

An Alice in Wonderland maze, complete with its Mad Hatter, was as simple as you could get, but I found myself where I really wanted to be. Lost. In a good way.

Food outlets during the evenings were packed…but we somehow squeezed into the rock-out diner. I'd never really seen Charlotte (at six years old) rock-out but, wearing my oversized jumper, she head-banged with the best of them. She was way ahead of me at the same age.

The end of each day brought us the Disney Parade with its pirate ship. Captain Hook hammed up playing the good old villain as all of the characters evolved in front of us.

As did a (real) magic carpet.

The dust that had always been there had finally settled on me. I was able to fly again.

'I do believe in fairies. I do, I do, I do.'

A new call to arms. Charlotte's (not mine). As I watched her run around the new garden ad nauseam repeating Peter Pan, she breathed a new life in to things. *Tinkerbell* became DVD of the week and for months to follow. *Dirty Dancing* too, the 'lift' being a feature we lovingly worked on.

And then 'the' book on the shelf moment.

'Dad, there's a book on the shelf with your name on it.'

Having seen it wedged between Dylan Thomas' *Under Milk Wood* and *The Oxford Dictionary of Quotations* she found it amusing that someone had the same name as me. Having pointed out that the book was mine, her excitement levels rose. All of a sudden she had her opportunity, one of those rites of passage at school, for their 'show and tell'. *Immortal Harlequin* took on yet another new life. Not for the critics, not for the sales but (as with Carl) something very dear and important to a single person. *Immortal* became a badge she could wear with pride. Once again, I was reminded of why I'd written it.

'Of course you can take it to school.'

Easiest promise I'd ever made. Not the first. Or the last.

She was good with phrases that, even when they were out of the context they had come from, they still made sense.

'Love is always,' was one of them.

I'd never hidden my mother's easel, box of old oils and some canvases. Charlotte, armed with a pot of pink paint, had taken the canvases outside and created her own simple masterpieces on them. A beautiful buttercup shaped thing as a smiley face. A man shaped thing. A passion flower. All very random, but taking on a good shape, good meaning and purpose. She had learned well. Able to paint inside the lines. One day she would step outside them too. Until then I wouldn't sacrifice a minute. I'd watched her first tentative brush strokes at a very early age. Five years later, she was drawing with the best of them. Happiness anything but an illusion.

I smiled every time I looked at her.

Her first ever end-of-year school report came in after a year of holding myself back, quietly tending my own little projects, to allow her to get those little feet firmly planted under a school desk. The words on her report that pleased me the most? Not (just) the obvious fondness for art and books. More the school's perception of her being socially astute, well grounded…and happy.

I'd served and spent my time well. And emerged better, wiser, and kinder. And with renewed energy.

I tested all that energy, and my limits, with a crack at the Reading Half Marathon. The ranges became my best friend over many a day as I ploughed around them. The Reading Half was a fairly flat course, only the final stretch being the steep uphill towards and into the Majedski football ground. Happy with one hour forty, twenty-five years had only cost me fifteen minutes. I was hoping for maybe only five but I'd take everything I got.

School sports day had always been fun, even at infants. At junior school no different but, with the circular 300m track containing no stagger a first bit of coaching from the sideline to ensure the inside lane was taken. Never one to celebrate any success too keenly, the strangely decisive first place was readily taken. They had all been told that it was the taking part and there were no winners and losers…but you had to feel sorry for the poor girl out in lane four who heroically battled round finishing last, a good thirty metres behind everyone else.

Football became Charlotte's sport of choice, albeit the coaching thereof meant it was little more than just a hoof about. It was now, things being settled and football being something we could share, that I introduced her to Spurs. A problem shared is a problem halved. My hope was that she would get in to it and, whether through Panini stickers or other, use it as one of her weapons of choice if, as and where necessary.

2011 was coming to a close with a variety of things falling in to place.

The old arbour that'd once morphed from a symbol of solitude and loneliness, to a lovely place to both relax and dream, had moved with us. It had now become a football goal in a pivotal, sunny place of our new garden. We had already burst a few beach balls on the two roses we'd also brought. It had taken a couple of hefty lads a long while to shift but, relaxing beneath it now, it was the perfect place to reflect on a whirlwind eighteen months. Candles on the lawn flickered away. The night was cool. Still. No insects.

Everything fitted perfectly. The Moroccan lights, relics of a far removed holiday to Marrakesh, found themselves in use, to good effect, for the first time.

Burst balls. But not bubbles. The new little garden had become an oasis of enjoyment and calm. A new chapter. A new labour of love.

The last remaining strands of the Indian summer were being kind. And in the moment I realised why. Why her?

Why Seabreeze?

The last year and a half had been hard to digest, hard to define. We had been little shooting stars crossing fleetingly. Nothing about seeing her had been normal. Over a set of seasons she had flitted in and floated out, like a butterfly, showing me all of them. She'd brought order to my world, a bridge over troubled waters and lifted a load.

One of the hardest lessons in life is letting go. Whether it's guilt, anger, love, betrayal or loss. Change is never easy. We fight to hold on, we fight to let go.

After some very powerful Celtic poetry at two thousand metres up in the sky on a shared spiritual trajectory she had given me something far more though. My mum, who had always been there, no longer haunted me.

There was, finally, acceptance.

Seabreeze had emotionally and mentally rinsed me but at the same time had lovingly and endearingly given me the most precious gift of all.

Closure.

Take It Easy
2012 - 2015

The old needle in the eye trick. I saw it coming all the way. Like something out of a 007 film.

'Do you expect me to talk?'

'No, Mr. Bond, I expect you to cry.'

That wasn't happening. I don't do crying. I am bigger than this, this repair yet another hole in my eye cryotherapy shaped thing. I'm impervious to pain, both emotionally and physically.

Shit that hurt. Maybe I'm not bigger than this.

That is the thing about having your eyeballs stitched up. Anaesthetising injections (several) to get under each layer. And then (once they've worked) the actual cryotherapy (a weird sort of freezing Waterman pen as an alternative to a laser job). All very revolutionary and, when the anaesthetics haven't kicked in, fucking painful.

I had opted for the local rather than a general. Precious thing sight…if you can see it, you can deal with it. Perhaps the general next time though.

They gave me the choice of a male or female nurse to hold my hand. Can't move my head they said. Do squeeze the hand if something hurts or doesn't feel right they said. Should be fine they said. Birddog rule number one: assume nothing. Someone is there principally because IT IS going to hurt. There will be lots of squeezing.

'No offence, mate,' I said to the male nurse.

'None taken.'

I never got her name.

Possibly on her badge, except I couldn't turn my neck. So there we were. Up close, a short head apart, not on first name terms, holding each other's hand for a very first time. For a long time. Making the sort of small talk you'd expect on a first date, but typically over a chilled white. Transpired that day was to be her last day at work before the gold on her finger…her wedding in two days' time.

'So…we're over before we've started?' I said, trying to seek humour in a situation where crying should have been the only practical and real alternative.

'It was lovely while it all lasted,' she said, her enchanting demeanour saving both me and the situation.

I guess she knew the op hadn't gone quite to plan.

'Take a look in the mirror,' were her final words.

She meant specifically. Generally might have been more apt.

A day later, the reflection wasn't great. The completely scarlet, blood shot eye took some three weeks to eventually go pink before settling back close to something like it used to be…white with a bit of brown in the middle.

My previous dabbles in online dating had led to something very specific but had taken me way off piste from where I had originally set off. Time now seemed right to try it once again…with a better, fuller understanding of me and where I was at. I hoped, now heading towards my fifties, I knew. It was going to be another interesting read on playback.

Back online and my friends, the Dangerous Dans, were all still there, all still replicating each other. Only this time, having been on so many 'hair-raising' adventures, it seemed all their photos (sunglasses, hats) were pulling a lot of wool (and badly dyed hair) over the eyes. The ladies by contrast were now mostly mirror selfies or cropped photos next to some bloke in a hat, badly died hair and sunglasses.

Fantasy and illusion might be completely overrated but seemed to be à la carte here. The whole online dating scene had matured in to something quite bland…everyone either hiding who they really were or over-egging it.

'I love laughing!' Doesn't everyone?

'I like going out and staying in!' Ah, so you like existing.

'Looking for a partner in crime!' Busy chap.

'My friends say I am...' Yeah, but they're just adjectives (the words, not the friends)…point is, nothing's proven until you get to know someone.

All so full of clichés leaving me, well, as sick as a parrot.

As samey as it looked and felt, I was already doing that classic dating no-no. Don't insult anyone, complain about my own experiences or criticise.

'At least 6ft.' Oh ffs!

That blank profile description box eyeballed me again. And, once more, the first line was going to be the hardest. Second time around, the truth still hurt.

Spurs were mirroring my dating life. Lots of small wins, no trophies or titles. Close, but no cigars. Harry Redknapp had been getting the best out of a team that included both Bale and Modric. Mauricio Pochettino, the relatively novice Southampton coach, took over.

Back to another random e-mailer. Another 'match up of the day', dictated and shaped by the dating sites algorithms. Life was short. My energy and reading ability were getting shorter and I stopped dating.

Whilst whiling away the hours, it was around now that the missing 6 October Old Ride prep school letter became less of a mystery. Facebook had championed the social media mantle started way back by Friends Reunited. Last reviews of Friends Reunited's site, before it dissolved into history, revealed little on Long Close peers, but plenty (almost too much) on The Old Ride. Police had sought, via the social site in its day, anyone who'd had any contact with specific masters, and that could either remember or were willing to come forward with details of exactly what had been going on. Masters running riot with the kids, all sorts of horrific paedophilic activity and many a lost childhood it appeared. The school had turned out to be some perverts' paradise. The science teacher was given eight years for being a serial abuser; fifty-four charges against eighteen kids. Boys were forcing themselves to eat soap to attempt to get off classes. The headmaster was described as a violent, raging lunatic. Letters, I knew now, had to be left unsealed to ensure they either didn't spill any beans or would identify the targetable children. I wonder if I'd hit a nerve in my letter that hadn't passed censorship that 'lost' Sunday. Scoring goals for fun was all I'd typically ever written about. Either way, this new revelation that particular masters had been abusing kids ad nauseam had gone public. I must've missed it when I was there, only seen what had been going on from an outsider's view. But the revelations told their own story. The school system (particularly boarding) in the seventies and eighties should have been a safe haven for expressiveness, personal growth and learning.

Reading all those social media messages reminded me of little things I'd forgotten. For me, my year had been about football. For a large proportion of others though there was one aim…survival. The clues were apparent, not least that no-one had wanted to be there. Runaways, odd movements at night, kids disappearing for 'punishment', some coming back with sweets (normally banned), others coming back crying. For me it had been a place to lose myself in running around and writing about doing so.

Football, without me knowing it, had been my saviour.

The Old Ride didn't survive the notoriety and come the turn of the millennium had been closed down.

At the same time as I stumbled across these revelations, the papers would soon be flooded with further discoveries concerning footballers and specific coaches dating back to much the same period. Paul Stewart was one of those able to stand up and be bravely counted.

Football did, however, sadly lose Gary Speed, the Wales manager. Described as 'closed' by his dear wife, a glass half empty person by his mum. The first game after his suicide was at the Liberty Stadium in Swansea. His wife picked up the pieces. He'd been ill for a very long time. A time bomb waiting to explode. There but for the grace of god went a lot of us.

We were about to fully enter the age of social media and what it does to the mind.

Ninety-nine percent of all fans are appreciative of what makes sport…its essence. You win you lose, you go again. The rest, the trolls, those with a strange mental disposition of their own go straight in to the abuse. One percent ruins it for all. In the old days, hooligans. Now it was online.

I hadn't played football for years. Watching Charlotte, who enjoyed it at school, fresh from our fantasy football garden sessions, would have to do. The school's approach seemed to be very much one of 'it had to be played, but no-one is going to invest any time in it'.

Once a game starts there is little control over what goes on. Change happens once the need has been established.

I turned up to watch Charlotte play in a tournament. In their first two games her school were trounced 9-0 and 5-0. The scores didn't seem to bother anyone, try as they might. Their 'coach' didn't know much about football, it was the taking part that mattered. Results were immaterial.

It was after the fourteenth goal had gone in that I'd had enough of rolling my eyes. Having turned up the year or so earlier as athletics coach, it was now football manager. As that second game finished I pointed out one simple thing to the team. Their keeper was making great saves, but then lobbing the ball straight back down the middle towards the halfway line. The other schools took their soccer seriously and had good players. Anything that went down the middle was coming straight back, more often than not via the back of the net. I suggested to the keeper that if she threw it out towards the halfway sideline, rather than down the middle, and everyone bundle it from there, they might get a better result for their last game. The game management changed and the balls were thrown to the sides. They bundled well.

The third and last game ended in a respectable 0-0 draw. It felt like victory and the girls celebrated as if it was. I smiled the smile of someone who'd just won a massive victory of their own. 'Not down the middle' became our private joke.

Office life became all about staying one step ahead of the recession. Looking after the financial assets was one thing, securing them from Covent Garden's burglary contingent another. Got the tee-shirt for that years ago. Highlights this time asking the strip club opposite to see their CCTV.

Birddog's new business development back then (Brand on the Run) involved the monthly meet around the eclectic pool table in the Billiard Room at the revamped Sanderson Hotel. It had become famous, a step up in quality from its origins as a carpet warehouse…and my pre-university work offices. Nothing remained of old that I could recall except perhaps, at a guess, the spa would have been roughly where the open-plan development area I had been a part of used to be. I resisted going to look for my stapler…or getting a round of tea in.

Birddog was both a unique company and team in those days…reaching a peak of sorts, both in terms of delivery, revenue and its staff numbers. Scot, the managing director, thought he looked like Steve McQueen, Mark was a dead-ringer for Tom Hanks. I made a good Donkey from *Shrek*. David Niven hadn't joined at this stage. The biggest team outing of the year was to our PA's wedding, an interesting Jewish/Catholic affair, the reception for which ended up at the Film Museum over at Waterloo. Among the dancefloor music later in the evening 'I've Had The Time Of My Life'. And the *Dirty Dancing* lift. I knew it was going to be my last proper 'dad dance' with Charlotte and one more lift it was. We were going to go down in style.

By now a Pilates instructor (who looked like Jane Fonda in *Barbarella*) had become the girlfriend. Two or three good years, nice holidays and a lot of road trips backwards and forwards to Eastbourne where she lived. She came with a cute dog Dylan, a Cavachon, who hated postmen, but was otherwise warm, loyal and very protective...and he became Charlotte's best friend. He reminded me in so many ways of Robin.

Charlotte's thoughts turned to a different animal. It was *The Lion King* and junior school play time. She got to play Sarafina with her own sole line, 'Hmm, what do you think Sarabi?' We had come a full circle (of life) since Moly. Not as dramatic as 'Up the Mole!' but nostalgic and I found out that Sarafina in Swahili meant 'bright star'. Life is a circle of happiness, sadness, hard times and good times.

I couldn't have scripted this bit better.

2014 brought a half-century for both Jon and I. My fortieth had been fabulous. Ten years on from Charlotte's birth and *Immortal Harlequin* and, in advance of further celebrations in July, I organised match day dinner hospitality (messily so), fittingly at Harlequins, for their end-of-season game against Bath. I'd tried to get Charlotte into rugby, but the arrival of a trio of Belgians (Toby Alderweireld, Jan Vertonghen and Mousa Dembele) at Spurs had kept her persuasions sweet. Securing tables and tickets for thirty or so people however, meant Charlotte had the mascot's role and walked out onto the pitch side by side with Chris Robshaw, Harlequins and England captain. Hard not to notice Gavin Henson, in the tunnel. No-one should be afraid of changing and he looked like he'd grown up hugely since the papers had savaged his drunken train ride home from The Stoop some eight years prior. I saw him leave then and wished him well now.

A great day and reunions all round. A proud father and all of my old school, university, work, football and hockey friends in the shadows of Twickenham as well. A reminder that Jon and I never quite got to do our bucket list 'Forty before Forty'. A one promise to ourselves left, to finally see a rugby international at Twickenham together. With some birthday money, I bought myself a very expensive bottle of pink bubbly and vowed to save it for a special occasion.

Jon's actual fiftieth next up. A dinner at Banwell Castle, just outside Weston. A proper Englishman's castle, proper job and a sleepover in an original Tudor four poster. Given the home of Thatchers Cider to be along the road, it was a nostalgic trip down cider drinking lane for good measure.

Bringing up kids leaves little time to catch up properly for any new adventures. The last for a while being a box at Bath rugby ground with Jon and Jules.

Late summer of 2015 and Charlotte and I were about to move back into Farnham. Doing school runs and driving at night were difficult anyway and, with secondary school on the horizon, running around and trying to stay a step ahead would make them even more so. The Cottage on the canal had treated us well, and left us with lovely memories.

Trying to move was both a complicated and frustrating process. Given the house's quirky uniqueness it was always going to take someone to buy it who could see it for that. Viewers came and went. In order to sell it, we had to take the first offer but, with the only house in Farnham that we liked (including resident tortoise) falling over on exchange, we had nothing to move into. We would have many a week on the road, staying in hotels, to tide us over.

Change, as difficult as it would be, was coming.

The Last Resort
September 2015

The Rugby World Cup was close and Twickenham tickets for Wales and Australia, in the group stages, would finally complete the 'Forty before Forty' bucket list that Jon and I were going to do (the last time I had caught up with some Aussies at a World Cup it had all got messy). Late to our own party, a big game on a big stage, a once in a lifetime opportunity, we were pretty much there; to make the event more special, we'd stay over at the Marriott at the ground.

Life was frenetic. Charlotte had just started at secondary school…and the going was tough for her. New curriculum (trying to do all the 'software coding' brought tears, mostly mine…just as well I hadn't got that back in my day), peer group ins and outs and seniors trying to be the 'big I am'. All not helped by a very protracted cottage sale. Farnham had changed quite a lot over six years. Mostly new houses cropping up wherever a tiny bit of space allowed. My old running fields near Beavers were being built over. The right place for us, another idyll, was a way off. We took what we could find…a small town house in Red Lion Lane, right in the centre, in the shadow of Lady Hamilton's former estate (all things 'Nelson' seemed to follow me). Offer accepted and, for a final month or so, it was hotel after hotel.

Saturday 19 September and Charlotte and I were staying at The Village Hotel in Farnborough, scene of the 'dance me through chemistry' evening of a few years before. The hotel's cute sports bar looked like a proper pub, not unlike The Village Home in Alverstoke, scene of Jon and my early drinking days…or even Farnham's The Plough, the scene of that memorable Liverpool versus Juventus Champions League final game, also shared with my best mate.

Jon was struggling back home in Weston with a broken ankle, care of tripping down the pier on a Pink Tie Charity night. Saturday lunchtime he sent a picture sat at home, plastered from the foot up, England shirt on, ready for the day's big rugby games…Scotland versus Ireland and South Africa against Japan. The ankle was a bit of a set-back but hopefully our Twickenham game together, more than ten years overdue, was still a runner.

Settling down in the corner of the packed sports bar at the Village Hotel with Charlotte, we ordered burgers and fries from a '50s diner menu prior to the South Africa and Japan game starting. Nobody puts us in the corner, to coin a phrase, but it was chock-full in there and we were tucked behind the main entrance doors in our own little space. A simple table, a small TV on the wall, aided and abetted by diner style cutlery, condiment holders and some flickering candles. Barely room to put a glass of coke (ice, straw, no lemon) and my pint of cider. With all of life's distractions going on around us though, it was just perfect on the night.

We settled down to one of the greatest games of rugby most of us have seen, willing the underdogs on at the end as they opted to twist rather than stick. The match finished and Japan wrote themselves, magnificently, into the history books. The texts with Jon started flowing…

…not much fun on the road, but what a great game.

…the Japanese backing their rich attacking flair.

…looking forward to a catch-up in a few weeks' time.

Whilst Charlotte and I would continue our quality time with the next game, Scotland and Ireland, Jon settled in for the evening with Siobhan and Jules to watch *Avengers: Age of Ultron* (partly filmed by coincidence in Farnham).

We swapped more texts, full of reflection and nostalgia. Our last of the evening was to do with the curtains being drawn over my latest relationship. He hoped I would work something out, for better or worse.

I made him a promise that it and I would.

I like to keep promises.

A LIFETIME

Dear Jon,

Writing the words for your Best Man's speech was one of my trickier moments but, being by your side then, one of my proudest.

I speak here today knowing that this will be a tougher gig, but 'by your side' is where we all now are.

One of your finest of all too many qualities was your ability to talk in the warmest and most engaging of ways. Back in the days when nothing seemed to matter and when we didn't have a care in the world, you wrote letters so eloquently too. Those letters (some three hundred plus) still evoke the loveliest of memories. So…

…by return, here's a last one…for the road.

People don't die unless you forget them.

Talking to your many friends…sharing their rich stories…the absolute truth is that you are, and always will be, unforgettable.

A beloved son to John and Joan, the best of brothers to Julie, visiting your family home as kids we all remember the welcome, the loveliness, the hospitality extended by all…warmth and hospitality you always extended on, over the years, to us all. To Siobhan, the best of husbands, your wedding was the loveliest of days. To Jules, whose charming nature is a credit to, and a reflection of you, you are the bestest dad. Ever.

A Portsmouth schools swimming champion, how you swam!

Swam the Med, Maltese island to Maltese island. Swam with dolphins a mile off Stokes Bay in that long hot summer of 1976. Chased by, and outrunning, an elephant seal in the Antarctic, playing cricket on its ice, as a diver you swam beneath it. How you loved the sea, travelling to places most of us have never heard of.

You loved cars too, Formula 1's specifically. The Monaco Grand Prix with your loved ones for your fiftieth a magic carpet ride for all.

You also loved Bond and we all shared your disappointment at being pipped by Daniel Craig last time round but…when we go looking for a proud naval officer in to fast cars, gadgets and boy's own *adventures…you will always be our 007.*

You did the simple things well. Not least…friendship.

Asked to help tutor a schoolmate at maths, because you were better, you did. He got the better results, but his lifelong friendship your deserved reward. On leaving the Navy, you made up the grades at university with a First of your own.

You had time for everyone. You are the guy that was always there when it did matter and when someone needed to care. Your old friend Alun puts it best: 'One could not have a more honest, loyal and faithful friend. It was an honour to be his.' A sentiment we all share.

There is a moistness in the air. Autumn is with us and rugby, your other great love, is back. As we grew older we joined the ranks of the playing disinherited but the game, friendships, memories, these remain.

Your last game South Africa and Japan was, in your own words, fittingly one of the best games you'd seen…a game that showed that, even as time draws to its close, a spirit of adventure…your spirit of adventure…can, and will, carry you home.

An officer, a gentleman, a proud family man…and faster than an elephant seal…is how we will always remember you.

Best wishes wherever the wind and the sea take you.

Keep swimming…and take care.

Love,

All of us

The Sad Café
Autumn 2015

Five minutes were all I was given to sum up a lifetime of great memories and a deep friendship. What would I have given for added time? Even if just a second.

The morning after the South Africa and Japan game was a very lonely day in The Village.

A message came through as Charlotte and I were about to go to the swimming pool to say Jon had died the night before. A blood clot. Two hours after I had promised him it would all be okay in the end.

Charlotte swam her lengths unaware of the tragedy and emptiness that had suddenly befallen. I sought quiet and solace in the confines of the poolside steam room. I'd been here many times before, this sauna; small, white, almost the same size as an ambulance. It was empty and quiet. Almost too quiet. And, unusually, it was firing on all cylinders and extremely hot. The steam was thick, a proper pea-souper, and left me gently drifting through the mists of time. The condensation on the cold door rolled down like rain softly falling on a window on any other early autumn day.

Hot. Damp. On my own, surprisingly tranquil. Peaceful even. And where I started the inevitable process…of both shock and denial.

For the brief time I was in there composing myself, the sound of silence was broken only by the ghostly echoes of a past that came softly calling. Memories of a time gone by, the last time the music died.

After showering, Charlotte and I left. I told her in the car in the hotel's car park.

Then we both let it go. Let it go properly. And cried and cried and cried.

Back home my first call was to Alun in Dubai. No reply. A message to call me back. He guessed what was coming.

In the days that followed I met Paul, conveniently and surprisingly working nearby, back at The Village. We sat in the foyer opposite their internal Starbucks. The flames of the faux fireplace flickered slowly by our side. A video call with Alun reunited three of us, the fourth musketeer being missed whole-heartedly.

The trip to visit Siobhan and Jules the following Saturday was as messed-up as could be. Travelling through Shepton Mallet, Jack Garrett came onto the radio...something about spirits going. It sounded apt in the moment. A bridge was draped with a white bedsheet saying 'Happy 40th Siobhan'. All very weird. I doubled back to take it all in to make sure I wasn't seeing things. I wasn't.

The following morning Jules and I went to pick up two weeks-worth of Sunday newspapers. On any other Sunday, Jules and Jon's normal routine. The shopkeeper put them out and enquired if everything was okay.

I choked. I just couldn't find the words.

The silence was eventually broken by a boy becoming a man.

'My dad died.'

Two things happened for me in that moment. Firstly death suddenly, sadly, became very real. No Twickenham. No more drinks buddy. Jon, the very last of the good ones. Gone. Along with all the dreams we had and things we still planned to do. Secondly, I realised Jules was his dad's son right through to his core. Extremely mature for his age. He had my back. He did his dad proud. I'd always have his.

The weekend passed in a blur, a sadness in the air.

The return home later on Sunday was another of those lonely journeys. Rain falling. The enormity of everything hit me halfway along the A336, just outside Warminster. I had to pull into a pub car park and gather myself. As I did, a magnificent shaft of sunlight broke through the dull, grey clouds, forcing me to take in the scene, daubed in its early autumn glow. And at that moment I realised where I was. The Royal Oak. Thirty five years, cheddar and cider came flooding back.

Having absorbed the moment I continued my journey, getting scarce a few hundred metres along the road before, once again, doubling back to make sure my eyes and mind weren't deceiving me. The rays of sunshine were stronger. And all the more poignant.

The journey up. The journey back. A weird road trip full of sentiment and symbolism.

Giving Jon's eulogy, as Siobhan had lovingly asked, would be my first stand-up since being his Best Man.

With little time to think, the words still came easy. Jon was that sort of friend. Easy to do anything with. Either to talk to or to talk about. As the days progressed, the whole process started to mirror the weeks leading up to one of those big games…where the longer the week went on (and the closer the day came) the nerves, the angst and pressure became that little bit greater. Nothing else mattered. Think. Prepare. Train. Sharpen the focus. And go again. Time and day-to-day became irrelevant. The only thing that mattered was delivery and the performance. Sport never guarantees you either a good or your best one.

This wasn't a game though.

A first draft. About three pages. A read through. Eight minutes.

'You've got four,' said the chaplain mid-week. We'd met before…as she had conducted the wedding in Dartmouth.

'Four?' I enquired, knowing that really wasn't going to be anywhere near enough to describe a man for all seasons.

'Yes…two reasons…partly because we are on the clock at the crematorium and partly because if, as happens more often than not, you crack, stumble and fall, I'll be finishing it off for you.'

No pressure then.

I needed to do two things. Firstly, look her in the eye and convince both of us stumbling and falling wasn't going to happen. Secondly, to have Jon's back for one final time, and buy a little more time for everyone.

'I've got this. Give me five.'

I'd bought us all a minute of extra time. Every second, every word, had to count. Right down to the last of each.

Five minutes to tell the best of stories.

Not knowing whether I would turn up in the biggest of moments was probably the least of my concerns. Reading the words of a script, with my eyesight, was going to be the far bigger challenge.

There is not much you can do with five minutes, when eight aren't going to be half enough. Eight became seven. Seven, six. Six, five.

Spirits of adventure. Swimming forever. Those long hot days where nothing ever mattered. Elephant seals. Wanting to go back to being young. Letters. Simpler times. Rugby. More letters.

The memories when they came back hurt all the more.

And so my final words to my best friend became what they had always been. A letter. His letters, his words, had stood me good for his wedding. My words, my letter now. Just the one though. A last one. One for the road. A 'Dear Jon'. But a fond, dear Jon.

The sad night before the funeral and another road trip. A brief Solstice Park KFC stop (which wasn't there the last time I had come through with Jon and Paul cycling on our way to Stonehenge) and then onwards to a hotel to break the journey at Shepton Mallet. A dry run of the speech the night before. Five minutes. Perfect on the night. The next day an entirely new and different proposition. I reminded myself of doing exams. Slow but sure.

And that you are only as good as your last one.

A fitting full English (toast and jam) to start.

One final practise run.

It is really hard to capture everything as time, and final minutes, slip away. Hard to write, harder to read, let alone deliver on. Many a time of running, either towards or away, taught me you can't prepare yourself for the day, what is in front of you…or how else your brain is going to test you. Time to stop running, if just for now, and face the music.

People began to slowly arrive at the crematorium chapel in Weston. Family. Mine. Jon's. I recognised Uncle Bernie, whose boat we'd stayed on all those years ago in Falmouth. And Jon's many friends, most of whom I recognised from times gone by.

The crisp, early autumn air evoked those rugby playing school days down on the Marsh. The inherent sadness also reminded me of a quarter of a century, and half a lifetime, previous. Another little chapel. Another crematorium. And with that familiarity came a sense, and strength, of purpose. It had taken me a long time back then to get over the worst of autumns and the sorriest of Christmases. The mountains of Murren had given solace and closure and let ghosts go. This one might take time too, but the next hour came first.

The briefest of telephone calls came in to say the house I'd bought had completed. It had been rolling on almost as an aside. The keys would have to wait for a quieter day.

I sat with my thoughts on the edge of the second row, close to the lectern and by the huge stained glass windows. All on my own, whilst the chapel filled up behind me, until Siobhan's sister and her family joined me.

The music came. 'Nobody Does It Better' brought Jon and his close family in. As fitting as any piece of music and place to start, the crammed room testament to it and him.

The Reverend Caroline began the service with her own kind, endearing words.

And then my five minutes. My turn to break a lifetime down into reasons and seasons. The reason why getting on for nearly one hundred and fifty people were all crammed together in this small room. Not just family, but hordes of

186

friends, every work acquaintance and more than that. Five minutes for Moly to bring everything he had.

I wasn't a substitute for this one though, hamming it up with my one line, one night only pantomime performance. And I wasn't wearing a mask either. Nor was I a substitute coming cold off a bench to miss the game defining tackle. Unlike the Best Man's speech there were no expectations, but like the Best Man's speech everything still came down to this one moment in time. In death, it was time for the performance of a lifetime. Not mine, someone else's.

A slow walk over to the stage, up to the lectern, to the microphone. A look across at those gathered. Silence as I took an envelope from my jacket pocket and took out the single piece of paper.

And then clarity.

For five minutes something deep changed. No mists, no fog. I saw everything. Every tiny detail. All the expressions. The back of the room. The front row where the emotions and the grief ran deepest.

The hurt. The pain. The sadness.

And my words.

For the first time in my life, on the biggest of stages, my eyes didn't let me down, betray me or deceive me. The ball was very big and I wasn't dropping it.

'Dear Jon…'

And then it was over. I could read it many times again, but never with such fluidity. I have no idea whether, in the end, it was five minutes or not. It was a life's time, though.

A final line in the final second.

'Love, All of us.'

With that, our last letter was sealed in its envelope and placed on the coffin.

Back at my chair I got a quiet, reassuring nod.

Then I was on my own. Needing a friend.

Another Paul, a neighbour and close friend of Jon, read out Tennyson's sailors' poem *Crossing the Bar.*

As I concentrated on the stained glass windows, holding it in, sealing my emotions, wondering if I'd done enough, the rest of the service passed me by.

Fleetwood Mac's 'The Chain', Formula 1's theme music, echoed one last time. The service, and a final curtain, drew to their close. Outside an England rugby ball, made of red and white flowers, took centre stage.

The wake was at Banwell Castle, a stone's skim from the Thatchers Cider factory and scene of a memorable fiftieth.

A Thatchers it was then. And one more for the road.

In the weeks that followed, the last of our bucket list, that rugby international at Twickenham, came and went. Wales tripped over themselves against the Aussies. Fernando and Jane (his wife, not Fonda) filled the empty seats and stayed over at the Marriott with Charlotte and I. At a pre-match dinner we pointed out the poignancy to Jhon, a Mauritian waiter, how appropriate it was that he should be serving us (Jon always had a thing about misplaced 'h's).

We received an ice bucket and a lovely bottle of wine later with a poignant message, 'On the house, from Jhon.' Very on point. A toast, and with Jon there in spirit(s), in a small but endearing way the bucket list was pretty much all but complete.

Later that evening as our party drowned their collective game sorrows we found ourselves sitting with the parents of Alun Wyn Jones. Tim Jones had been recovering from throat cancer. As he reminisced about all things Welsh, you could feel the immense pride Tim, a hugely engaging man, had at watching his son perform at the highest of levels on the biggest of stages.

Charlotte was undergoing the step up to secondary school and all of her own life changes that came with it. Barbarella faded away into the distance, another love come and gone, another relationship that didn't last. There were a hundred reasons why this one didn't work, in the end though mostly because I was on my own. The office walls of my two jobs (Birddog and Sunbury, down its long, empty wing) seemed to take on slightly greyer tones, but they remained no less welcome and somewhere to hide.

The house move happened. The new one, a 1970s mid terrace with no specific character or definition, was as good as things were going to get. Right in the heart of Farnham, it at least was an easy walk to Charlotte's school. Better for her and for me in minimising that school run. It retained a very seventies feel, unmodernised, heavy wood panelling and anaglypta on the walls and ceilings. Water tanks in the attic were stagnant and full of bird shit. A small back patio rolled into a long and dramatically steep, hugely overgrown tree and bramble enveloped slope of a 'garden'.

Loss cuts deepest in the darkness of winter afternoons. Little things came in from left field, like a random *Dear John* DVD in the rental store, to remind me.

I had already waded through denial and many bottles of wine and was about to enter anger phase.

Pen and ink letters used to be the greatest medicine for battling insecurities and fears, hurt and pain. Not primarily all mine although there was always that cathartic element to writing them. How often had I written postcards from the edge, over many a year, helping people battle demons? A legacy of listening to my mother, I had been a magnet for fractured souls, allowing them to slowly open up over time as they started to trust me. Knowing I'd never judge them for who they were, where they were or even how they had got there. Giving them the courage to continue on in their own personal life journeys, expecting little back in return, except the opportunity to while away lonely, late evenings via loads of rambling, flowery words. Hoping someone else felt better for it, rather than making myself necessarily so, whilst never really letting go of any feelings. How I needed a letter, or some sort of demonstrative sign, now.

I had no plan. I desperately needed another anchor.

Glenn Frey died in January 2016 and Don Henley went on record as saying the Eagles would never tour again.

Tottenham. Just you left then. Why you?

Spurs did not lose a game at home and finished second in the Premier League at the end of the 2016-17 season, an all-time high. Their highest position since 1962-63.

With that, all their walls came down.

'White Hart' pubs seemed to have been a part of me, all my life. I'm sure there would be more.

White Hart Lane, however, was reduced to rubble.

Red Lion Lane all but followed.

I had spent too long staring at the characterless walls. In a fit of anger all the anaglypta was ripped off, the kitchen stud walls smashed. Pretty much anything able to be pulled down was. Until not much of any worth was left standing.

Men are generally ashamed of anything that makes them feel vulnerable. We hide at all the times we need to admit it most. Like a mole, I wasn't really seeing the light of day.

Some mornings I would wake up and feel okay.

Others seemed grey and empty, colourless and hopeless.

You can't run away from the truth as it will always find you. Those three words, the ones that men find hardest to say, expressed how I felt and where I was at.

I needed help.

Wasted Time
Summer 2017

There is no quick fix for grief. I'd been there before. You wear it as best you can. Once again it knocked me hard. Two relatively quiet years later I was still angry. I'd pretty much lost sight of myself. And not just the past few years. Most of my life. Once again the shadows had come to stay.

Moving house, loss of a loved one, relationship failure. Pretty much every emotional downer at once. At least there was Birddog but with just McQueen, Hanks, Niven and I, Donkey, remaining the company was going down its own long and winding road. One of the last acts was a Brand on the Run peer and beer session at the Union Club in, of all places, Greek Street…hosted by a chap who in his day had been head roadie for both Bowie and Queen and, with a resonant dollop of serendipity, Supertramp at Earls Court. Singing into Freddie Mercury's Live Aid mic that he had brought along gave me that wish straight out of Aladdin's lamp…I was finally back in the '80s and twenty-one again.

Voluntary redundancy gave me four out of four on the emotional downer classics, leaving me back out on those streets bar a day or so a week in Sunbury. Time for a long period off (most of the week, anyway). All summer long, six months, or as long as it took.

Bargaining progressed to the depression phase.

'You better let somebody love you, before it's too late.'

The words rung through my head.

Life has its way of moving things on if you give it the chance. Luck will find a way, Barry once said. And you can make your own.

With the house (painfully…builders!) knocked back in to shape, all that remained inside was a paint job. Plain white and a new slate. Which just left the garden to look forward to. Or at least up at. Very (very) steep. Almost a cliff from top to bottom…and also sloping left to right. Like Wiggy's toupee all those years ago. Very overgrown with it.

This was going to be a massive task but how I needed a challenge. Building retaining walls which, metaphorically, I had always been good at. I was going to be in for a long haul, literally. If life (and oil rigs and straws and dress pins) had taught me just one thing, it was 'go large'. Being mid-terrace meant bringing the railway sleepers (no scrimping, a good hundred or so) through the house on my own to then try and landscape them upwards, never ending tier by tier, terrace by terrace.

Clearing the many saplings and brambles gave me the opportunity to light a fire and survey the steep mountain of soil. A pile of building materials faced me every day when I got up. It took a couple more weeks before I then went out to stare them down. I was unable to dip my toe in to start. Loneliness can blind you, but the warm May heralded the onset of summer and made my solitude easier.

Help came in the form of Robin. Or rather a robin.

As the days progressed I noticed Robin sat in the trees watching with both alarm, concern and some dismay at the paucity of activity. As I sat there, staring myself out, he was the first to dip a toe in, gradually hopping out of the trees. After a day or two he inched his way beside me…trusting, expectant and hungry.

Dear old Confucius once said that it takes a first stone to move a mountain. What is buried beneath that stone is, however, the real problem.

Normally that's feelings and emotions.

It was the first worm that did it.

Sometimes being there is all you need to show someone the way or to help them onto it. Worm by worm, marginal gain by marginal gain, my little Robin lightened every load I shovelled. He gave me a new purpose and became a new friend. He made me get up for breakfast early doors and I would sit outside sharing it and the worms with him (I was more yoghurt or bacon sarnie than worms).

Dig. And dig. And dig. Inch by inch. Trench by trench. Foothold by foothold. The dug soil dragged up the slope. Sleeper by sleeper, steeper and steeper, higher and higher. Reaching for the sky.

Between us we made progress and built our bridges. Me shifting the piles of earth and Robin picking off the titbits. Recovery was in progress. Four months later and we were done. The days became shorter but brighter and I'd had a lot of time to reflect. Without distractions or complications something in my mind changed.

I'd spent a long time hoping to find a relationship that clearly defined what love really meant. Not really thinking straight...or being able to. Spending far too much time in relationships that I hoped would cure a pain. And probably knowing that, when I entered in to them, something wasn't quite right. I had settled for them, willing to sacrifice a little in the hope of gaining a lot. A typical Cancerian, going into a shell and making myself unlovable, because I feared love. Real love.

I never knew whether Robin was a he or a she. Just the very real early bird that got the worms. Life is about what's real. Moving on is not all about self-help books available by the dozen. It is about timely and pivotal events...people, things, animals...that come into your life unexpectedly that you let in, that create enough of a spark to enforce change. Robin, my faithful digging friend, was now gone but had provided that kick up the arse. The once empty house (and tangled garden) was now a lovely home. Easy for Charlotte for her new school. Result all round.

The cherry on top of the icing on the cake was a small one...a gin palace standing proud on top of the cliff (now terraces), way above the height of the house, where I could see and survey the meadows and the town football pitch beyond; the end of the summer, '80s music on and beer in hand. The years may have rushed by but the view from the 'palace' took me back in time. Back to those old summer night football playing days.

Tottenham were about to start the new season with a different perspective too.

White Hart Lane was down, the last match at that old stadium against Manchester United. A 2-1 victory should have been the meaningful bit, but seeing all the old legends was unique. All those who had come and gone. Those who were special but suffered their own destructions, mentally like Gazza, or physically like Ledley King. The victory was special, as well as the parade. Sport gives you memories. Something to hang on to. On the day it rained a little and then the sun appeared. For White Hart Lane's final bow, the cherry on the icing of its cake was a rainbow above.

All that remained were dreams about tomorrow. Spurs were now (for as long as it took) going to be playing their home games at Wembley. It was time for new heroes.

Football players are never going to be quite good enough, according to all of the social media armchair managers, no matter what strengths those new players might have and no matter what they might bring to the table. In Tottenham's case it was Mousa Sissoko, bought from Newcastle for a club record thirty-odd million, who took a lot of the flak. And Fernando Llorente, the back-up forward bought from Swansea. 'Why?' howled the 'fans'. Charlotte smiled. These were new names, players who came with a clean slate who she could talk about at school. Her birthday present to me that year had been two tickets to a Tottenham game of my choice. Logically, for me, it had to be against Swansea at Wembley. Personal history attached to both teams…with the old Wembley my first ever Tottenham game, the new Wembley hers.

A return to 'Wembley' for me for the first time since the Eagles. Tottenham went into their match off the back of a good result against Dortmund in the Champions League. Expectation was high for Charlotte's first game and with it (for her) an opportunity to watch Dele Alli play.

The game, unfortunately, was one of those where the minutes did go by like hours. Swansea had zero shots on target. Tottenham had seventy-five percent possession and twenty-six 'shots', although only eight on target. Looked good on paper, but all very dull and unimaginative at face value. Created chances, dominated the game, maybe a little unlucky, but Tottenham failed to score at 'home' for the first time in thirty games.

Houston, we sense we might have a problem.

The best bit came two-thirds of the way through, with Kane scooping a shot over the crossbar when it was easier to score. Llorente, on to make his league debut, offered an extra and different attacking option. The 'fans' didn't see or buy it. Spurs were ultimately frustrated by a disciplined Swansea and lost ground on a title pursuit.

Tottenham's journey this season was already becoming flawed…just as they gave everyone hope, they kept losing the purpose and the roadmap.

For me, my purpose and roadmap was a treadmill and back to running…and slowly starting to play hockey again. More road trips, this time with an extended crew…Daz, as always, Chris, Nige and George. Something of a five-a-side hockey team of sorts in there…Chris in goal, George at the back, Nige and I in the middle and Daz upfront.

In one of the first games back a hamstring went, badly, early. With a club shortage of players the following week, it meant a lot of strapping and a statuesque fill-in role, goal hanging in their 'D'. No running, just making a nuisance of myself. For the first time in a lifetime, not running actually turned out to be the best result…I scored four goals, my biggest match tally ever.

Standing still seemed to be the new running away.

The good things moved slowly and gently forward.

If Chunky had done a great job in the old days of passing on a literary education, Simon Pegg was doing the same job for the youth of today. Or at least Charlotte. Her interest in *Shaun of the Dead* segued into *Pride and Prejudice and Zombies* (not as bad as it sounded) and from there to Jane Austen's house in Chawton. With it an appreciation of the classics she never knew existed.

Jules' music education was evolving, starting as he was to listen to rock. I bought him a turntable and gave him my copy of 'Freebird' by way of kick-off. Getting his dad's old records out of the attic would be A-level standard.

Tottenham may have been frugal in the transfer market, but Toby and Sanchez, a pair of young gerbils, joined our household team. Charlotte picked them and after a stressed journey 'home' for them, they settled in nicely to our little family. They kept each other amused and, for us, were just 'always there'. For Charlotte, company after school and for me, keeping me sane of a long evening when she was with her mum. And, like Robin (both), their marginal gain was massive.

Tottenham, however, crumbled against Juventus exiting the Champions League last sixteen in the process. Chiellini, one of the Italian players, rubbed it in.

'It is the history of Tottenham. In the end, they always miss something.'

Like a crusty old lasagne, or stale cheese, old habits die hard.

It was back to work as well with a part-time consultancy role…helping get a company back on its feet. Early on I realised it was going to be a monster to steer into calmer waters and would exhaust me both mentally and physically. On top of Sunbury, I was now working all hours.

I felt like Cinderella…with just some friendly rodents to talk to and never getting to the ball.

THE SEASON

The Long Run
July 2018

I met Belle six months ago.

As this July closed we made it to a Mad Hatter's Ball at Hartley Wintney Cricket Club. Pink bow ties and flamingo dresses the order of the day, the event scrubbed up nicely and the party band, MadHen, were insanely brilliant.

Making it to the ball is one thing, but every fairy tale has its villain…and this particular one was no exception. In this instance (based on the somewhat incredulous stories being thrown around the dinner table) it actually was Dangerous Dan! The irony of life imitating art.

This real life Gaston bided his villainous time at the bar until, when neither his seemingly long-suffering girlfriend nor I were around, played the soft hands over Belle. At this point there should, quite rightly, have been some gauntlets thrown down and a duel (fight! fight! fight!). Belle was way quicker out of the blocks though with a withering look that would have made a T-Rex run down a rabbit hole. Oooh! That was like a razor jab to the goolies and the solar plexus all in one. Both surprised and impressed, I had that feeling you get when someone scores a 'worldy' right in front of you. Gaston-lite slimed off into the shadows to presumably turn into a pumpkin at midnight. I'd seemingly got a new drinking buddy, a token that didn't pass easily or lightly.

One-time air-traffic controller, former midwife, holistic guru, and now teaching assistant. To buy time, she'd been around the job sphere almost as much as me. She did head massage, Reiki, believed unicorns were real as well as being into the whole angelic thing. She'd also been the glue that held a lot of people together. As retrograde goes, she went to that Apollo Extreme concert...and supported Wolves.

Belle was also back finding her relationship feet as well, it not having been easy. She came with Aurora (of Disney

Sleeping Beauty princess fame) who was one week older than Charlotte and who had cerebral palsy. Aurora loved art and films, especially Disney (good on her!) and liked to allocate the roles therein. Everyone was given their character, their personality, her own favourite being Aurora. Her mum was Belle (occasionally Mary Poppins). I had always been used to being Gregory, Donkey or a poor man's Martin Kemp. In Aurora's world however, sometimes I was Robbie Hart from *The Wedding Singer*, although she did agree on Donkey. Other times I was The Rock. It was always nice to be one. Mostly though, I was Beast. Very appropriately so. At fifty-three, there had been an anger inside and those petals were wilting. I had been locked up in my own wing for far too long. Everything about Aurora seemed to resonate too.

In six months we had already been on a few adventures.

Both Belle and Aurora were there the time I broke my nose, split my lip and lost a tooth, all care of a badly swung opposition stick after five minutes of a night-time hockey game. The first time they had seen me play hockey. Aurora thought the explosion of claret out on the pitch, and in the make-shift dugout stitch-up area just after, all terribly good fun. Best movie she'd ever seen and she laughed her head off. I played on (no substitutes).

'Ian! Ian!' was all I could hear for the rest of the game. It was Aurora cheering me on. I'd got a fan. What was not to love? And as I didn't do hospitals it was even funnier for her watching the Steri-Strips being administered at tea after the game.

The funeral of my Aunt Maria, sad occasion that it was, was still an early chance to meet the extended family. It felt as if Belle had been centre stage for way more than just the few months.

The consultancy work I'd taken on just before meeting Belle had developed in to a bit of a nightmare, well before Christmas, but as the new year had progressed she'd often popped over to help out after her own morning's work. It was a proper team effort and she helped save many a day. Or at least make them better.

She also got to meet Siobhan and Jules on picking us up at Heathrow after we had been over to see Alun in Dubai. The pre-arranged holiday had been a great chance for Jules to wax lyrical and try to outgun Al on everything rock.

'That's one my dad used to play.'

The list went on. Belle wasn't a Dorothy or a Susan. Just her unique self, a rare diamond with a heart of gold. Days were worth getting up for.

July had started with a Watercress Line outing with the girls. Aurora loved trains…the older and the more Thomas Tanky the better.

The following Saturday was LowdeFest, a music festival with overnight camping…getting the (future) Glastonbury vibes going for Charlotte and an opportunity for Belle to chill and relax. England were playing Sweden in the World Cup quarter-finals on the big screen aside the music stages. Dele Alli slotted for England's second to wrap up the game and Charlotte and the crowd, ably and madly assisted by 29 Fingers (on stage at the time), went bananas. The hot and gorgeous day ended with Rick Parfitt Jnr.

'Here is one my dad used to play,' he said, bringing the night to a close and the house down.

The end of the month brought adult time and a stay at the Enid Blyton-esque Knoll House, a quaint throwback to *Famous Five* days (where the stories were, in part, written). Nothing had seemingly changed…the rolling hills, hidden paths down to the beach and croquet on the lawns.

Dinner at the fabulous Shell Bay was gorgeous.

She was taking me places I'd never been.

Turns out she knew The Westin Beach in Florida. We had both been. By a quirk of fate…at the same time.

It may have been six months since Belle and I met, but she might just have grasped, with the Johnny Sexton inspired

Ireland Grand Slam in the Six Nations and the end to the Premier League, where time (often) went. For Tottenham, the players and the song remained the same…up and down during their first full season at Wembley but ending with a win in a nine-goal thriller against Leicester City that dear old Wandsworth Common would have been proud of.

Almost before anyone had a chance to grab their breath, the end of July's pre-season warm-up tournaments began. Spurs beat Roma 4-1 (Llorente and Moura sticking hands up early) and a 2-2 draw was then salvaged with Barcelona at The Rose Bowl. Times had changed. Gone the nostalgic days of friendlies with Stevenage, the footballing equivalent of a snog behind the bike sheds when compared to Barca in Pasadena. The season was about to begin but how we all needed some old time ethics, heart, soul…and romance.

The romance started, joyously, with a penalty shootout up in Scotland endearingly ending East Fife 4, Forfar 5.

Ethics were slowly starting to find their way back. Social media had long since empowered players and with it their interactions with supporters. They'd taken control of their own narratives, cultivating their own brands, reducing the distance between themselves and their fans…making them almost separate and bigger than the teams they played for. Social media had also given rise to anger, rage and tribalism even more polarised and extreme.

With it all came concerns over emotional wellbeing. All EFL clubs would carry the MIND mental health squiggle logo in the coming season to highlight the issues.

At the top of my garden, over many a hot evening, the summer continued to roll. Cut and trimmed, I had slowly watched the plants grow according to both the weather and seasons. The slopes and walls were resplendent. Birds were everywhere, both in noise…and shit. Everything seemed in order, the perfect place to create memories.

Romance (complete with snogs) up in the Sky Bar was most definitely alive too.

No More Cloudy Days
August 2018

The Sunbury job continued to provide a help horizon. My room was still brown, still small, and still very square. Still tucked down its own private wing…but now had a slightly different hue. Belle still came in on afternoons at the other consultancy place after doing her own work and plugged away, keeping the invoice pile low.

Just being there helped…the little things, like a welcome bar of chocolate or a bunch of grapes.

She was good in other ways too, like the secret trips she arranged. Notting Hill, the blue door, the bookshop, gin at The Distillery, Portobello Road and the picnic and open air cinema screening of *Notting Hill* in Holland Park. Life was changing.

Nobody should be all alone against the world outside.

Red Lion Lane had now become the playground. Disco lights (and the three foot flamingo) made it quirky. Kicking inflatable beach balls around the living room, I could have been that eight year old again. Spurs needed a new central midfielder. I wasn't available (too much fun in my land of dreams). Sissoko (who reminded me a little of me, in so far as his ability to be in all positions at all times) carried the team's sole hopes in this regard. More pre-season friendlies ended up with a 4-1 loss at mighty Girona. The warm-ups had been a bit of a curate's egg.

Maybe I might have to lace the boots up again.

In other fantasies, Aurora was off to Disneyland with her dad, giving Belle a little break. It was heartening to be a part of Aurora's magic kingdom and it reminded me of the time when Charlotte and I went and the blast we had…the revolving tea cups, Tinkerbell, Peter Pan and an army of Lost Boys. 'Again! Again!' she cried as the carousel came to its (first) end.

A few days at a holiday camp down in West Sands with Belle, Charlotte, Daz and his family became another trip down memory lane. Static caravans, racing cars, fairground attractions, crazy golf, amusement arcade and barbeques as well as Take That and Little Mix tribute bands. Good fun had by all.

Charlotte and I took half an hour out to go on the all-weather court to practise football. All went well until a load of ten year olds walked on to claim the terrain, challenging us to a seven versus two game. Lots of wannabe footballers (one Bournemouth Academy) against just us. A challenge is a challenge. That and the honour of my daughter being at stake. Oh…and for the first time in my life I was the big lad at school. We won 9-1. I embarrassed (and also reduced Charlotte to fits of giggles) when I back-heeled from over the halfway line then ran round with my shirt over my face. Fair play to all the kids who took it all in good grace (they shouldn't have put me on the lower numbered side).

'Were you a professional footballer once?' one asked.

'Yes…when I was your age, my friend.'

There was something about not having to grow up.

Charlotte, Belle and I followed my field of dreams by taking the big tent and a road trip to the Gower Peninsula, near Swansea. Three Cliffs camping site was up there with the best, set on its headland overlooking Three Cliffs Bay, with long beach walks and rope swings on the way down to Tor Bay and Oxwich. Charlotte, wearing a Barcelona shirt, sitting on the rope swing over a South Wales beach never looked, in my fading eyes, lovelier. Days were all rounded off with jaunts to quaint pubs and a fire pit by the tent. It rained once, briefly. The trick of the camera captured Belle, quite literally, with a rainbow above her.

Peaceful, lovely, timely. Wales, land of my mother, was for me a time and place gone by. One of endless summer holidays as a child, castles in the sky, beaches, sand dunes, cycle trips, rites of passage…but also never more beautiful in this moment. Porthcawl too, where both The Breaksea and the old funfair were still as I'd remembered them. The harbour had been modernised. New coffee and art shops. Somehow through the mists of time, it all looked the same.

Reasons. Seasons. Lifetimes. And those lonely teardrops that never came.

All chapters of my life lead to now, the present.

It's pouring with rain when we get there. 'There' being past any semblances of coal mines. Past The Liberty, Swansea's football ground.

Margam Crematorium is a place I haven't revisited in nearly thirty years. I don't remember the funeral cortege to the park all those decades ago that well. All I remember is being there. Little has changed. The steel mills still shroud it. Otherwise it's as tranquil as it ever was.

We find the car park, close to the main buildings, and all those closed memories come back. Stepping out of the car, we are roughly facing where Mum's ashes were spread. It's hard not to see the white feather.

Whilst locating the grid coordinates in the admin office, we are interrupted by the hymn for an ongoing cremation service. It's 'Abide With Me'. We've been here before.

Back by the car again, about ten paces forward, into the Garden of Remembrance, lovely as it is, and we are pretty much on the spot.

Belle stands back, graciously allowing Charlotte and I to stand in silence. She can see I've been hurting. Charlotte's doing the crying for both of us…meeting the grandmother she never knew, for the first time. I hope in the future she never stops crying when she needs to…experience has told me, it's better out than in. I'm just absorbing the moment. Allowing time to stand still for as long as it lasts.

And, in that moment, I see who she really is. Belle. A loveliness, a still calm. In just over six months I have taken her to a funeral and a cremation site. She's different. I've no idea what is going to happen when time starts revving up again, but she keeps taking me places I have never been. And she's the only person I've taken to meet my mum in nearly thirty years. Today, I feel like I am no longer on my own, the last of that lifetime's worth of barricades having finally been cleared.

After Swansea, Aurora's back and the four of us are off to Knoll House to stay in their family lodge. Aurora loves her swimming and after a fab afternoon in the outdoor pool it's a movie on our big screen projector. The Rock's in it.

On our way home we stop at The Sandbanks Hotel to claim a dinner that was our previous New Year's Eve 'best family' prize. And it's now a proper family affair.

Thereafter it's just Belle and me at Kolymbia in Rhodes, skinny dipping and all under a moonlit boardwalk at night. Something very romantic about being all alone in the Med at two in the morning. There's a first for everything.

The entertainment programme is good…none more so than on Monday evening which is going to be a test of all things romantic; at the same time, downtown, its Spurs and Manchester United.

Football is a little like a Disney film…epic quests in the struggle of good against evil (or in football's case 'money'). Tottenham have been pencilled in for failure this season, making transfer history for all the wrong reasons. The first premier league club to sign precisely zero players. Despite two wins from two to kick the new season off it has been very scrappy…things don't seem right.

Having been open about his struggles with depression prior to the 2018 World Cup, Danny Rose reveals that he was actually labelled 'crazy' by a club interested in signing him. Social media goes off on one. There is uncertainty at the club and a whole world of problems lie ahead.

Not least with the logistics out in Kolymbia.

Belle's quite happy to take a wander around the resort and see what the nightlife (and sports bars) are like. As it is 'The Sports Bar' is just a big screen over the market square. Could be worse…as could Lucas Moura who heralds his arrival on the big stage (Old Trafford, not Kolymbia) with two fine goals to add to Kane's one. Second chances don't come around very often and Moura's making the most of his. He could be special this guy.

As, I am fast thinking, could this girl.

Just like Moura the night before, The Jackson 5 tribute band (all the way from South Africa) could be something too on the hotel's large, outdoor entertainment stage. The problem is there are only four of them. And, as anticipated well in advance, they are going to need an 'extra' to fill the stage. I've been an extra before, chasing ambulances. It was emotional…but not post a lot of alcohol consumption.

This opportunity, and I know it's going to be me (perils of having the front row seats and walking back with a large Estrella and some nuclear cocktails) is going to be a test of a history…nay, a legacy even…of crap nightclub dancing and shutting the world out. The very considered audience (of ooh, about three hundred holiday makers) could well be my biggest gig.

As expected, I get the twelfth (or fifth) man call. This bit (for them) isn't going to be scripted though.

This is no 'Baa Baa Black Sheep'. My new found, one night only, five-a-side team will need to step their game up.

Fear is a funny thing but I'm still on a high from Moura the night before and, up on a package holiday music stage, I shut my eyes and I'm away with the disco fairies. The rest of 'my' band are wondering what's going on behind them. And not in any Marvin Gaye kinda way. I resist doing the 'moonwalk'. Mainly because I can't. The only thing missing from my holiday camp repertoire.

They used to hate me…love me, but hate me, all my old teammates, in most of my sport playing days…because I'd just run around and do my own thing, like Sissoko, looking to bring out the best in the team. Nobody got that it was to make everyone else look better. I would subtly lead from the back and let others take the glory in front.

On a balmy night, on the biggest of European (holiday) stages, here I am making Marlon, Jackie, Jermaine and Tito, proper sweaty as the guys are, look like true professionals. For about five minutes I'm lost in music. Completely out of sync with my team…but the crowd are on fire. Not like at a Meatloaf concert. In a good way. The 'Four' give it up to me when they make sure I can get off the stage without falling when the shepherd's crook is due.

One of my better five-a-sides.

And I finally got my disco day in the holiday sun.

The massive applause after (to them) raises the roof. It is a huge round (applause as well) from me, for making me realise, at the end of the day, any day, lovely or otherwise, there is safety in numbers. There'll always be someone who has got your back…or in their case…my front.

Belle shows it back to me on her phone.

Not all of it. Just that sunshine, moonlight, good times, boogie bit. Awesome rhythm and moves.

With me doing something more akin to 'Thriller' in the background.

'Don't give up your day job,' she says. Probably just as well, as I like having her around for that.

Don't be afraid to fall in love again I was once told.

That fog is lifting.

With a whole new season just kicking off, and football about to come thick and fast, I hope it won't cloud all that has gone by to date.

Match (up) of the day is on. It's hard to pick a side.

Belle versus my nauseating obsession with Tottenham (whose current squad might have passed their peak). Both would be first choices in the playground team of life.

In chasing the ultimate prize, what price victory?

It has been three years since Jon left. Autumns have come and gone and I've watched the garden die but go through its own cycles of rebirth, knowing that spring is just around the corner.

Tottenham are going through their own reinvention. A September loss to Watford suggests they might be falling off the early season pace quicker than all the leaves on the trees. A similar fate against Liverpool in a not bad, but not good enough, performance suggests the wheels might be coming off too. Their league form looks like it plateaued in 2017 in the last season of White Hart Lane.

A trip with my girl gang to a fun dog show does little to sway the mood. It's Champions League kick-off week.

'If we get to the Champions League final can we go to watch it? Love you, hands round the back and back again.'

Charlotte still keeps challenging me in all the best ways.

Aware that Spurs have only ever made it to the semis of Europe's most prestigious tournament once in their entire history, and still lost that with arguably their greatest ever team, I know it isn't going to happen.

'Of course.'

I know it's a promise I am able to keep because I know Tottenham just aren't good enough to force both my hand and my wallet. Inter Milan score two late goals to take the first game of their group stage and my thoughts are, sadly, vindicated.

Tottenham and I know each other inside out.

Respite of sorts comes in the league with their win away to Brighton, scene of South Africa and Japan…contrasted by their lowest ever Wembley attendance. Barely twenty-six thousand get out of their beds for a dull League Cup draw against Watford, Tottenham needing penalties to settle the fixture. This season is starting to turn as dark as the days are closing in. Small mercies come at the end of the month with a win against Huddersfield.

Jules brings some relevance back to the weekend dinner table. He remembers the elephant seal. A mental image to hold on to. If not get chased by.

Belle has seen all the chinks in my armour (even after a few months, many times over) and seems quite happy welding them back up. I have taken her to the top of my highest walls. Now I'm taking her to a Take That tribute in one of The Village's function rooms; same room and same scene as 'dancing through chemistry'. The group looks nothing like Take That (there are only the three of them and I resist joining them on stage) but somehow they still manage to conjure up a fab party vibe and spirit (aided and abetted by racks of tequila and Porn Star Martinis). It's a proper hair let down. If I retook a chemistry practical in this moment, I would be fully in my element. It's an A-plus evening.

Reality bites the following Wednesday. Against a record ever home crowd topping eighty-two thousand, Messi and Barcelona storm Wembley and Spurs' Champions League fantasy and my promise are pretty much done. The Spanish outfit, led masterfully by the Argentinian magician, run riot. Tottenham are more than part of an enthralling game, but know their European lights and nights have been dimmed as Barca ease to a 4-2 victory. I have still got my Swansea photographs of Charlotte on a swing, by the beach, to hold on to.

What's left of October plays out like the early part. The wins against Cardiff and West Ham emphasise pretty much where Tottenham are. The season has been either black or white to date, a two-thirds win-loss set of statistics, with no draws. Conclusions? They've been very much hit or miss, laboured and (or) scratchy. The effort is there, but no-one is really standing up and being counted. No momentum to build on, no consistency. That, and…why are we talking about statistics? They got me nowhere. Anyway, two-thirds (relatively speaking) is better than a half.

PSV are the next Champions League opponents and the dog's dinner continues. Tottenham get their noses in front, but allow an eighty-seventh minute equaliser.

'Our chances of qualifying are nearly over, it will be so difficult,' says Pochettino.

Manchester City rub it in with a win in the league. Small mercies come with League Cup progress and a victory over West Ham. Son Heung-min (Sonny) scores twice and the much (fan) maligned, but infinitely professional and whole-hearted Llorente also gets on the score sheet.

Diversions from all the trials and tribulations of football come from a few (non-night) games of hockey, as well as a nostalgic step into the past with the showing of *Christopher Robin* at Farnham Maltings.

Pooh Bear gets his game face on. His voice resonates.

To close the month it's an adult weekend for us at the Haven Hotel on Sandbanks with dinner at Shell Bay. An adventure amongst the curiosity shops of Swanage tosses up a 'Drinking Partners for Life' keyring. As trophies go it's poignant and I give it to Belle. Bert, a stuffed toy sloth, literally jumps out of a seaside Grab Machine and becomes a member of our extended family. The weekend has been good.

I could quite easily have all my adventures with Belle.

It's November and Toby and Sanchez, the other members of the family, turn one. As naming rights and Tottenham defenders go, they could have been Jan and Juan but the former names stuck. As gerbils go, their names suit. With Charlotte away at her mum's half the week, and Belle at her house, they provide a welcoming noise at the front door when I come in, and a comforting scratch against a quiet nights' monotony. They keep a house a home.

The very human Toby and Sanchez have a game up at Wolves to contend with. Kane scores his first goal in four games and Tottenham gain a 3-2 victory in a match they were 3-0 up. A little light via the Spurs regular shades of darkness.

Two days later and it's a crunch game against PSV back in Europe. Lose and Spurs are done. With little over ten minutes to go they are all but down and out. Kane scores two, one in the last minute of normal time. The light, if not flooding in, is much brighter, more so with Inter drawing against Barca. Spurs are three points behind qualifying with two games to go. A European extension on a bigger stage (the Estrella is in the fridge) looks like it is going to go to the wire, particularly with Tottenham having to travel to Barca for their last game and needing to get points.

Also going to the wire is my early morning hockey game over at Yateley the following weekend. I've never been late for a game in my life. Missed that one school rugby game, but never been late. Usually, as any of my teammates (past or present) would vouch for, at least a half an hour early. Belle's sat-nav has taken a detour via the wilds of nowhere (actually Basingstoke) and time is spent. Five minutes to the start and we are at least fifteen minutes away. Tension and my angst rise. I'm aware we only had a bare minimum eleven and for the first time I can remember I am about to let another team down. Memories of that game, that school rugby game, invade my thoughts. I struggle to keep it all in. Changing in the car is a tight fit but, as always, the girls are amused. Belle has a lot of endearing qualities…not looking out of place in a *Fast and Furious* movie is one of them. We arrive and the game has already been going on for a short while. The opposition took full advantage of a man down and insisted on a prompt start.

I get onto the pitch and it all comes out. First touch of the ball, a quick self-tap from a foul on the half-way line, a charge into the D and I've roofed it. Five minutes later and

I bury a second and with it forty years of being haunted by a different game I never started.

'Ian! Ian!' loudly rings out from the touch-line dugout. Over and above my loyal daughter, who has been to and seen most games, Aurora is having a ball.

I remember pretty much all of my goals, hockey and football, but these five minutes resonate much deeper. The game is so much simpler when you either don't have time, or do not actually over-think it (guilty of that for many a season). A third goal in the second half gives me a hat-trick and we go on to win 6-0. After the game I tell the guys this is (finally) my last game...as the next two months are later games in the dark and prudence dictates I won't be playing. It is the right way to finish. Things couldn't get or be any better than this moment. I was late. Scored three. The end.

It wouldn't have been the pitch I would have chosen to go out on. I've played on too many to mention. Favourite? Probably the Bar Pitch at Crystal Palace. Not because of its aesthetic qualities or its playing surface. Just where most of the memories, good or bad, come from...memorial games, eye haemorrhages, my best hockey goal and non-goal. And where I've played at least one game with most of my many hockey and football teammates.

It lasted a week.

The following weekend Jules and Siobhan visit us. The Lamb is rammed for the England against All Blacks rugby match. We've got our seats early on in what is an absolutely foul day. Walking there gets us soaked. As we settle, Daz sends a text over to say they only have nine players for the hockey with push-back in ten minutes. Could I make it? I decline. I'm done. And spend the first quarter of the rugby chewing my lip. I've got to go. I do. I run home, get my kit on and get to their game. It is five o'clock and pitch black, even with the astro lights on. It's a monsoon. Pretty much as good as it gets for me. They've found two players and are 2-0 up. I return to The Lamb happy I tried. It is small, insular, sweaty, noisy, warmer and very much the place to be. The rest of the rugby and the company are fab.

Desperado, an Eagles tribute band, are at The Maltings that evening. Jules, Siobhan, Belle and I soak up all the hits. Wembley Stadium, on a summer's night it isn't, poignant and evocative it is. As is the Abba themed party the week after at The Lighthouse in Woking. It is a bananas affair, unicorns and rainbows all over the place. Tottenham beat Palace and Chelsea. All the clouds are lifting and, if physics taught me anything, it is that momentum starts with small actions. Not everything is text book though.

As November closes, it is the penultimate Champion's League group game against Inter. It is win or bust. At 0-0, going into the dying embers of the match, Spurs are just ten minutes from going out. Eriksen scores and the nerves are about to get shredded. Heading into injury time, Inter have to go for it. Tottenham bodies are being thrown all over the place. The game ends. One group game left.

Tottenham have to go to Barcelona to match or better Inter's final game against PSV. It's been a different autumn but the last month of the year already looks tasty. If Spurs (and PSV) play out of their skins a journey begins.

The new Tottenham stadium, whilst not falling down, isn't going up as quickly as intended. Fire warning system problems, software issues, increasing costs and lengthening delays. It's been a long process right from 2001 (when the need was first identified) and in 2003 (when land was first acquired). They've always been there for me though.

I've tried to stay one step, one year, ahead of Charlotte. Spurs have helped there too. I know she'll probably grow out of them...but I hope we get something special to really remember before she does.

You can't turn back time, but hope to find a way to fix the future so that it sheds a different kind of light on the past. In that regard, we're all in this together.

I wonder what December and 2019 will bring.

Witchy Woman
December 2018

Decembers have become busy. Christmas…and now one more birthday to add to the list. Somehow sport, somehow running, doesn't seem as important as it once was. It's also a year on from meeting Belle. She's been a game changer.

Her profile, that year before, had been refreshingly simple. The meet, back then, all very festive, all very *Love, Actually*.

Her lovely words had suggested something, something undefined (thank you again, Billy). And, as online profiles went, more than a dollop of charm and intelligence. There seemed a delicate fragility to her but also an air of mystery; her single picture hauntingly beautiful (decorated lovingly with Snapchat filters). The biggie though, the real biggie…a love of all things *Dirty Dancing*, *Ghost* and *Roadhouse*. As gifts went, she could've been all my Christmases at once (Pooh bear ride-on aeroplane excepted).

I read her lovely words two or three times to make sure. She mentioned Italy quite a bit. Venice, Sorrento, the Alps, Capri, Parma and Bologna were places I could relate to and talk about if we ever met. Coming in left field though, she confused me slightly.

Something else was going on that intrigued me over and above that Snapchat aura. Her eyes, which couldn't cloud my judgement, carried some sort of emptiness, a void, that left her (like a jigsaw puzzle down a piece) incomplete. She looked more vulnerable than her forty something years.

The longer I analysed her features, the more questions I raised…but the more interesting she became. Everyone is made up of segments which, when integrated, make us the people we are. She was no different...segments of sadness, of anger, excitement, fear, hope. I couldn't quite work out what the missing piece was though.

Tendency to be over-analytical. That was me. I had left that out of my previous 2008 profile for good reason.

I curbed my challenging side to suit and I found myself being gentle with any questioning. I held back trying not to get too close, too early.

Maybe in this one case I was afraid to.

I nevertheless looked forward to seeing her name pop up on my computer. She beguiled and enchanted in equal measure…and those battered old eyes liked what they saw. They wanted to see more.

I needed a flight of fancy. Belle turned my engine on.

I did wonder whether I would be wasting my time. She lived a way away. A good few years younger than me. Nine it turned out. Yet we had made that initial connection. My circumstances were often off-putting to some, depending obviously on what it was they were really looking for. I was always upfront and honest so people didn't get the wrong idea. I had never made any attempt to hide the fact I had a young daughter.

Why me?

What made me different to anyone else?

Once again, I hadn't been featuring highly on any other dater's list of elusive Mr. Rights (or even Mr. Half Rights). I knew nothing of her circumstances that sat on the back of my mind, but she got me.

A little more as each day passed.

It was the photo with Aurora that gave me the first clue as to the questions she wasn't posing but that I was asking. There was something simple in the picture, entirely missing from every other profile I had seen. A refreshing and very deliberate honesty. Aurora looked a sweetie.

It coloured in her canvas all the more.

Here I was starting to love finding out more about her, as much as she would reveal; and each little bit I found out added more definition to that canvas. Without having met her, I felt an affinity, a feeling of being close to someone.

Why her? She was making me do it again. Writing pages and pages of utter gibberish, turning me in to a tongue-tied wreck. How come I could talk about football like it was the simplest of equations (O-level standard), yet thinking and writing about love and romance was quantum physics?

I knew I couldn't hide behind the computer for ever, giving her the best of my Byron or Burns. And nor could she. Face-to-face conversation can never be beaten as the definitive prelude to any reasons, seasons or lifetimes. Only then do all the main senses start clicking in to gear....sight, sound, smell, touch.

I smiled.

Either we didn't spark and the words would just drop away. We'd both lose. Or things kicked off a little, we gave more of each other away only to find neither was in the right head space. We'd both lose.

Or a journey begins.

Six days after profile exchange and lots of emails, a date.

On the day before the date, time just ran away from me. The consultancy job had resulted in the week from hell and needed a local stayover for the night. Work finished, I went back to my hotel accommodation at about seven. A shower and a bit of food the pre-match warm up.

Time for a first call to add the voice...and a next layer.

Stand up toilet break first.

And…the phone rang.

Pretty much done, so I answered, knowing I could call a bit of a bluff, waste a little time, run down the clock…and buy about thirty seconds by dribbling towards the corner.

'Are you in the loo?'

The voice was a kind 'all's well in the world' one.

Her opening line was utterly memorable too.

An hour later we were still chatting away, me having resorted to using the toilet (for a seat), not wishing to break the moment. The conversation kept flowing, well into the night. Opening up was easy.

It was a direct train from work up to Waterloo the next evening. Christmas time, under the clock on the concourse. As romantic as any first night date could be after a prior evening of toilet humour.

The scene straight out of Simon Pegg's *Man Up*.

This had been a strangely different week of preparation. No thinking ahead to the big game a week in advance, the nerves, expectation and anxiety building.

The train was five minutes late but, after texting to buy me the time, it finally drew in. Rush hour on a Friday night was guaranteed to have an awful lot of people under the clock. I hoped she'd be the one I wanted her to be.

Through the big crowd I couldn't miss her, even from a distance, with my eyes. She smiled and for all the online foreplay, there she was. Every inch, and unmistakably, the same in real life as her online pictures.

As the time on the big overhead clock caught its breath, so did I. Being comfortable around her had taken no time at all and it was one of those evenings where you wanted time to stand still.

I had hoped to impress with tales of the old book, tales of national magazine underpants centre spreads. Possibly not the relative ins and outs of the online Gerbil Forum. It turned out I didn't need to and she wouldn't have been that impressed anyway. No more Clark Kent or Superman, no more Henry the mild-mannered janitor or Hong Kong Phooey. Just me. No need for a full on 'here I am' Haka.

Just a simple hand in hand walk along the South Bank to the Winter Festival. Drinking mulled cider round the fire pits, the sparks flew. An eerie warmth shrouded me in the dancing shadows and the flames…a kind of chemistry that could, and would, only make sense to my past.

Beautiful, quirky…spellbinding even. A free spirit and a very rare combination of graces and energy. Charming and utterly lovely with it. She had me mesmerised into a night which continued along the South Bank, up on the carousel and some tapas at Don Felipe. What's not to love about a tasty Spanish in the right moment to round things off?

The following week it was chat, chat, chat. I wooed her further with my favourite clip from *Crazy, Stupid, Love*…the one where Jacob (Ryan Gosling) takes his shirt off.

'What's your big move?' Emma Stone's character asked. 'I've Had The Time Of My Life' goes onto Jacob's record player and they do the *Dirty Dancing* lift.

'What's your big move?' Belle asked.

Good question. Emma's was scripted, Belle's wasn't. I didn't really have one. Except, once upon a time, the *Dirty Dancing* lift; with Charlotte. I sent her my *Man Up* DVD.

I learned more about her. She was a real fighter. Told Aurora wouldn't ever walk or talk, she now did both with assurance. Reassurance and intimate praise do wonders for anxiety. You could see how good a mum Belle was in that and all regards. Any figure that represented love, guidance and safety, that allowed someone to be a better version of their self, was worth way more than they had probably ever given themselves credit for.

Two weeks after that first meet, it was Christmas Day. I was on my own that year, the young Toby and Sanchez for company (the gerbils, not the footballers, for the avoidance of doubt), for the first time since 'pass the sausages'. This one felt different (the year, not the double-entendres, again for the avoidance of doubt).

She had given me a hamper of goodies to tide me over. She barely knew me…but she could see right through me. She had gone from being a terrific mystery to simply full of tidings of comfort and joy. She had integrity, honesty and my back. On this most special of days she gave me a voice.

She also gave me one of those presents you want to slowly unwrap, curious and excited about what lay within. It was a gorgeous, flowery, summer shirt, the like of which I hadn't seen since my greatest ever flowery, summer shirt took two beers on the house for Jon and I.

I had in mind something I wanted to do for a long time. Like, since I had given up art at school. Paint. Belle liked unicorns. And I felt like painting her some kind of fantastic beast. All Christmas day I painted and painted and painted.

That Christmas a year ago flowed in to New Year's Eve at The Sandbanks Hotel and a first chance for Charlotte to meet her. The hotel's American '50s styled party was full of proper families. And we were just making up the numbers. Until we were given the first place in their competition for 'best family'. Interesting, as we'd only been a pretend one for a few hours. Chemistry practicals were turning out well. Everything resonated and it felt like we were on the same page.

I realised, little more than a month in, it was decision time. A crossroads. Run…or stand (the test of time).

An evolving canvas had taken shape. But I had no idea what was being created. No idea how it would end up.

A masterpiece…or a bowl of fruit.

That was a year ago.

Back in the present, as 2018 draws to a close, Spurs are desperately trying to squeeze life back into their season, as young as it is. A solid 2-0 win at Leicester precedes the big one…Barcelona away to try and progress to the knockout stages of the Champions League.

Tottenham have to match or better Inter Milan's home game with PSV. Barcelona go one up after seven minutes.

With just five minutes left, Moura connects with a Kane cross. The game finishes 1-1. It's also 1-1 in Milan where they are still playing and going into injury time. In the last minute of added time, the game all but done, Inter's Icardi should score to take Milan through. Nick Viergever puts in an unbelievably heroic last ditch block to save the day.

Only one point from their first three group games but Tottenham squeeze into the knockout rounds by the skin of their teeth, gaining seven of the last nine points. Won two, drawn two, lost two. Saint Nick is Spurs' unheralded and very unsung seasonal gift giver, utterly professional to the end. Tottenham should give him a shirt. I'd be keeping the new flowery one though.

'One of the most important goals of my life,' says the still lost-in-space Moura.

'One of the best displays by a foreign team in the Nou Camp for many years,' says pundit Guillem Balague.

'It's a massive, massive achievement for the club,' says Poch.

Also at the start of this month is the Naomi House Santa Run in Winchester, which we do with Daz and his family. Unfortunately, Aurora's sports wheelchair has a puncture at the eleventh hour, but it becomes a mission to get her round the five kilometres of cobbles in her standard NHS one…a feat we achieve and creditably well placed. I can see lots of new competitive challenges lying ahead. We also need to find somewhere to watch a match against Arsenal. On our way back from Winchester we find a cellar bar in Alton which has the game on. We park up with Tottenham bossing it…but when we reach the bar a few minutes later, Arsenal have turned the match on its head and the game is all but gone. Normality, if there is such a thing for Spurs this season, resumes a few days later with a 3-1 win against Southampton, the goals being shared upfront by Kane, Son and Moura.

Friday and it's the Tropicana Nights '80s party at the G-Live in Guildford. Belle's going as Maverick and I've got my Rob Lowe tee-shirt on. For one moment in time I am back on those streets of Falmouth, soaking up Wham! and the rhythms of the night…only in this present there's a Big Daddy, an Officer and a Gentleman, Sloth and more neon and lycra than on a middle-aged man's Sunday afternoon cycle fest.

It's our one year anniversary. Frankie says relax. We do.

In a search to find someone to like me, love me, maybe even fall in love with me, I have found that person who has, in a relatively short space of time, given me a deeper understanding of what it is (and indeed takes) to be affable and human. Someone who has both been there before and learned to laugh through and past it. It's been a good year. Magic, even.

Charlotte's birthday is Capital Radio's Jingle Bell Ball at the O2. It's Rita Ora and (unlike Tropicana) a whole host of people I don't recognise, although some of the music I can just about recall. It's then down to Bournemouth for the weekend with Belle's parents and a Christmas send-off for Aurora. Days are really starting to feel like they have a beginning, middle and end.

In the right order.

Spurs beat Burnley in the league and then Arsenal in the League Cup. December's football seems back on track too.

Christmas with my family on 23 December, poignant a day as it is, is matched by a whopping 6-2 win at Everton. Santa's come early. Christmas itself is Charlotte, Belle and I staying two nights at Pennyhill Park, near Ascot. We're on fire winning their Christmas Day quiz, care of Charlotte's current pop knowledge (mine not having progressed much since either the '80s or her birthday). To add to the festive spirit, Spurs thrash Bournemouth on Boxing Day. They're on fire too, up to second in the league.

After Christmas, Aurora is back for a Santa double dip. She's not interested in X-Boxes. Any box of delights will do. Anything simple. An orange. A puzzle. It's like going back in time and being a kid again.

For Belle's birthday the four of us hit Harlequins at The Big Game at Twickenham. Seems like, fireworks and all, Aurora has got a front row taste for all things rugby. And she's marked out Tim Visser every time Harlequins have been on TV. 'Tim! Tim!' becomes her new fan appreciation of choice. Beside the West Stand before the game, quite by chance, an injured and non-playing Tim walks right across our paths and is more than happy to pose for the photos. His mum would be proud. Sport is taking everyone places they've never been.

With the Champions League next stages looming, Spurs bring everyone back down to earth, scoring one early but conceding three late to lose to Wolves.

Belle's happy though. She's been, and had, a good one. In the Littlewoods Football Pools game of life, there's a very good chance I might have finally called a result. This could very well go to extra time (hopefully not penalties).

Love Will Keep Us Alive
Spring 2019

2018 ended a strangely different one as relationships went. Both Tottenham and Belle. As time and the season evolved we found out more about each other. Erratic would have been one of the words to describe Spurs; working it out on the hoof, others. Of Belle? Liked her. Loved her. Falling in love with her.

Tottenham start the year beating Cardiff in the league and then putting seven past Tranmere in the FA Cup, their biggest win of the season. Llorente, in a guest appearance, reminds us all he might have something to add, pitching in with a hat-trick. The 1-0 first leg, semi-final win at home to Chelsea leaves it all to play for in the League Cup.

This is Tottenham though. Like life, for all the ups they give us it seems there is an equal and opposite down. They go down to Manchester United. We aren't in Kolymbia any longer (for all The Jackson 5 purists, probably just as well). To add to the bad news, Mousa Dembele, the heartbeat of the team, one of Charlotte's Belgian favourites, sadly gets transferred to Guangzhou R&F in China.

Reality and sadness bite right at the start of 2019 with a return to Cardiff with Belle to see Fernando and Jane for the funeral of Jane's mother. A delightful rugby family, the service and the occasion are evocative and poignant.

As mid-January, and the blues, set in, it's a Sunday trip to the Bombay Sapphire Distillery. The bus we take drives past our stop, leaving us short of time to get back (on foot) to our scheduled gin tour slot. It is about a mile, so we are going to have to leg it. Belle lasts both a good pace and my home-made cocktail admirably. Running the miles doesn't seem as far with a friend by your side.

Stopping over at, very appropriately, The White Hart in Whitchurch afterwards is very deliberate as they have a TV and Tottenham are playing Fulham. Llorente blunders an early own goal but Winks bails him out to win it deep into stoppage time with the most unexpected header. This night becomes a strange school night too, the locals all ganging up to take us on at pool, including a bloke who looks like Lewis Collins from *The Professionals*.

They are. We aren't…but we give as good as we get and take our figurative beating well. There's a new calm.

I smile an awful lot more when she's around.

Tottenham's hits and misses continue, losing to Chelsea in the League Cup semi-final second leg. For the first time away goals don't count, otherwise Spurs would have, at last, made a final. It is penalties instead…Dier and Moura miss theirs and the chance is gone.

Redemption comes, in part, against Crystal Palace in the FA Cup. Underlying problems both on and off the field are still apparent against Watford in the league, as the month closes. Two late goals from Son and Llorente scramble the win, but the crowd of twenty-nine thousand is the lowest home league attendance of the season. Wembley is pretty much empty on a wet Wednesday.

Valentine's month brings a first snowfall of the year. Spurs labour to a 1-0 win against Newcastle but the greater and more enjoyable event sees Aurora and I build a snowman. She launches a snowball from across the garden, scoring a direct hit to her mum's head. Wouldn't walk, wouldn't talk they said, she'll be a cricketer yet.

It's festive season all over again as Belle, Charlotte and I return to Pennyhill Park for a few nights, the first prize we won at their Christmas Day quiz. The England rugby team are also staying there for their game on the Sunday against France. It's a very interesting dynamic watching them train and then mingling with them after as they wander around. They are all in completely different zones. Some choose to burn rubber down the driveway, some are lost in their own thoughts, whilst some engage with the public. Eddie Jones doesn't mind a photo. Jonny May is the only player who is completely locked out…and is fastest out of the blocks on the Sunday, scoring a hat-trick of tries in half an hour.

Tottenham are out of the blocks to beat Leicester as a prelude to their Champions League Round of Sixteen. On Valentine's Eve it's a love-in as they rout Dortmund in the first leg. The big Spaniard notches the third and it's hard not to fall for him. He's making up the numbers but doing his job with a resolute honesty, integrity and passion.

Post Valentine's weekend it's a trip to the gin themed Salcombe Harbour Hotel and the Salcombe Distilling Co. where Belle and I make our own bottle of gin. Giving so much of herself away in the little things she says and does, the more she reveals.

Her real beauty lies in not knowing how good she is.

Tottenham give quite a lot of themselves away, losing to both Burnley and then Chelsea. They snatch a draw against Arsenal but their progress in the league is faltering. Nerves going in to the second leg against Dortmund?

That first half is full of collywobbles. Just after half-time Kane scores to pretty much put the game beyond doubt.

'It is a great achievement for Spurs to be in the quarter finals,' says David Moyes capturing the spirit of the season with a minor love-in.

'I make Manchester City favourites to win the trophy in Madrid in June, because they have got the best squad and an unbelievably driven manager,' says Mark Lawrenson.

Tottenham draw City in the quarters.

St. Patrick's weekend brings England versus Scotland and Wales against Ireland in the Six Nations finale. The Raven in Hook, Daz's local, plays host. With it comes some new drinking buddies, Baz and Pedro the dog. Wales play the game of their lives to commandeer the title, Grand Slam and all. Alun Wyn Jones is captain supreme. It's evocative and when the game is over he looks to the skies. His father would have been proud. I saw it in his eyes with mine.

In celebration we have tequilas (not Pedro, obviously, but he made himself available for any Mexican stand-off).

It's down to Belle's local for the last day of March and a key game with Liverpool. It's an even contest, with Spurs getting more in to the game the longer it goes on. Palms to face when Alderweireld scores an own goal in the ninetieth minute. Portsmouth make up for it in part straight after by winning the Football League trophy at Wembley. There has been a warm glow to that stadium over these last couple of years. Tottenham's brief stay there is nearly over.

There's more nostalgia to the month. Not least because I'm given an opportunity for a few games of hockey as that season ends. The first is a crushing 9-1 local derby victory against a side that have proven difficult to beat over the years. The second in a team missing a few key players, not least in goal, where we have a young lad who has stepped in at the eleventh hour to play a first game of adult hockey. We have no centre back either and I find myself wholly out of my comfort zone partnering George there. The kid pulls off a great early save and I get my defensive bearings. I am seeing the ball very large and I have got a game face back. George and I weather the storm and we go on to win 4-0. My first congratulations go to the youngster in possibly my best (and last) game ever.

I have played pretty much every sport there is, team or other. Mostly in an Average Joe's kind of way (about the only one I haven't, ironically, being dodgeball)…football, hockey, rugby being the main ones. I've enjoyed them all, eyes notwithstanding. For those, I know, I'm now done.

Sport is about many things, not least family and friends.

'You were a rock mate,' one of their players says to me. I look over towards Aurora and smile.

In The City
April 2019

Martin Kemp is doing an eighties night in Winchester. It's a massive cavern of a hall with cheap booze by the gallon. Through hazy eyes we could easily have been transported back to a Glen Disco with er, Spandau Ballet on video on the big screen. Amidst all the '80s neon and lycra (everyone else, not me) many of the people weirdly think I'm Martin. It must be quite dark in there. That, or a few too many of the dangerous sounding, looking and tasting cocktails.

Martin cruises through the evening, unlike Sonny who has struggled since Harry Kane came back from his injury. From being main man, Son has suddenly become a bit part sub. Kane is scoring again, but Tottenham can't buy a win. Someone needs to take the team by the scruff of the neck and turn this weird season round. The restless dynamic and inconsistency that has plagued their system has come back. Their travails are well documented: Lloris is currently a bit of a calamity in goal; their fullbacks are playing below par and the misfiring midfield too heavily reliant on Sissoko to keep bailing them out; Eriksen's head is elsewhere; Dele Alli's only played five league games in 2019 and ended up being subbed in three of them.

One point from the last fifteen, the poor form has seen them catapulted out of the top four qualifying positions to leave them just a point ahead of sixth.

All that and a lack of player investment in the last year are beginning to show. The safety certificate on the 62,062 stadium has, however, finally been approved. All shiny and new, the expectation for Tottenham's inaugural game there is massive. It has been a long time since they first adopted this bigger commercial mindset.

The dress rehearsal is a cast of legends, most of whom I have grown up with.

There is a certain irony, for me at least, that my home was once Crystal Palace. Tottenham have since built a football Disneyland but the Palace game has become a must win if any real momentum is going to be derived heading into the business end of the season. The stadium has the largest bar in Europe. Just as well, as the supporters will probably be needing it.

'Glory, Glory, Tottenham Hotspur!' booms out as their red tape is cut and yet more legends parade forth.

The first forty-five minutes of a new dawn and anxiety and waves of dread pervade. Spurs are being, well…Spurs. Straight from the kick-off any bright lights almost fade into gloom. Through the dullness of a drab first half however, out on the horizon, Sonny is still shining. In the fifty-fifth minute he scuffs one in and the collective sense of relief is palpable.

Spurs go on to win 2-0 but it is a result of mixed shades. The three points are long overdue but a one billion pound stadium, and its attached business plan, are going to need more than a few pies being sold…maybe even some sort of miracle.

Manchester City are on the cards for three of the next four games (the Champions league quarter-finals home and away, with the league game at City to finish); the cup games are fortuitously split by a game at home against struggling Huddersfield. Hard to gauge which is the more necessary: league points to guarantee Champions League qualification and revenue next year; or a full-on, bust-a-gut effort against the favourites in this year's tournament itself.

To take up the worry time, Daz and Lisa stay over for a weekend curry and quiz night at The Plough. It's changed. Same four-square walls, furniture moved around, different people, no football. We struggle on all the music questions without our pop queen, but manage a creditable second.

Tuesday night arrives and with it the Champions League quarter-final, first leg. The pressure is all on Spurs to find a way of maximising home advantage and, crucially, try not to concede any away goals. The game is poor, with neither team at their best. Sonny breaks the deadlock with the only moment of class and Lloris saves a penalty. Kane is injured however with what looks to be a significant foot problem. The game finishes 1-0 to Spurs but everyone goes in hope, more than expectation, up to Manchester in a week.

Huddersfield provides light relief, notable as much for a rare Wanyama strike but, more significantly, Moura filling in for the injured Kane. He duly scores a hat-trick and then celebrates playing kickaball on the pitch with his son once the game is over. The crowd see a lot more to him than has been present in the cameos he's been afforded during the season to date. He's got two feet and can use both. He also looks like he's all heart, passion, faith and kindness. Family too. Welcome to the Spurs one.

Celebrations over, its midweek again.

Second leg survival in Manchester.

Charlotte and I head over to The Lamb expecting a classic of shredded nerves and fingernails. Spurs' home leg lead is wiped out by Sterling before we've grabbed a table. Sonny equalises before I have ordered the drinks and he's picked up another before I have taken a sip. Spurs are leading 3-1 on aggregate. What could possibly go wrong? Apart from there being eighty minutes left. Ah, and Bernard Silva and Sterling scoring again. The momentum has shifted. 3-3 on aggregate, with Tottenham holding the precious away goal advantage. We need to leave the pub. It's getting raucous, it's a school night and Dave's got his licence to consider.

A short walk home, TV on, Aguero scores. 4-3, City up. Spurs have weathered the hurricane admirably but City are relentless. With it, added drama. There are Belgians all over the place but De Bruyne, absent from the first leg for City, is making all the difference in this. Sonny gets a card! He's out of Spurs' next European game which, at the moment, there isn't. Time is rolling. Spurs look like they are running out of ideas. They get a corner which comes over…

…and Llorente's arse has somehow become the pivotal moment of the season.

The ball drops amidst everyone and the big Spaniard is, well, the big Spaniard and throws something, everything, at it. Nobody knows what it has come off…but it's a goal as far as Tottenham are concerned and they're off celebrating.

Hold on. VAR is being an arse about his arse.

Repeated montage after repeated montage. Slow motion angle after slow motion angle. What is not in doubt is what it came off last…Llorente's hip. What is in doubt though is whether he's feathered it with his non-existent gloves. We need snickometer. We haven't got it. The hulking lump has however made his body shape more natural and fluid than a T-1000 Terminator. There's nothing clear and obvious to overrule the goal. Every Tottenham fan suddenly wants to kiss those magnificent cheeks.

The ninety minutes are up. It is 4-4 and, with the away goals, Tottenham are so, so close to something exceptional. Charlotte and I are on edge. And there are still five minutes of added hope, misery, pain and joy (depending which side you are on) left. This epic match is FAR FROM OVER.

Added time and City ramp it up. Ninety-three minutes. Eriksen misplaces a pass; it's scurried into the Tottenham area. Sterling scores to complete his hat-trick as the crowd and the City bench go bonkers.

Utter deflation on Spurs'. Heads in hands. Heartbreak.

Tottenham were so close…but wait…

…they still might be in this.

VAR has been called in again. Aguero is unfortunately, but clear and obviously, offside. Tottenham are now going mental. Poch is undressing. Hopefully there are no YMCA tribute acts in the stadium. He doesn't look like he cares.

The whistle, eventually, goes and they're through to the Champions League semi-final. Nothing Spursy about this.

They have out Cityed City. Proper warriors. Skins of teeth maybe, other body parts more prevalent.

The journalists have a field day and adjectives are flying.

'Dramatic.'

'Exhausting.'

'Unbelievable.'

'All-time classic.'

'A credit to the sport.'

'Anything but one-sided.'

'The second leg had been one of the most chaotic and enthralling the competition has witnessed.'

'This is why we love football,' says Poch.

Game four of my Tottenham top five goes into the bag.

And breathe.

Cycling in Alice Holt Forest with all the girls, Aurora on her specialist bike, is a brief chance to chill in all the footy madness. Because of Spurs I laugh a little more and smile a little more; because of Belle I laugh and smile a lot more.

City regain bragging rights with their 1-0 league win but we are happier with a semi. A squeaky win against Brighton restores Tottenham's momentum. They are nervous days though with the looming visit of Ajax, on an absolute high, having just put Real Madrid to the sword.

Come the first leg of a tense knockout, Super Jan does exactly that…gets himself knocked out. There is claret all over Vertonghen's face and he staggers off. The supreme form of the relentless Dutch team continues. Spurs are also sucker-punched, losing 0-1 (ceding up that vital away goal).

Holland has always given me fond memories: first crush (one of the heyday 'Famous Five' was Dutch); De Hems; the Dam to Dam. Tottenham…it's now down to you.

The second leg in Amsterdam is still alive but Spurs, as ever, are making a real meal of it. Less lasagne, more sticky toffee pudding.

Heartache Tonight
May 2019

It's the Army versus Navy rugby game at Twickenham. A relative calm before a month of sporting storm…if calm and Army Navy game can ever be used in the same breath. It's busy. Belle is bemused by it all. Less so the rugby, more so the trashed people and streets.

It is also the same day as Bournemouth and Tottenham. Tottenham go down to nine players with more than half of the game to play. It's 0-0 for pretty much all of it but their endeavour and heart sees them almost to the end. Dele Alli leads from a depleted front-line…running and running and running. A mile more than anyone else on the pitch…and then, in the cruellest of blows as the game goes deep in to injury time, Bournemouth score the winner from a header. Having imploded, it is the wrong sort of preparations for the biggest game in Tottenham's history in four days' time. Tottenham are at their Spursy best. Filling us all with hope, threatening highs, only to bounce back down to the trough of despair. Spurs aren't good for my relative state of mind.

Footballers can all kick a ball, whether over the fence or into a goal, in the garden or on the greatest of stages. What separates the good from bad is their decision making skills, particularly under pressure…managed as much as that is by feelings…whether going on in the background, or on the day. A consideration for some time has been that football's approach to mental health has been a dereliction of duty. Mental health isn't taken seriously enough. Players all come from different backgrounds, have hopes and prospects and fears and, if they make it, financial security…albeit short lived. No support structure afterwards. A cut and run.

The military services would say the same.

Prince William and associated other stars launch Mental Health Awareness Week. In a radio broadcast, the Prince urges listeners to talk about their problems, in a bid to stay mentally fit and healthy. He asks the nation to pause…and listen to a person in need.

The next day, Sunday, it's a christening at a local church and then nibbles at the village hall after. Arsenal are playing and the BBC Sport updates are crucial. In the end Arsenal trip over themselves and, whilst not guaranteed, that fourth place remains in Tottenham's hands.

Tuesday 7 May and time for two of the heavyweights of European football, Liverpool and Barcelona, with the first of the semis. 3-0 up from the first leg and it's the Spanish outfit who want to control the pace of the game and make it slow. Liverpool do not accept the challenge and create their own tempo. Each goal that Liverpool claw back is a heavyweight blow. Their fourth is the knockout.

'You'll Never Walk Alone,' chant the fans as the game climaxes. It is deafening…bringing back memories of that other great Champions League night…Istanbul and Jon.

7 May, the eve of Tottenham's biggest ever game, is also thirty-six years to the day of the ambulance.

The road's been long.

The following night arrives. It's as good as virgin territory for Tottenham. Only once before have they been in the semi-final of Europe's biggest competition, 1962, before I was born. Even then the greatest of Spurs sides, fabled and never readily compared to, weren't able to get over the line.

Heading in to the game Tottenham are only one down, albeit the Ajax away goal. The task might be far easier than Liverpool's was but…well, it's Spurs. This young Ajax side, fearless and relentless, have already embarrassed two other European goliaths, Real Madrid and Juventus. Tottenham, my Tottenham, Tottenham, our Tottenham, have lost five of their previous six games. The City game sucked the life out of them. The pressure has mounted, as revealed against Bournemouth. Mind games aplenty.

The Ajax supporters let off fireworks outside the Spurs players' hotel in the early hours to keep them awake.

A restless night, then down to The Lamb for Charlotte and I. Unfortunately for us it is ukulele night and the place is packed with a variety of stringed instruments. The TVs are on but there's no sound, with only a small standing area at the back.

Ajax are both slick and rampant. There is an intensity to them and it goes from bad to worse. 1-0 before the game, a further two deft goals mean Spurs are effectively losing 3-0 at the half. They have come undone and there is a massive gap between where they are, to where they want to be. The Champions League adventure is all but ended and another season is slipping away.

It's a school night and our particular adventure is all but over too. Watching football should take you through all the emotions. In the here and now those feelings are merely of frustration and disappointment. Time for us to walk home.

We substitute ourselves to a chorus of duelling banjos. The magic TV has to make do again. The only thing magic we are going to see tonight is the signed Paul Stewart 1991 FA Cup video below it.

After that terrible first forty-five minutes Kane, who has not even been on the pitch, is in the Tottenham changing room…'going mental,' says Trippier. It's deliverance time.

Spurs have to take more than a little chance.

They need a lift. What's your big move, Poch?

The meander back along our lane is a slow one with more than a few heavy sighs. We arrive home just as they come out for the second half.

Football is played with the mind…but Poch's big move is old school basics. Bring out the biggest lad you've got to intimidate, bully and take the ball off the smaller kids.

Enter the Dragon…well that Spanish bloke all the way from Swansea. Llorente has come on in place of Wanyama.

The six foot five (would go down a storm on a dating site) old master does exactly that…

…starts to bully the Ajax defence as soon as the game restarts. Starts to give them an education. The welly boots have come off. You've got to kick the ball with your feet, but you have got to play with your heart. Spurs have come out in the most uncontrolled fashion, now playing with a freedom and abandon. Anything technical has gone. In its place instinct. This is the Spurs we have loved for decades. This is the 1960's team all over. This is what we remember. The echoes, the memories.

The Spaniard plays what's in front of him. Fifty percent pass completion but as always though, there's passion and a fire that belies his languid approach. And a menace. The long balls, all the flick-ons. It's invigorating. It's lifting. It's generating momentum. Something in the searing heat of this moment you have to love…a 1970s throwback playing the game an old-fashioned way. The Tottenham way.

Their guard is now well and truly dropped and they are coming out swinging.

Both teams are going toe-to-toe only, on this night, like middleweight boxers…Eubank, Watson and Benn at their best. Both teams are speedy, slick, fluid, skilful, jabbing and counterpunching in a relentless pursuit of each other.

The Ajax supporters are doing their bit, as they start to sing their anthem, Bob Marley's 'Three Little Birds'.

'Don't worry…about a thing…'

No one wins a game off the pitch…and that is why we love football. Amidst all of the high stakes drama, there is a monumental prize at stake. The players just have to trust in their own playing abilities. Bring their own walls down and isolate themselves from all the sponsors, agents and public relations companies and play for the badge.

Fifty-five minutes and Lucas Moura does what he does best. Latches on to a through ball and steers it in.

A few remarkable minutes later and Llorente makes an

absolute nuisance of himself right in front of goal. There is pandemonium in the Ajax area. Andre Onana, their keeper, tries to grab both the ball and his own player's foot. There is no daylight to be found in a packed and chaotic penalty area but, like a mole digging in the dark, Moura's crept in and stolen the ground from both of them. He thinks fast, he shuffles his feet faster, better and way quicker than any sleight of hand. He's got his back to goal, ball at his feet. HE'S GOING THE WRONG WAY! Oh wait. WHAT? No-one expects the spin and shoot.

YEEEEEEESSSS!

He turns to all the travelling supporters up in the gods and waives his hands to raise the decibels. The mood has changed dramatically. Tottenham have got thirty minutes to find another goal to grab an aggregate draw and an away goal win. Ajax probably just need one more to all but put the game to bed. 'Next goal' really does win.

Tottenham now have no discernible formation, except Sissoko covering about five positions. I smile an evocative smile. Ajax are still looking slicker and more troubling with their rapier counter attacks though.

Both teams are running themselves ragged and into the ground, but the basics of any team game are on show to the fullest…heart, emotion, desire.

The amount of times the post gets hit by both sides, it seems like a third for either of them on the night just isn't coming. This game is dripping in drama. It's already been a top five Spurs game. Now it's in the lap of the gods.

The pressure increases. I bite my nails. A lot.

And then, with the gut-wrenching action unabating, ninety minutes are pretty much up. Time draws to its inexorable close.

That's life. That's what all the people say. You're riding high in April, you're shot down in May.

The board for added time goes up…

Nightingale
8 May 2019 21:51

Hello five minutes my old friend.

We've all been here before. The expectation. The still of time. Emotionally drained supporters. Hung out. Wearied. Rinsed. Exactly five minutes of added time. No more. No less. And when it comes down to it, that final whistle, what would we give for just that one additional second?

The night is closing on the Johan Cruijff Arena, but not the memories. It's been a journey, this season. Tottenham have always been that 'big' club in name only. Always been 'Spursy'.

As Chiellini once pointed out, 'It's their history.' Wrong. The past is not a closed book. History can be rewritten.

Their heritage is the Bill Nicholson way. The supporters want passion, they want emotion. They want to smell the soul of every player. This is a team that has come from the very brink of elimination to still be in the dying embers of a Champions League semi-final and, regardless of result, as the final five minutes play out, they have done us all proud. They have somehow kept themselves in with a glimmer, a hope.

The chances come often for both teams in such a short, frantic, passage of time. They are playing with a complete intensity.

93:30: Tottenham have a corner.

'This is it,' I say to Charlotte, as spent as anyone.

'This is it,' says commentator Darren Fletcher, as spent as anyone.

Lloris runs up. The ball comes in. Llorente's shouldered header sails over. It's a lonely jog back for the goalkeeper.

94:00: Onana is booked for taking way too much time collecting the ball for the goal-kick and trying to buy thirty seconds of what's left on the clock.

94:30: Onana kicks straight down the middle. No! Not down the middle. I mean, yes! Down the middle!

94:49: The teams trade headers. The ball is back to the halfway. Davies gets his toe in to divert it to Son. It is tight and crowded around the centre spot and Son has to play it way back to Sissoko.

A bumpy journey, both in Europe and on the domestic front. It's been an epic comeback from the brink. They just wouldn't go away. They have been minutes from going out. Now they are seconds from actually doing so.

94:54: Sissoko launches an American football style 'Hail Mary'. With a hint of back spin. Like he has been practising it all season.

It comes down close to the edge of the Ajax box with a scary accuracy direct to Llorente. Could go anywhere now. Except the Spanish master of the moment deftly deflects it on the volley.

94:58: 'Here's Dele Alli…'

Alli feigns slightly and then rolls the ball into the path of an onrushing Moura.

94:59: 'Here's Lucas Moura…'

Moura hits a first time shot just as De Ligt gets a toe to it, making the ball veer off to the right side of the goal.

95:00: Onana dives, in vain though, as the ball goes past him. The ball is up to the goal line.

Hugh and I have been here before.

95:01: *'OOOOOOHHH, THEY'VE DONE IT! I cannot believe it! Lucas Moura with the last kick of the game. The Ajax players collapse to the ground. Tottenham Hotspur are heading to the Champions League final with a goal that we just couldn't believe!'*

There are screams and complete disbelief in front of the magic TV, in the ground, everywhere.

'He's done it, he's done it. OMFG. OMFG,' we shout, palms to forehead.

The Ajax team are, literally, down. Onana is on his back blinking, as if waking up from a dream.

The drama. The theatre. The significance. The emotion. The timing. Five minutes plus one magical, mystical extra second.

It goes mental out there for what seems like an eternity but the game, agonisingly, hasn't finished.

There is time for a restart and its back down the Spurs end. Lamela's dribbling away from goal, losing it, winning it back. It's up to Sissoko (now playing up front) who finds himself pretty much on his own wide right from the Ajax penalty area. He is closed down, he dribbles briefly, he falls over, he's spent. Even his engine has finally gone. No-one cares. The whistle blows.

We let it go in our house. We let it happen. We jump up and down. We run around the sofa like rabid dogs chasing tails. Romance never dies and Tottenham's melody remains unbroken. I do several windmills.

Erik ten Hag, the Ajax manager, stands a silent man in the moment; it's hard not to admire his fortitude and grace.

Pochettino's on his knees.

Lucas Moura's been mobbed.

Harry Kane's leg is better.

We scream the house down.

We are still running. Around the sofa. No-one is hiding anymore. We are still screaming and laughing and hugging each other. That…and crying. Tears of joy.

Every little thing's going to be alright.

It's gotten late. Very late. I text Belle to say I'll call in about ten minutes. Something important I need to say.

Tottenham have defied the odds. Every game has been crazy. They've only gone and done it. They've taken it right to the limit, got everything spot on. For Ajax, pretty much everything went wrong. I'm lost in the moment now.

Pochettino's crying now. 'Thank you football. This type of emotion without football is not possible. Thank you to everyone who believed in us. To describe this in words is difficult,' he says.

It was a proper game. No rolling around. Touches of class. The right way to play from both teams…in the spirit of adventure.

'Football is my life,' says Moura, crying. It's in his heart, it is in his history. At which point it was impossible for me to keep holding tears back again as well. Ricky Villa is now in shared company. I was just a spotty teenager back then, when he gave me my previous most treasured Tottenham memory (and about to start a lifetime of being haunted).

I'm with my own teenager now and the darkness has all gone. We can say, 'We were there.'

The interviews take place. Everyone is crying. Everyone is riding an emotional wave. The masks have all come off and it really is one of those nights. They built a Disneyland and now they are peddling in dreams.

The post-match analysis goes on. And on.

We watch those last five minutes. Over and over. Epic, Mickey. We dance into the night. One night that is going to last forever. All summer long, at least.

It is pretty much time for bed come one in the morning. Charlotte's already gone, happy. I wind down to an eighties music channel.

'I'm All Out Of Love' comes on.

Shit. Shit. Triple Shit.

In the chaos, I forgot the most important call of my life.

The next morning Belle gets her call.

'I love you,' I say.

'Say it one more time.'

'I love you.'

'Ditto.'

My quest to find 'I love you girl' is all but done.

Work's off the menu. Head's elsewhere, playing that game round and round. We watch the match again in its entirety the following night.

Social media will break all but the best. The right thing, like the papers, is to ignore it. Jon and Gazza shared that moment. Social media (the negative, spiteful side of it at least) has, for the moment, taken the day off too. Twitter's reaction to the pivotal goal seems to mirror ours. Plenty of running. Around sofas. Moura, indifferent they once said. Sissoko, worst purchase ever they once said. Llorente, why, they all asked once. These three, these players most of all, who have displayed patience, faith and taken their chances, have also shown the old fashioned qualities of persistence, diligence, heart and soul. Added to team spirit, bottle and self-improvement they've quite rightly become legends.

Going into the weekend, Belle and I travel down to The Christchurch Harbour Hotel for the town's Food Festival. It feels like we are dining at the top table…and the Estrella tastes good.

Tottenham have the one regular season game left and, looking sluggish, come from behind to get their necessary draw with Everton to secure the next season's Champions League adventure. Every five year plan has a reason as well as a beginning, middle and end. With Tottenham it hasn't necessarily been in that order.

We're back to Christchurch at the end of the month for the Mudeford Seafood Festival. Belle adopts a home-craft fairy called Molly Mae from one of their lovely 'creative' stalls. Everything happens for a reason.

Tottenham are going to be in the Champions League final next weekend in Madrid.

We aren't.

The logistics of school and the prohibitive travel, ticket and hotel costs make it all but impossible. About ten grand a person all in (via an extremely tortuous, several days long, trek). More importantly…

…there are four of us. We are watching this together.

Promises are still promises though.

Peaceful Easy Feeling
June 2019

We've reached end game. The biggest night in Tottenham's history, one of those moments of my life…and I can't find anywhere that will let the four of us in. Health and safety. That promise that we'd get to 'see' the Champions League final, is a promise which I seemingly now can't deliver on. I'd never thought Spurs would have been able to have put me on that spot.

Finding anything, let alone somewhere, special for this night…two adults and two teenagers…has become a huge problem. As much as I'd love it, we would never get in The Lamb. No-one else wants us.

The last resort. The Village Hotel, Farnborough.

They've got hotel rooms too (obviously). A call to make sure we are all fine to get in for the day, evening and night. Rooms (tick), Champions League on TV (tick), no problem with special needs (tick), no problem with kids (tick). Two rooms please for Saturday 1 June. Actually, make that three rooms, as Fernando and Jane are coming too. Daz will pop over with the kids to complete the set up.

And breathe. We're sorted. We've made it.

Tottenham have dragged me through all of the chapters of my life. Been to the mill and back. Mostly in the company of people that matter and times of life…1972 UEFA Cup (family), 1981 FA Cup (boarding friends), 1984 UEFA Cup (university mates), 1991 FA Cup (Jon), this season's quarter and semi (Charlotte).

A fifth decade of Tottenham in finals. And it all comes down to tonight; the only thing that's certain, not one of us has been here before. Us, randomly, in the newly revamped Village. Specifically as well though the team, management and supporters, collectively or individually. The only team to win a trophy in every decade since I was born…and this, the very last opportunity now, the most unexpected. There have been magical seasons with '18-19, in its topsy-turvy all over the place way, more than most. A season of agonies. Lost nineteen games…yet somehow ended up in the top four. And the Champions League final. Consistent in their mediocrity through most of the time I've supported them, this particularly iron-willed squad have taken us all through another season of historic overachievement. Performances have been something of a Picasso. Not so easy on the eye, fractured at the best of times but, as both away at City and Ajax, utterly priceless. The true value and endeavour won't be appreciated for a while.

They've brought a whole list of things to the top table. In the absence of money they've brought back authenticity instead. Emotion and big hearts worn close to sleeves too. All that and tears. This season they've been a team.

Is there one bit of magic, one defining act, left?

The Village has changed. Wholly revamped, more modern touches everywhere. By the large front doors, huge letters, *Live Love Life*. Both prominent and poignant. Inside, their own walls have very much come down. The old sports bar has gone, replaced by what looks like a very grey open-plan business centre, an accountant's or salesman's paradise. All very modern. No soul.

On the other side of the foyer a new, open-plan sports bar. Big, modern, Americanised, multiple TVs. And a sign.

'Champions League final tonight. OVER 16s ONLY.'

Shit. Shit. Triple shit. Again. What?

Less than three hours to go and we've a huge problem. Not just huge. Like, very huge. The hotel is really sorry but health and safety and licencing. Hang on. I phoned, asked the right questions. You said, 'Sure, no problem.'

Charlotte, for the first time I have ever seen, kicks off. She's got this. Making sure she IS going to see her final.

'We have got friends from Spain (ahem, Wandsworth) over to watch it.'

'Um…we should be having it on in the business centre for hotel guests.'

'You're sure of that?'

'Yes…I er, think so.'

As if to prove the point, Fernando and Jane arrive. Daz soon follows. Safety in numbers. The final will be on.

7 p.m. arrives. One hour to go to kick-off. The business centre is opened. It is grey and cold. All very corporate. No atmosphere. The huge screen at the far end by a small bar shows Sky News. The conference style tables have all been laid up for others who have also started turning up.

We are given a table in the corner by the door, where an old wall TV used to hang (now a wall-to-wall bookcase and a new, huge TV). Nobody puts us in the corner. But…

…of all the corners of all the bars in all the world, we've been here before, Charlotte and I. It is our corner. Comfy sofas have replaced those old diner style tables and chairs where we had parked up, once upon a time, watching the timeless romance of Japan and South Africa unfold. Those napkin and ketchup holders, the cutlery, the candles…they are unmistakably still the same as on that night. And on the big TV we have another game of relative importance and no little significance. We've been unexpectedly transported back to another time. In the same place. The goose bumps, those memories, those ghostly echoes of a life gone by still resonate. Time, for a second, stands still.

What weird alchemy is this?

If I hadn't taken it on board before, I do now. On the night of Tottenham's greatest achievement this isn't about Spurs and my endearing love for them anymore (although it is they who have gloriously made this happen). Football miracles by Liverpool and Spurs remind us why we are in love with this beautiful game, whoever we support. Fifty-odd years of supporting Spurs are coming to a climax, but tonight is more important than that. Success on the field is something but life is not about the big moments, just the shared ones. It is about togetherness. Charlotte, obviously. Belle and Aurora, Fernando and Jane, Daz and the gang.

And in absentia, family and Siobhan and Jules as well.

We are a team. This feels like one.

Charlotte had championed the earlier issue, in her own way with the management…who have now kindly given us some champagne on the house for the toast to our twelfth man and absent friends. I have brought my fiftieth birthday expensive bottle of pink that I was saving for special too.

The game has barely started before it is all over. A piece of gamesmanship (worthy of any Sunday morning game on Wandsworth Common) gifts a penalty to Liverpool in the first minute, setting a boring scene for the remainder of the match, which passes in a blur. For the two sides that made the most crosses in the league, were in the top five passers, played possession and positioning with power, athleticism and fitness…they are serving up a dog's dinner of a game. Spurs have shots. Lots of them. Statistically one of the best games they have played. But their beating hearts are still in Amsterdam.

It doesn't end up being the result we all wanted but the miracle had already been achieved.

'It is better to fail aiming high than to succeed aiming low. And we of Spurs have set our sights very high, so high in fact that even failure will have in it an echo of glory.' Bill Nicholson's words were never more apt.

Lloris, too, speaks of defeat not as a failure…it is a big win for the club and a giant step forward. A sixty thousand plus stadium, a superb squad, no distractions and a world record profit. If a measure of success is money in the bank Spurs have done well, but this season was much more than that. It was the perfect love story. All twists and turns, all heart and soul. Like the last days of the best summer ever Tottenham have left behind an unforgettable romance.

For me there is more. I had that promise to deliver on. Getting us to the Champions League final on time was just the side bet that Charlotte went and owned for herself.

The day, the month, the season, the year and the place, this shared field of dreams, turns out to be that promise. A longstanding one. To Jon and our last text.

To let somebody love me.

Why you, Tottenham? For all of our ups, for all the downs, you have taken me way deep on this journey, this long and winding road. We've come full circle. Why you?

Time doesn't heal…it accommodates. And in effectively understanding that, I realise why. Why you, Tottenham?

Closure.

This time not high in the Alps, way more down to earth in the company of good friends. I accept Jon's gone now, except in my memories. I wonder if he will ever show his hand again though.

The following weekend after all the fuss is over, Belle and I visit Fernando and Jane for paella, champagne and Spanish wine on the Friday. Then it's a Saturday trip down memory lane to Portsmouth for D-Day 75 commemoration events, with it a cocktail festival. The Red Arrows fly past. An IBIS hotel has never felt better, overlooking St John's College as it does. We are back in time…it's the 1980s and Belle and I cruise all the pubs full of the 18-30 brigade and show them how it's done. There isn't a care in the world.

Two weekends later and it's the 'Twilight Run' over at Farnborough Airport. Charlotte's gaining sponsorship for her school trip to Sri Lanka. She is doing well at school and offers up her best maths exam advice…always do all of the questions in reverse…when your brain's both fresh and in gear, because there are more marks to be won in the latter stages. It leaves me wondering if I had followed that simple advice all the years gone by how much the past would have changed. Like the blue bit of that old red-blue rubber that never did its erasing job though, I wouldn't scrub a thing.

If I had just the one word of wisdom for my former self it wouldn't be about how to tackle either some Pythagoras or a tricky winger.

I'd just say, 'Believe.'

Back on the runway, the one-time air traffic controller is doing a great job of trekking the track and steering her own daughter home.

It's the last week of the month, a month which has built and is reaching a crescendo. Saturday 23 June sees a catch-up with an old hockey friend over from the States. Great to see him and chew the relative Spurs and Arsenal dynamic. Then Belle and I are off to Wembley one more time. The Eagles are in town for one of those tours before their last but one tour. Since the last time I saw them they've lost an integral part along the way, but kept spirits flying.

It's a warm night, a perfect setting. Deacon Frey's doing his father proud, going through the back catalogue.

'Here's another one my dad used to play.'

He's loving the minute and the moment. The rest of the band are giving him all the time he needs. A Wembley full house is lost in all the nostalgia. And the Queen of Hearts, fully in the moment too, has still proven to be my best bet.

For once, 'Desperado' isn't the last song of the evening. It's last but one, ushering in a finale encore.

'Best Of My Love' plays us out.

On the way from the stadium the subway to the rail link is rammed. It could be any old football game, but this is a night for music…and as we are held en masse awaiting the controlled stop-start flow, someone starts singing.

'Don't worry 'bout a thing, cause every little thing gonna be alright.'

Everyone…the fans, the stewards, the police all join in.

'Three Little Birds' is on echo.

I've finally lost my mind.

I've no idea how it all ends. How the next season turns out. Undeniably this has been a great one. Belle understands the value of time…particularly someone else's. She's got things she needs to do for herself now as well.

I do know there is one last promise…to Mum.

Time for me to man up.

Childish things can stay though. As long as they like, for many seasons to come.

Before that next step, large or small, there is a holiday to Mexico with Jules and Siobhan to get organised. We need to do some planning, so it's a couple of hours in the car to get to theirs.

With it, a lunchtime stopover at The Royal Oak. Might possibly have a ploughman's.

And one for the road.

Afterword

As I write, a year on from Spurs' extraordinary Champions League adventure the world has changed.

They are 'still' the reigning runners-up but, with football as we know it very different for the foreseeable, they face perhaps their biggest challenge yet. They will have massive problems financing the new stadium without crowds and in the absence of all their other cancelled big events.

Like so many others, their business plans will have gone out the window.

Everything is relative.

In the middle of a global pandemic, the world has come to a shuddering halt. Hit the buffers.

We've been in a virus lockdown and time, time that we won't get back, hasn't become more precious…rather, all the more cherished.

I (ironically), like most, am sat on a sofa with a bottle of wine and a DVD. Reflecting, observing, listening.

So far, the only thing I have learned is that even Penrod 'Penry' Pooch, otherwise known as Hong Kong Phooey, was never (ever) 'Henry' the mild-mannered janitor either.

We never heard his alter-ego, Penry, correctly.

Just as we absorbed strange times in those early 1970s with all the general strikes, the kids of today are also absorbing a transitory but strangely different way of life and, with it, a greater perspective. As a kid back then I would while away all of my time recreating the greatest goals I had seen, the originals still existing on some media somewhere, mine lost to time and memories. It took me forever to perfect 'that' Hoddle volley against United (if I tried it now too many bits would fall off). Which is why (in this extended absence of 'normal' football as an outlet for emotion and passion) there is a kind of magic watching the kids in this present, with all this extra time they have, recreating best shots and moments to savour…and preserving them for posterity.

Enter the gerbils. Reasons, seasons, lifetimes.

For me they weren't talking animals from the very best of Disney but, when I returned to our house of an evening, I could always say, 'Hey, boys.'

They would scratch, dig and run on their wheel with the best of them. A quiet, constant comfort as evenings moved into night.

Depression has so many faces and happens to all of us regardless of wealth or class. It affects everyone differently.

Adolescent girls are twice as likely to suffer from mental health issues. I hoped I'd protected Charlotte well, up to at least secondary school. To give her a decent shot there, I gave her Tottenham as her shield.

Then it was out of my control.

Juggling social media, rigours of exams, growing in to adulthood and friendship groups creates its own world of problems. She has found some really good ones in the pals category, long may they continue. With all the jostling until everything settled though, Toby and Sanchez both played their part.

These days we value the little things more, in whatever shape and however small they might come. We cherish life itself, never taking anyone or anything for granted.

Sometimes however we run out of road or pitch.

Or time.

Toby sadly died two weeks in to lockdown (the Gerbil Forum suggesting a stroke). Fleeting, transitory, he played a great game over a couple of seasons. Whilst there are, have been and will be far greater tragedies in these strange and difficult times, like all the best pets though, he was still a part of the family.

I don't know what I did with my garden but I'd created a safe haven, a magical little paradise full of flowers. There is a perfect place in it, a border where you can always hear the birds singing and where the sun shines longest, right up until it sets. A lovely place to lie…and to be at rest.

Which segues us back to all things Patrick Swayze.

Like Dalton in *Roadhouse*, at the bottom of the steps up to the Sky Bar, Toby is now in charge of who comes in or out. And as with Sam in *Ghost,* the film's last line resonates.

'See ya,' says Molly, tears streaming down her face.

Relevant. But not (quite) the point.

'When those you love die, the best you can do is honour their spirit for as long as you live. You make a commitment that you are going to take whatever lesson that person or animal was trying to teach you…and you make it true in your own life. It's a positive way to keep their spirit alive in the world, by keeping it alive in yourself,' said dear Patrick, sadly aware of his own mortality.

Animals give you unconditional love.

On the little rocket we built to bury Toby in, Charlotte wrote, 'You always were a great listener.'

Seeing it written, I realise how important he was for her. We always need someone who has got our back. I didn't realise how much he had hers.

May we all be great, and even better, listeners now.

Thanking him for being there for me. Thanking him for taking on the baton and being there for her.

The boy done good.

Printed in Great Britain
by Amazon